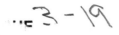

OFFICIALLY
DISCARDED

"I go make medicine," Steve said. "Maybe you don't think I make medicine. Pretty soon you find out. I go sing Grasshopper Song.

"Long time ago it rain and rain. You can't see no river, just mist. By and by Grasshopper, he come out. He walk down to river. But ain't no river. Just mist. It rain and rain. Grasshopper, he sit by river and sing his song. He say, 'Ai-ai. Ai-ai. Ai-ai.' Then he say, 'Puff.'

"And then he blow like this. Mist, he break and he go down river. Rain, he go away. Sun, he shine. Grasshopper, he go back and he say, 'When mist, he come on river and ain't no sun; and rain, he rain and rain; everybody sing my song and say, "Puff".'

"Then mist, he go down river; and sun, he shine; and rain, he don't rain no more."

In the Land of the Grasshopper Song

**TWO WOMEN IN THE KLAMATH
RIVER INDIAN COUNTRY IN 1908–09
SECOND EDITION**

by
MARY ELLICOTT ARNOLD
and **MABEL REED**

**Foreword to the new Bison Books edition by
André Cramblit
Introduction to the new Bison Books edition by
Susan Bernardin
Afterword to the new Bison Books edition by
Terry Supahan**

UNIVERSITY OF NEBRASKA PRESS • LINCOLN AND LONDON

First Nebraska paperback printing: 1980

Reprinted by arrangement with Andrew Genzoli and Marian E. Genzoli.

Library of Congress Cataloging-in-Publication Data
Arnold, Mary Ellicott.
In the land of the grasshopper song: two women in the Klamath River Indian country in 1908–09 / Mary Ellicott Arnold and Mabel Reed; foreword by André Cramblit; introduction by Susan Bernardin; afterword by Terry Supahan—2nd ed.
p.   cm.
Includes bibliographical references.
ISBN 978-0-8032-3637-0 (pbk.: alk. paper)
1. Frontier and pioneer life—California—Siskiyou County. 2. Karok Indians—Social life and customs. 3. Siskiyou County (Calif.)—Social life and customs. 4. Siskiyou County (Calif.)—Description and travel. I. Reed, Mabel. II. Title.
F868.S6A7 2011
979.4'21—dc23   2011021432

This Bison Books edition follows the original in beginning chapter 1 on arabic page 11; the text remains unaltered.

Foreword to the New Bison Books Edition

André Cramblit

In the Land of the Grasshopper Song is the story of California's past and also of its future and is tied to the history and future of the Karuk people. The intertwined story of Mary Ellicott Arnold, Mabel Reed, and the Karuk people is one of learning. The two women learned that their misconceptions about the Natives of the Klamath River had been built on romantic stereotypes, ignorance, and fear. For the Karuks it meant learning about the onslaught of a new era that would take them from their isolated lives on the river into a world that would eventually show them electricity, automobiles, television, the atomic bomb, man landing on the moon, cellular and computer technology, and human probes on Mars. That is quite a leap for one society to make within three generations. What we as readers learn is that there is a fine line of culture that defines us as people. As white women, Arnold and Reed did not know that their western sensibilities would be influenced, changed, and, heavens forbid, improved by the very people they were sent to "civilize."

Western miners came to the Klamath River looking for the mother lode but did not find their El Dorado. But they did find much more than they had hoped for. They discovered cultures, languages, ceremonies, salmon, acorns, baskets; and they discovered the center of the universe was at Katimiin. What they didn't think they would find was that the Karuk people had all the riches they needed without the allure of gold.

The pages of this book allow the outside universe to peer into the center of the Karuk people. At the same time, the book gives us as Karuk people the opportunity to examine another perspective of our history previously known through the family stories shared as a part of our oral tradition. It is a vehicle of discovery for even the casual reader. The story of these two women, who entered a society they did not know, mirrors the story of the Karuk people, who were also connecting with a new, unfamiliar way of life. The Karuks were entering a new century, a new world brought on by the reality of contact. The truth that unfolds within the pages of this book reflects the nature of this change that was occurring in the Karuk people, as well as the transformation experienced by the authors.

The impetus for the journey into Karuk country is not truly known, but the impact that it had on Arnold and Reed becomes clearer on every page. The story itself parallels the journey told of in Joseph Conrad's *Heart of Darkness.* The two heroines of this book travel upriver into Native lands and begin to discover the duality that exists within themselves: their ties to their western upbringing and their growing understanding of the cultural/spiritual world of the Karuk people.

To learn about the Karuk people you must first learn about the rivers, the mountains, the trees, the salmon, and the nature that surrounds us. This is a journey of discovering what is inside you by opening up your eyes to see the whirlwind around you. Arnold and Reed forded the rapids of the river to find who they were. They found themselves as teachers, learners, farmers, jesters, healers, carpenters, and emissaries of a new millennium. They learned from the Karuk people not only what it took to survive in the wilds of Klamath country but what it took to survive in the outside world.

This narrative takes place at the turn of the century, a time that had two diametrically opposite meanings for the people involved. For western society it meant the realization of manifest destiny, the conquering and subjugation of the West and the indigenous peoples that lived there. To the Karuk people it meant an end to a way of life as they knew it. It meant dammed up rivers, disease, alcoholism, boarding schools, and the loss of culture and language. In recent times things have begun to bloom, springlike. We have seen a renaissance with our dances and ceremonies being revived, our language being taught, and the growth of a strong sovereign tribal government.

These two women were on their own in the unknown territory of the Klamath. Initially they did not understand that the Karuk people were being forced into the outside world, where the collision of ways of life would result in an explosion of acculturation and genocide. They came to know that they were witnesses to the end of an empire (if only in and around the Klamath and Salmon rivers). Their journals, notes, and writings draw the reader a picture of a people, a cosmology, a civilization at the end of the time when they controlled their own destiny.

One of the things the book illustrates to me is the dramatic change that has occurred since it was written. What was once several days' journey from the Pacific coast to the heart of Karuk country now takes but a few hours in a car driven by my wife as I work on my laptop before I get to the tribal office so I can get on the wireless network to check my e-mail. This ride follows the original Indian trails, now highways, and takes me past the same landmarks seen by Reed and Arnold. I, too, slide into the Hoopa Valley, rush across the river at Weitchpec (now by bridge), drive past Somes Bar and Katimiin (my own family village), and I can look across the river and see the village of I-ees Steve, the home of my great uncle Leonard Super. My uncle saw a wide range of things change in his life, from the time he took his parents to see the Pacific Ocean for the first time in their lives (even though they had grown up less than sixty miles from it) to the launching of the space shuttle. He also told me about the medallion that was given to him, which came from two school matrons who had once briefly visited the Karuk people.

This is more than just a story. This is more than just a book. This is more than just a diary of two women who went out West to teach the Indians. This is more than just a historical overview of California. This is more than just the culture conflict between American Indian and white people. This is about reality—the reality of two worlds coming together at a time and place where each would have to learn to live with the other.

As a member of the Karuk Tribe I have a personal attachment to this book. It discusses people I have heard about through the personal stories of my relatives. It describes places that I know, including my home village of Katimiin. While the book is not written by a tribal member, nor from a wholly Karuk perspective, I often recommend it to friends so they can get a basic understanding of what life was for my people shortly after contact with western society. This is a rare book that presents a Native people without romancing, objectifying, and stereotyping the subject. It is not a story to be told but rather the reflections and observations of two visitors to an extraordinary new land.

This personal narrative was written by two ordinary women to document a people and place at a specific point in history. Arnold and Reed acknowledged their own biases and ignorance and were open to learning from their river friends and neighbors. This is a very refreshing difference from the usual work of anthropologists. The typical writings of these academicians are full of preconceived notions slanted to support their own ethnocentric educational philosophy, which was colored by a privileged western male orientation and the self-assurance that they were always correct in their judgment and interpretation of the culture of their studied peoples.

Hopefully we can see ourselves in the story of these two women and their experience of life on the river with the Karuk people. From their experiences with the Native people of the Klamath and Salmon rivers we can learn the lessons of history. Ideally the tale would allow us to find a way to live in a world of personal, community, social, national, and international upheavals. The inherent value of this book includes the keen insight of what it takes to see each other from both a distance and under a microscope, to examine how our own values shadow our vision. The ability to see ourselves as part of a continuum of people that connects each of us one to another has allowed the Karuk people to exist from past to present.

My great aunt Violet Super always said that once you drank of the Salmon River, you would always return. The beauty of Karuk country remains a part of all those who travel the rivers. By sharing the story of Mary Arnold and Mabel Reed we are all returning to the Salmon, and reflecting on and reliving the history of both the Karuk people and the United States at a time of change.

Let the song of the grasshopper clear the mist of time and allow you to share this story of connection and learning.

Introduction

Susan Bernardin

In 1980 Andrew Genzoli, a local historian, newspaper columnist, and educator in Humboldt County, California, facilitated the reprint of a beloved regional classic: Mary Ellicott Arnold and Mabel Reed's *In the Land of the Grasshopper Song: Two Women in the Klamath River Indian Country in 1908–09.* It was fitting that he was the one to do so: his review in the *Humboldt Times* had first alerted area residents of the book's publication in 1957. Moreover, his inclusion of Arnold and Reed's mailing address ensured that readers could reciprocate the authors' stories by offering some of their own. Among Arnold and Reed's papers are several dozen letters by readers who sent updates and reminiscences of family members mentioned in *Grasshopper Song.* This reissue of the 1980 Bison Books edition acknowledges the region's unabated interest in this book, underscored most recently with the text's adaptation by the locally based, internationally acclaimed theatre company and school Dell'Arte. Its touring production of *In the Land of the Grasshopper Song* included the very communities where much of the action in the book unfolds—Karuk ancestral homelands, at and near the confluence of the Klamath and Salmon rivers.

This edition of *In the Land of the Grasshopper Song* offers a new foreword, introduction, and afterword that together underscore the book's complex and ongoing role in Karuk tribal history, as well as in broader regional and national stories of cross-cultural relationships. These three perspectives recognize the extraordinarily challenging circumstances that awaited the two women in the communities of Karuk tribal members and settler families. The daily challenges of Karuk adaptation, survival, and continuance witnessed by these two outsiders make *In the Land of the Grasshopper Song* a living text of lessons still vital today, over a century later. While the foreword by André Cramblit and afterword by Terry Supahan suggest contemporary Karuk perspectives about *Grasshopper Song*'s ongoing legacy, this introduction briefly addresses readers' long-held questions about the authors and *their* story: what brought them to northwestern California in the first place, why they left after only two years, and how they determined to write this book nearly five decades later.

Following years of fruitless attempts to interest either university or commercial presses, Arnold and Reed financed the publication of *In the Land of the Grasshopper Song* with Vantage Press in 1957. Although read by anthropologists and writers such as Oliver LaFarge and Ruth Underhill and reviewed in *Publishers Weekly*, *Grasshopper Song* did not reach a wide audience, its circulation largely limited to Arnold's own distribution efforts. In fact, until the Bison Books reprint in 1980, copies were scarce, especially after *Grasshopper Song* went out of print a few years after publication. Its release, however, capped over fifty years of astonishingly varied activism that was shaped in large part by Arnold and Reed's two-year tenure in the lower Klamath River region of northwestern California. Their very presence in the region cannot be understood apart from ruinous federal Indian policies of the late nineteenth and early twentieth centuries.

Just sixty years before the women's arrival, catastrophe ensued after miners and other newcomers moved into far northern California. Like much of California, the origins of Humboldt County and neighboring counties are inseparable from the extermination of Native peoples through massacres, roundups, and removals. Local and regional campaigns against Native peoples following statehood in 1850, including a sanctioned system of de facto slavery, were reinforced by broader federal policies aimed at the same end: the eradication of culturally and linguistically distinct sovereign Native nations and the appropriation of their lands.

Arnold and Reed arrived in the region courtesy of the field matron program, established by the then-named Office of Indian Affairs in 1890 as part of its sweeping efforts to assimilate American Indians, efforts that included the infamous Dawes Allotment Act of 1887 and compulsory attendance at Indian boarding schools. Part of a broader cultural project that Amy Kaplan has labeled elsewhere as "manifest domesticity," the field matron program recruited white middle-class women "to instruct Indian women in duties of the household; assist and encourage them in bettering their homes, and taking proper care of their children; and incite among Indians generally aspirations for improvement in their life—morally, intellectually, socially, and religiously."[1] Although Native women also served as field matrons, the decades-long program favored those perceived as exemplars of Christian piety and domestic virtue.

Widely held assumptions about Native women as "beasts of burden" and "drudges" had already propelled white middle-class women to the forefront of national Indian reform. Members of the Women's National Indian Association (WNIA), founded in 1879, viewed themselves as rescuing Native women from the throes of savagery. In the words of influential WNIA leader Amelia Quinton, "To go among the women of these destitute tribes to minister to their great sufferings from barbarism, to enlighten their physical, mental, and spiritual ignorance is a work imperatively needed."[2] These activists used what the era's policymakers deemed the "Indian problem" to their advantage, capitalizing on their prescribed role as "proper" women to enter fields of employment on reservations and in boarding schools. The field matron program highlights the paradox of white middle-class women finding personal and professional fulfillment outside their own homes by entering the homes of Native families. At the 1892 meeting of the Lake Mohonk Conference of Friends of the Indian, Emily S. Cook declared that field matrons "give the Indian woman an idea of what can and should be in a home." She equated their role with that of a missionary, and she anticipated "a contagion of home-making on the reservation."[3]

Cook could not have expressed the situation more accurately in suggesting the contagion spread by policymakers' zealous dismissal of Native family life. Not surprisingly, many field matrons arrived in Native communities with little understanding of the values they encountered and little preparation for *actual* needs, especially in healthcare. *Grasshopper Song* recounts Reed and Arnold's two-year experience as wayward field matrons in 1908 and 1909. This regional classic offers a startling point of view notably absent in most written accounts by non-Natives from this era: well-humored stories of relationships, conflicts, and interactions among many locally well-remembered families—Karuk, Hupa, Yurok, and non-Native—many of whose descendants still live in northwestern California. While Arnold and Reed's work was dictated by their participation in larger systems of cultural appropriation and assimilation, the two women also forged relationships within communities in Karuk homelands, relationships that at times defy expectations of colonial encounters.

The two women's difficulty in communicating the complexity of their experiences is expressed in the very form of the narrative. Simply put, *Grasshopper Song* is an astonishing hybrid text: part travelogue, part ethnography, part frontier bildungsroman, part feminist western. The authors' subversion of narrative conventions available to them parallels their refusal to fully abide by the conventions of their position as Victorian ladies and as field matrons. *Grasshopper Song* not only gleefully subverts the era's expectations for white women, but as a reverse acculturation narrative, it holds up Karuk values as vastly superior to the ones the two women were paid to disseminate.

Lifelong activists, Reed and Arnold were perhaps more poised than other women to refashion their public role as domesticating agents of the U.S. government. Mary Arnold's papers, along with over one hundred unpublished pages from the original manuscript, help us understand why she and Reed first enlisted as field matrons, far from their homes in the Northeast. Both women were born in 1876 and grew up in two close-knit families in New Jersey. At age sixteen, the two women decided "to share all our respective belongings to the dismay of both families."[4] In an autobiographical statement included among her papers, Arnold notes, "At the age of 16 I made three important decisions: 1) Not to marry 2) A lifelong association with Mabel Reed 3) a business career." Their lifelong partnership included several years of farming on the Reeds' fifty-five acres near Raritan: "[We] reduced our skirts to knee length. . . . Took plow in hand (in that day and age considered not a seemly occupation for young ladies)."[5] Although the farming venture proved unsuccessful, Arnold credited their experience with giving them "iron constitutions" while freeing them from the "ills" of being "mid-Victorian ladies."[6] Notably, just two years later, they left their jobs in model tenement housing in New York City to go "adventuring" in California. Their visit with Arnold's cousin Annie Bidwell, widow of John Bidwell, one of the first Anglo settlers in the Sacramento region, would prove transformative. Annie Bidwell, a prominent leader in the Women's National Indian Association and the Northern California Indian Association, introduced them to C. E. Kelsey, agent for Indians in northern California. After asking him for jobs in the "roughest" part of Indian Country, the women found themselves traveling up the coast to Eureka, where they began a grueling trail ride of several days through the coastal mountains to the confluence of the Klamath and Salmon rivers.

Among a handful of white women resident in the region, they joined a dispersed network of field matrons in the Yurok communities of Weitchpec and Requa and the Hupa community at Hoopa Valley Reservation. When Reed and Arnold had to dispense with their "best" shirtwaists and "elaborate, trimmed hats" on their grueling journey to Somes Bar and Katimiin, at the center of the Karuk universe, the authors also dispensed with the traps and trappings of white femininity. Their sly awareness of clothes and manners as culturally enforced norms underlines their subsequent actions as field matrons. When it was necessary to impress some settlers, the women played up their status as white ladies; when it was necessary to gain credibility among others, they impressed by virtue of their ability to ford rivers and navigate treacherously steep trails on horseback. While Arnold and Reed pleased their supervisors so much that they received As on their field matron "report cards," they also came to respect many Karuk values and perspectives as superior to those of their own culture.

More specifically, both women shed conventional attitudes they had carried toward American Indians, recognizing instead their own responsibility to "mend their manners." As they observed with humor and insight the ironies, paradoxes, discomforts, and ugliness of cross-cultural coexistence, they also saw that their presence in the region was no game. The women ultimately found no humor in the clear constraints of their position *as* women in a so-

ciety with little interest in the future of Native peoples. Writing of
their unease during their travels elsewhere in the region, where
"women have not much chance in this white man's country," Arnold and Reed echo statements they had made regarding the Karuks' lack of legal recourse in securing rights to their land. While
aware of the privileges they wielded as "white ladies," Arnold and
Reed were also clear about their powerlessness to change local attitudes about Native peoples or the legal system. It was this very
frustration over their ineffectuality in providing meaningful and
sustained legal redress that propelled the two women to turn to
other outlets of social activism, closer to their own home.

After leaving the lower Klamath River region in 1909, Reed
and Arnold brought their humor and considerable managerial
and accounting skills to a startling range of activist and progres-
sive initiatives, making them leaders in the cooperative movement.
They first spent several years creating healthy, budget-conscious
dining options for students at Cornell University, then later managed a major cooperative organization in New York City that en-
compassed up to eleven cafeterias and a large office building. After
a meeting with Father Jimmy Tompkins, a leader in cooperative
movements in Nova Scotia, they moved to the Canadian province
to help finance and design housing developments for coal miners. So admired were the women that one of the developments was
named "Reedsville." From there Arnold and Reed turned to cod
fishermen in Newfoundland and lobster fishermen in Maine, helping them to launch credit unions. Late in life, Arnold indicated in
autobiographical notes that their seemingly disparate career choic-
es were linked by their self-fashioned role as outsiders coming into
communities, working to help people reclaim their self-sufficiency.

In 1942, decades after they left northwestern California, Arnold and Reed started writing what they called "Indian letters":
their account of their time as field matrons. Ostensibly based on
letters home—only a few of which survive—the book took shape
while they were busy directing and producing a film titled *Turn
of the Tide*, in which lobster fishermen share the economic challenges facing them. At the same time, the women were asked to
visit the Japanese American internment camp in Poston, Arizona,
to evaluate the possible involvement of cooperative organizations.

Taken together—the drafting of *Grasshopper Song*, the filming of *Turn of the Tide*, and their trip to Arizona—Arnold and Reed's varied tasks in the 1940s underscore the surprising range of their efforts to advocate for diverse communities. Moreover, at every major installment of their careers, Arnold and Reed turned to different genres—plays, books, even film—out of a desire to build broader community participation in and understanding of peoples' legal, economic, and social concerns. That they felt compelled to make sense of their experiences with Karuk tribal members in a book published after nearly fifty years of activism elsewhere suggests the enduring inspiration they had gained early in their careers. In the last years of their lives (Reed died in 1962; Arnold in 1968), both women turned once again to activism aimed at publicizing disastrous federal Indian policies such as termination and regional disasters such as the building of the Kinzua Dam and ensuing flooding of the Seneca reservation in Pennsylvania. Their correspondence with leading American Indian intellectual D'Arcy McNickle shows their interest in community development projects on the Navajo reservation. Arnold was especially active in the Friends (Quaker) Indian Committee, and she developed lectures on Indian rights for schools and community organizations.

When Arnold and Reed started receiving letters at their home in Moylan, Pennsylvania, from relatives and friends of the many people featured in the book, they experienced an unforeseen outcome of their writing: the responses of those they had written about. As a book about the complexities of community relationships and the possibilities of overcoming cultural divides, *Grasshopper Song* has generated feedback that continues today, both from Native and non-Native residents of the region. Beyond simply writing back, some residents even met Arnold and Reed. Beloved physician and community leader Dr. Richard Ricklefs, from Hoopa Valley, and his wife, Elsie Gardner Ricklefs, a former Hupa tribal chair, visited Arnold at her home in Pennsylvania in the early 1960s. In a representative letter to Betty Allen, Arnold writes:

> After we had left the Klamath country, it was as though the mountains had actually closed behind us, cutting us off from our friends and all the people and places we had cared about.

For a few years we had messages from our Indian friends (such as, "This is me, Annie" on a postcard). Then a long, long silence for over 45 years. And then suddenly, with the publication of the *Grasshopper Song*, letters and more letters. From all the old familiar places: Eureka and Arcata, and Blue Lake. Hoopa and Orleans and Somesbar. Yreka and Etna. And now yours from Willow Grove. We loved the people from the Rivers very much and though it was true that most of the time we "were scared enough to satisfy anybody," we loved the mountains and the rivers and summer and winter, the long, long days on the trail and, you can have no notion of what it has meant to us to have places and people come alive again.[7]

At the same time, the history of this book's reception in northwestern California extends the unforeseen outcomes of the cross-cultural experiences mapped out in its pages. When I first read *Grasshopper Song*, I found it valuable for the authors' subversion of gender roles and their surprisingly open critique of American settler society. Yet, when I first visited the area in 1996, I found to my surprise that *Grasshopper Song* occupies an important place in Karuk tribal history. I learned that many people have adopted this book on their own terms, claiming it as a vital source of family, community, and tribal stories. The often wryly humorous stories featured in the book tell about feuds, affairs, daily experiences, and lessons whose meanings remain vital today. The late Ramona Starritt, who knew many of the people named in *Grasshopper Song*, told me that the book is "funny in its happenings," remembering how much her family laughed over the incidents related in the narrative. As a young child, she met the field matrons, even remembering what food her grandmother had prepared for their visit.

When Arnold and Reed observed that many Karuks selectively adapted elements of settler culture, but "the influence of the white men came to an end" regarding core Karuk values, the women forecast the ultimate failure of the program that had sent them to the lower Klamath River region. While powerless in the early twentieth century to change the political and legal status of the Karuks with whom they lived, the two women left a written record of Karuk resilience whose legacy continues. Shortly after Reed died, Arnold

sent a letter to health educator Viola Pfrommer and D'Arcy Mc-
Nickle, to whom she also sent about $4,000 to support their efforts
in Native communities. Arnold's letter speaks of her deeply held
sense of accountability, forged during her two-year stay in Karuk
communities:

> This is the small part of a payment I owe the Indians. When
> we left Klamath country, I was a member of an Indian family.
> Not merely the people of Ieesrum, but all their connections
> up and down river, like the Sandy Bars. When it was "big wa-
> ter," and we had to cross the Klamath, the Sandy Bars put
> us across at the risk of their lives. At the "big dance" in Or-
> leans and Johnny Allen was out to get Steve, it was our job to
> see that Steve didn't get killed. Then we came away. We were
> pretty sure that some of our Indian friends needed money . .
> . but jobs in New York those days didn't pay much and we had
> no money to send. Then one by one our friends were gone
> and the debt remains unpaid.[8]

In her efforts to settle her sense of debt by passing funds on for
other Indians "in need of help," Arnold demonstrated just how
much she had learned and remembered from a mere two years living and working with Karuk tribal members.

Like *Grasshopper Song* itself, the story of bringing this new edition
to life has involved the forging of relationships. I acknowledge
with respect the many people who have helped to carry this story
along. I am very grateful to the late Marian and David Elkinton,
Dr. Richard Ricklefs, Ramona Starritt, Minerva Starritt, and Violet Super for sharing their stories about Arnold and Reed and the
book. I thank as well Phil and Sue Sanders and Leaf Hillman for
their stories and insights. At so many stages, Joan Berman, Special
Collections librarian, and Edie Butler, Special Collections assistant
at Humboldt State University, have shared their expertise, kindness, and encouragement. Merry Phillips's continuing hospitality
and friendship have been a gift. Rita Falls and C. J. Croce were a
vital part of this project's inception in 1996. The archival research
undertaken for this project has benefitted from the assistance of
Christopher Densmore, curator of the Friends Historical Library

at Swarthmore College, as well as staff at the Schlesinger Library, Radcliffe Institute, Harvard University. Grants from the McKnight Foundation, SUNY Oneonta, and the American Philosophical Society gave welcome support to this ongoing project. Finally, enduring gratitude to Jeanerette Jacups-Johnny for her good humor, patience, and friendship.

The spelling of people's names and place locations in *Grasshopper Song* reflects common usage in English of the period. Thus, for example, Mary Arnold and Mabel Reed use the terms *Karok* instead of *Karuk* and *Kot-e-meen* instead of the now-accepted *Katimiin*. For an introduction to the Karuk language and Karuk ways of knowing, see Julian Lang's *Ararapíkva, Creation Stories of the People: Traditional Karuk Indian Literature from Northwestern California* (Berkeley: Heyday Books, 1994).

Notes

1. Thomas J. Morgan, Commissioner of Indian Affairs, 1892 Annual Report of Indian Affairs.

2. Quoted in Valerie Sherer Mathes, "Nineteenth-Century Women and Reform: The Women's National Indian Association," *American Indian Quarterly* 14, no. 1 (1990): 1–18.

3. Emily S. Cook, "The Field Matron," in *Proceedings of the Thirteenth Annual Meeting of the Lake Mohonk Conference of the Friends of the Indian* (Washington DC: Government Printing Office, 1894), 58–59.

4. Mary Ellicott Arnold Papers, Folder 1, Box 1, Schlesinger Library, Radcliffe Institute, Harvard University.

5. Mary Ellicott Arnold Papers, Folder 1, Box 1, Schlesinger Library, Radcliffe Institute, Harvard University.

6. Mary Ellicott Arnold Papers, A-122, Vol. 8, Schlesinger Library, Radcliffe Institute, Harvard University.

7. Letter dated May 13, 1958, Mary Ellicott Arnold Papers, RG 5, Box 4, Ser. 2, Swarthmore Friends Historical Library.

8. Letter dated December 15, 1962, Mary Ellicott Arnold Papers, RG 2, Box 5, Ser. 2, Swarthmore Friends Historical Library.

Foreword

This story of Indian country in 1908-1909 is a true story, with everything put down exactly as it happened.

The Karoks, with whom we lived for two years, were a small band of about seven hundred Indians of Hokan stock. They were bow-and-arrow Indians and had no knowledge of textiles or pottery.

During the gold rush, in 1852, nearly a thousand white men came into the Klamath country; but when the easy gold was gone, about two years later, these miners left for richer diggings, and only a handful of squaw men remained on the Rivers.

When we came to the Klamath country, about fifty-four years later, the superficial effect of this great influx of white men was still evident. Karok Indians wore the clothes of the white man, built their cabins with tools, rejoiced in the rather questionable advantages of tea, coffee, and sugar, and gladly used white flour instead of acorn meal. They also used white nomenclature. The miners had called the Indians they worked with by familiar white names: Tom, Henry, or Joe. When the sons of these Indians grew up, they became Jim Tom, Pete Henry, and Little Joe.

But with these obvious changes in custom, the influence of the white man came to an end. In the sixty miles between Happy Camp and Orleans, the social life of the Indian—what he believed and the way he felt about things—was very little affected by white influence. The older Indians still had the spaced tattoo marks on their forearms, by which they could measure the length of the string of wampum required to buy a wife. And though strings of wampum were only used for ceremonial purposes, and Indians bought their wives with the white man's gold, Indian marriage still was the established custom on the Rivers.

It was true that none of the younger squaws had the traditional three tattoo marks on the chin. But in regard to birth, marriage, death, the status of women, feuds, *apruan* (similar to our witchcraft), the satisfaction of injury or murder by a fixed money payment, and other customs, the Indians on the Rivers in 1908 thought and acted as their fathers had done before them.

An Indian characteristic that impressed us very much was what we would call good breeding, a code of manners and feeling that stood out in sharp contrast to the lower social level of the average pioneer white man. Even more surprising, and something for which we were quite unprepared, was the intellectual capacity of the average Indian. Men like Steve and Bernard Jerry would have been unusual in any race or country. But the average squaw, well beyond school age, displayed a capacity to learn and an application and mental discipline not only far beyond the pioneer women we knew, but beyond our own friends and acquaintances of the same age back east.

The white men we knew on the Rivers were pioneers of the Old West. Old Bob Elliott and Dutch Henry had crossed the plains in prairie schooners and had never seen a railroad or listened to a steam whistle. Papa Frame, with forty other white men, had come into the Apache country in Arizona in 1845. Fifteen years later, Papa Frame and one other white man were the only ones left to come out alive. All around us was gold country, the land of the saloon and of the six-shooter. Our friends and neighbors carried guns as a matter of course, and used them on occasion. But the account given in these pages is not of these occurrences but of everyday life on the frontier in an Indian village, and what Indians and badmen did and said when they were not engaged in wiping out their friends and neighbors.

It is also an account of our own two years in Indian country where, in the sixty-mile stretch between Happy Camp and Orleans, we were the only white women, and most of the time quite scared enough to satisfy anybody.

We have felt that the value of this story lies in the authentic account it gives of the customs and habits of thought of Indians who could remember what life was like before the coming of the white man, and its picture of conditions in what was the last of the old frontier. We have therefore made no changes in the original text. What is given here stands as it was written in 1909.

We would spur our horses, after a long day on the trail, because the sun was going down behind Frank Offield's mountain, and would sit fearfully on our saddles in the gathering darkness because of possible panthers on the limbs of trees over our heads. (There was no reason, as we saw it, why all the panthers in the country should confine their attentions to the mailriders.) And when, finally, we did come safe through the thick chaparral to our own little house, we would thankfully close the door, eat anything we could find, and write down exactly what had happened since we set out in the morning.

We would then compare our two separate accounts in order to arrive, as nearly as possible, at a true statement of what our friends had said and done in the Indian country in the year 1909, in what was called the roughest place in the United States.

MARY ELLICOTT ARNOLD
MABEL REED

Moylan, Pensylvania
July, 1955

CONTENTS

Oregon Line

Happy Camp o

Yreka o

Klamath River

Siwillup o

C A L I F O R N I A

Lees Bar o

Ossi-puk o

Pich-pichi o   Kot-e-meen
                 o Somesbar
Orleans o

Forks of
Salmon

Salmon River

PACIFIC OCEAN

Klamath River

Witchpec o

Hoopa
Reservation

Hoopa o

Trinity River

o Eureka

Sketch map of the Rivers,
in the Coast Range,
Siskiyou County, California

CHAPTER I

The Unmapped Way, and How, Finally, We Hit the Trail, and the Mountains Closed Around Us

The clerk at Thomas Cook and Sons leaned his elbows on the desk.

"I don't know whether I can help you much," he said. "Not many people want to go to Somesbar. It is up in the northern part of the state just below the Oregon line. See, here it is on the map. Yes, that is the place, here in the Coast Range, about an even distance from Yreka on the railroad and Eureka on the ocean. But I wouldn't advise you to try the railroad. Good deal of snow up there now. I'd like to help you ladies out but we don't have much information about the country up there. It's mostly Indians; and they don't come to us when they travel." He gave us a very engaging grin.

"Tell you what I will do, though. Sell you two tickets from San Francisco to Eureka. Get you a nice stateroom on the *Pomona*. She sails Saturday. That's five days from today. Give you plenty of time to get ready. Then when you get to Eureka, it ought to be easy to find some folks who will tell you how to get up into the mountains."

The *SS Pomona* was a small boat and there were not many passengers. The rain pattered on the deck as we came up the gangplank. Tamalpais was only a faint blur in the mist. Although we did not know it at the time, we were to be in sore need of Indian Steve and the Grasshopper Song for several months to come. As we left the Golden Gate behind us and turned up the coast, a wave flapped against the *Pomona's* side and she began to roll. The shore was very close, with high cliffs and steep grassy slopes. We stood for a long time by the handrail, and then we sat on the steps that led from our stateroom to the deck. There did not seem anywhere else to go.

As night fell it grew very cold. We sat huddled close together for warmth, but we did not feel like going to bed. We were wondering how we would find our way up into the mountains. We wondered what Somesbar would be like. It had been easy enough to point to it on the map, but as we thought about it from the deck of the *Pomona* it seemed very far away, and we were not sure what we should find when we got there.

In any case, we had our appointments. We had looked at them again when we were in our stateroom. They were dated January, 1908. They said they were glad to advise us that Mary Ellicott Arnold and Mabel Reed had been appointed as Field Matrons in the United States Indian Service, Department of the Interior. These ladies would receive thirty dollars a month each, and traveling expenses, and they should proceed without delay to Somesbar, California.

When we left New Jersey to visit Cousin Annie Bidwell on her big ranch in the Sacramento Valley, we hoped we should see some Indians. There had been a small band of Indians on the ranch, but we had found them rather disappointing. We felt that Indians off somewhere in the mountains would probably act differently from those in Chico, in the Sacramento Valley, living in a neat little village surrounded by acres of fruit trees.

A Mr. Kelsey was staying with Cousin Annie at the time we were there. We learned he was Special Agent for all Indians in California, and we told him we should like to see what a really rough country was like. Mr. Kelsey looked at our pleated skirts, seven yards around the bottom, and down to within an inch of the floor, and his eye hardened.

"Shall I send you to the roughest field in the United States?" he asked.

I think he expected us to refuse. But of course we did not refuse. It was the chance we had been hoping for.

All the passengers were on the deck of the *Pomona* the next morning. We were across the bar and in the bay and everyone was saying that we had got off pretty easy. Right before us lay the town, and for some distance around the town were flat fields, gray and indistinct in the driving rain. But it was not at the town we looked as we leaned against the handrail. Behind the strip of flat country were mountains. Their dim outline, seen through the mist and rain, seemed incredibly high. And as far as we could follow them with our eyes, they seemed without break.

There was only one person in Eureka whose name we knew.

"Go to Mrs. Nealy," Cousin Annie had said. "She belongs to the WCTU, and I am sure she is an excellent woman."

Mrs. Nealy received us without enthusiasm. Did she know anyone who could give us some information about Somesbar, we asked. Did she know anyone who had ever been there?

Mrs. Nealy brightened up. She said that Mr. Lord went there very often. In fact, he used to live there. Mrs. Lord was obliged to bring up the children all by herself. There were six boys and a girl, and Mrs. Lord was a lovely Christian woman. Maybe we had better come into the back room and she would find out whether Mr. Lord was at home.

Mr. Lord was at home. We heard a loud friendly voice on the telephone. In a few minutes Mr. Lord came over. He sat down and began to tell us all about the country. We must first go to Hoopa and see the Indian agent, Mr. Kyselka. Then we could go on to Somesbar with the mail-rider.

"Of course," said Mr. Lord, "you know how to ride. A woman went up there some time ago and had difficulty in keeping up. I think the mailrider had to leave her behind."

We asked anxiously what had become of her.

"I seem to have forgotten," said Mr. Lord. "But I don't think you will have any real trouble. The trails are clearly marked and there are places you can stay. You should get along all right." He smiled and got up. "Good-by," he said. "I like that country. Maybe we shall run across each other some time, if you stay up there."

The next morning we took the train for Korbel. We supposed that Korbel must be a town or a village at the end of the line, but when the conductor called "This is Korbel; all out," we found there were only three or four large buildings, with the sign "North River Lumber Company" on one of them. One of the buildings seemed to be a sort of store, where we asked a clerk whether he could direct us to the hotel. He did not look up from what he was doing but said briefly we should go across the street.

We went across the street to another building and found a man working over some papers. When he saw us he showed obvious annoyance.

"You don't belong here," he said. "They ought to look out for you at the office."

We thought the office must be the post office we had noticed in a little coop in the center of the store. While we waited our turn, a young man went by and I asked him about a hotel.

"Wait a minute, he said, "and I'll get just the right man for you."

After a short wait, a lean and unhappy man appeared and said we might come upstairs. We followed him down a long hall with rooms on both sides. He put us into one of the rooms and left us.

We left our bags in the room and went downstairs again. The only person we could see to talk to was the man in the post office. He was busy sorting mail but he would look up every now and then and answer our questions.

He supposed the mailrider would come in about five that afternoon. . . . Probably he would tell us anything we wanted to know . . . No, he wouldn't go out again tonight . . . Certainly we could not take our trunk . . . Nor our suitcases. . . . He would advise us to pack in flour sacks. It might be they could find some for us in the store . . . He was sorry but he did not know how many pounds we would be allowed to take with us. Probably not many. . . . About the trunk? Why, he supposed it could stay here in Korbel . . . Of course, they would not assume any responsibility for it. It would probably be safe enough. . . . He was afraid it would be quite impossible to have the trunk sent upstairs. . . . Where was the trunk? He couldn't say. Maybe in the warehouse. . . . Yes, he supposed we might look for it, if we liked. . . . If we could find someone to let us in to the warehouse, maybe we could do our repacking there. . . .

The warehouse was dark and very chill. We sat on the floor and sorted our things into little piles. When there seemed to be enough things in any one of the piles, we stuffed them into a flour sack.

We took off the suits we had bought before we left New York. When you pack a pleated skirt that is seven yards around the bottom, it is wise to stitch down the pleats. We sat on the cold cement floor in the dim light and stitched down all the pleats. We put our suitcases in the trunk. Then we carefully folded our skirts and put them on top of the suitcases. Our hats were elaborate, trimmed hats that sat on the top of the head and were attached to the hair with a long hatpin. We wrapped them up carefully and put them in the trunk, on the top of our skirts. Then we sorted out our best shirtwaists and some of our newest high, white collars and packed them carefully around the hats. All the remaining shirtwaists and collars we tried to pack in a flour sack without mussing them.

We took the divided skirts that Mabel had made for us

in San Francisco and put them on. They seemed to be the
right length, just a little below our ankles. Mabel had
bought a sort of cowboy hat in San Francisco. I didn't seem
to have anything that would do so I went out and bought
a little round rubber hat in Korbel. We had picked out
serviceable-looking shirtwaists and white, starched collars
and we put them on. Then with some difficulty we got into
high boots. We locked the trunk and put on our hats and
sweaters.

We filled all the flour sacks from the little piles of cloth-
ing on the floor. There didn't seem anything else we could
do so we sat on the trunk and looked out of the warehouse
door at the buildings in Korbel. We thought we had better
wait there until the mailrider came in at five.

The man in the post office had told us that the mailrider was a half-breed. I kept thinking of all the things I
had read about half-breeds. But there were two of us, and
probably those stories were just written to sell. At least I
hoped so.

It had grown very dark and the rain was coming down
in earnest when we heard the sound of voices and could
just make out the dim shapes of a horse and wagon and
two men standing outside the door to the store. They
didn't pay much attention to our questions when we ran
over to speak to them, but we made out that the mail would
leave at seven in the morning. One of them said we had
better be ready. Then he went into the store and shut the
door.

We stood uncertainly for a minute or two in the darkness and rain and thought about supper. We should have
liked some supper, but no one in Korbel seemed to care what
became of us. At least we had a room with a bed in it. Maybe
it would be best just to go to bed and wait until tomorrow.

And then our spirits rose. We had made the first lap
of the journey. We were on our way. Ahead of us were the
mountains that we had seen from the deck of the *Pomona*.

And somewhere in the far distance, beyond the mountain's farthest rim, was Somesbar and the Indian country.

The road was level as we left the dim shapes of the buildings of the North California Lumber Company behind us and turned east toward the mountains of the Coast Range. Then the light grew stronger. We could see occasional cleared places with little cabins and patches of cultivated land. A few miles out of Korbel, the road became more stony and we began to climb. It was broad daylight by this time and a soft, fine rain blew in our faces. When, in the darkness, we had run over from what they called a hotel to a dim blur by one of the buildings, we had expected the kind of stage you see in pictures of the West, but all we found was a quite ordinary spring wagon. The back was piled high with mailbags, and as we came up the mailrider was stuffing in our flour sacks, and those flour sacks held every single thing we were taking into the Indian country.

The seat of the spring wagon was not very wide for three of us, and all along that part of my raincoat that was nearest the wheel I felt the water beginning to come through. I tried to tuck myself under the rubber blanket, and for a time it would seem to work, and then the rain would find its way in at another spot. As we climbed higher and higher, we began to catch glimpses of Korbel, far below us. Still higher we could see the full stretch of the Mad River Valley, with long streamers of mist along the mountains. The road grew very rocky, and we had to brace our feet as the spring wagon swayed and lurched when we came to a bad place. The rain was now falling in a steady, persistent downpour. We were thankful when the mailrider drew in his horses and said, "Bair's ranch. Stop here for lunch."

The mailrider drove off with his team, and we went up the steps of the ranch house and pounded on the door. No one answered, and after knocking repeatedly we opened the door and went in. There was a room to the right of the hall and in it was an enormous fireplace, in which several young trees were crackling. We stood as close to the fire as we could and turned as though we were on a spit, trying to dry out our skirts. Neither the rubber coats nor the rubber blanket had worked out very well. Just as we began to steam nicely, a bearded Englishman put his head in the door and lamented that there were no lady folks at the ranch but that we were free to use his bedroom.

The dining room was chill, and we were left to ourselves while the mailrider was evidently enjoying the comfort of the kitchen. We could hear talk and laughter and the clatter of chairs. There was some meat on the table but no forks to eat it with, so we passed it by and centered our attention on tea and bread and pie, which could be drunk or eaten with the fingers. This was a great mistake, for we learned later that the meat was bear meat, and whatever the method of approach we wished we had eaten it. After lunch, we went back to the great fireplace and took down our hair and braided it down our backs, and then went out. We found the mailrider saddling three horses in an open shed. Two other animals already had packs on their backs and were loaded high with mailbags.

As the mailrider leaned down and cinched one of the animals, we breathed a prayer that we should be able to mount without discredit. At Cousin Annie's ranch we had not dared to tackle her extremely spirited animals, but one day we had hired a small, stout pony for an afternoon. We took him well out of sight, in one of the orchards, and Mabel climbed on him and rode the length of the orchard and then brought him back to me. I climbed on him in my turn and gravely walked the length of the orchard and back. Then Mabel took another turn. All afternoon we mounted and dismounted and rode our little stint. But he was a rather small pony and the horses now before us looked extremely tall.

The mailrider straightened up and beckoned. Mabel went forward, put her foot in the stirrup, wavered a minute, and then she was in the saddle. I prayed hard, put my foot in the stirrup, hopped, hopped again, and then managed to get my leg over the flour sack fastened to the saddle. I was on. I found the stirrup with my right foot, and waited. The Bairs came out and waved to us. The mailrider turned his horse straight up the mountain. We were off.

It was raining steadily but we had no time to notice it. Before us was the mountain. There was no sign of road or trail. The brow of the mountain, up which we climbed, was bare of trees and brush. It was rocky, and through it ran ridges and ravines. Down these ravines flowed little watercourses. One of these watercourses seemed to be the trail, and up it we splashed. My horse would bunch himself, then with a heave would scramble up a steep incline. Every time he bunched himself I thought he was going to leave both me and the saddle behind. But by the grace of God we clung on.

The mailrider went first, a squat figure in oilskins, then came Mabel, and I followed. The watercourse was now a deep gully and our horses pitched and plunged as they tried to keep their feet in the rocky bed of the stream. We were going up Bald Mountain and on all sides of us was a wonderful smooth grassy slope. As we climbed and climbed, the valley, with Bair's in the mist below, grew smaller and smaller until, as we pitched down into a little cleft in the mountain, they disappeared from our view. We could now see other mountains closing in behind us. All signs of the valley had disappeared. The rain drove down, and I found I was beginning to be a little less scared. I know I must be less scared because I began to notice all the places on my raincoat where the water was coming through. My nine-dollar boots were not rainproof; neither was the hat I had bought in Korbel. The rain poured in regardless of the hat and found its way down the back of my neck. It clung there for a moment and then began to make a little waterfall down my backbone. I shifted in my saddle and tried to

get nearer to Mabel's horse, which seemed to be a very long
distance ahead.

Near the top of the mountain a strong wind whistled
past us and I had to cling to my hat, but farther on its
strength diminished. Sometimes the rain would turn into
mist, then the sky would thicken and grow dark again and
the rain would come back. I noticed that the mailrider had
gotten a long distance ahead. Then I saw that he had
stopped his horse and was waving for us to hurry up.

By the time we had caught up with him, he had left
the broad expanse of the grassy slope and was urging his
horse into a narrow little cut on the side of the mountain.
Below this cut was a clean precipice, as far down as the eye
could see. Some brush and a few little trees clung to the
side of the mountain wherever there was a little earth, but
in most places it was a sheer drop. Above this cut the mountain went straight up. You could almost brush it with your
shoulder as you rode. As we got nearer to the mailrider,
we could see that this cut along the side of the mountain
was a narrow trail, and that it was over this trail that we
were expected to ride.We also saw that the mailrider was
angry.

"You can't go on like this," he said. "You fellows have
got to make better time. I'm a half hour behind now and
at this rate we will take all night. You dig in your spurs and
come along."

He then gave his horse a sharp dig and started along the
cut at a quick trot. We expected to see him topple off into
the view. He did not topple over but in a few minutes he
was a very long distance ahead. The rain was very thick
by this time. On all sides were the dim shapes of mountains. The mist cut off the track over which we had come.
Even as we looked, the form of the mailrider and his horse
was becoming very dim in the mist ahead. In another moment we should be alone in the mountains. I did not want
to be alone with Mabel in the mountains. I gingerly dug in

a spur. My horse gave a little jump. I looked apprehensively at the sheer drop beside me and gave my horse another little dig. He began to trot along the narrow ribbon-like trail. For a while the trail was fairly level and then we began to go up and down. It was not one mountain along which the trail led, it was a jumble of mountains. We would slide down a sharp incline, cross a little creek, and struggle up the mountain on the other side. Then we would come out on another narrow cut, with the steep cliff above and the sheer drop below, and try to make a little better time. At first, I was too much alarmed by the character of the trail to notice anything else. I clung to my horse and prayed. My prayer was that he knew what he was about for I certainly did not.

Then I began to notice a large variety of aches and pains. I was very sore where I sat in the saddle. I was very sore all up and down the inside of my legs, where they scraped against the straps of the saddle. I tried to keep my toes in the stirrup, but I no sooner got them nicely planted than my horse gave an unexpected lurch. The next instant my feet bounced as far through the stirrups as they could go and I came down hard in the saddle. It was bad on the level. It was not quite so bad going up hill. But when we came down a hill I began to think that just quietly going off that sheer drop might not be such a bad thing.

After a time we left the mountainside and rode through pines. The air was chill as snow in our faces. The needle-like pines rose straight into the air until we lost sight of them in a slate-gray mist. Everything was still. I could just catch a glimpse of the mailrider's horse ahead as it flicked in and out among the misty trees. Then we began to go down. The slope became steeper. The mailrider and Mabel had disappeared. I forgot the number of my aches. I seized my lines and beat my stumbling horse to its utmost speed. The only thing in life was the necessity of keeping in sight the flying tail of the mailrider's horse. It was not that I particularly liked the mailrider but I hated to think that he might go off and leave us alone by ourselves in the mountains.

By this time I was beginning to get some notion of what I ought to do. When my horse was climbing, I clung to the saddle and rested my legs. When the ground fell away and I went down, if possible I kept off the saddle, rose in my stirrups, and beat my horse. I began to look languidly at mountains and mists and precipices. Speed was the only thing I thought about. And keeping the mailrider in sight.

Meantime, it had grown darker and the mountains were very dusky in the falling light. The trail ran through a little woodland, the trees standing out whitish and ghost-like. The mist was very thick. Only occasionally could I get a glimpse of the mailrider as he wound in and out among the trees. During one of these glimpses he turned and shouted at us.

"Keep up!" he cried. "Keep up! Don't get so far behind. Can't you fellows ride at all?"

I was beginning to have the gravest doubts about it myself. But for all that, I knew I did not like the mailrider. Darn him, anyway. What did he think we were? My own feeling was that we were riding a great deal faster than was either wise or safe. Moreover, if this pace was to keep up much longer, there would be no skin at all on several parts of my body.

Slowly the light faded. We came out again onto a narrow cut, where we could see the dim shapes of mountains. Then the light died out and night closed in. There were tall trees about us now, and we began to go downhill. The mailrider reined in his horse and waited for us.

"There is a good trail from here to Hoopa," he said. "You can't miss it. I'm going on. I've about missed out on my supper now."

Two long hours before, the one thing we had feared was that we might lose the mailrider. Now the one thing we desired was to see the last of him and his horse's tail. Suppose it *was* dark. Suppose we rode and rode and never got anywhere. It could not be nearly so bad as taking off all the skin that was left on our protesting persons.

"Go on," we said to the mailrider, and we slowed our horses to a walk.

It was very dark. The trail led down and down. The horses stumbled and slipped but we did not care. We seemed to have been slipping and sliding down that trail since the beginning of time. We lost all count of time. We tried to sit our horses so as to ease some of the numberless aches and pains that caught us in unexpected places, and clung on. The darkness, the trail, the sharp jounce in the saddle when we struck a rough place—these seemed to go on forever. Suddenly we became aware that we were no longer going downhill. Then we saw a light and passed a house. There were several more dark shapes of houses. A man loomed up ahead of us.

"Where are we?" we asked.

"Where are you?" he replied. "Why, you are in Hoopa. Over there is the house of Mr. Kyselka, the Indian agent. You can see the light in their parlor window."

We mounted the steps of the house very, very carefully. Our legs had quit having any relation to the other parts of us.

All evening we played cards with the kindly Kyselkas and their friends. In the excitement of getting off at Bair's, the flour sack with our shirtwaists and underwear in it had been left behind. We had no other skirts. As we played hand after hand, we dripped. The water formed in little pools at our feet. We could see the people near us eye it with disfavor and draw their skirts away. We did our best, but we saw the room and everything in it through a haze, and the people and the cards seemed a long way off.

And then, at long last, we were allowed to climb the stairs with our dripping skirts, and we were soon in bed.

"Hoopa is in an Indian reservation and there is a large

industrial school here," Mr. Kyselka told us.

We were sitting in his office the day after we had "hit the trail," and, to our surprise, we saw the first little gleam of sunshine since we had left San Francisco.

"But your field will lie outside the reservation," went on Mr. Kyselka. "It includes about two hundred square miles in the forest reserve, and for the most part it lies along the Klamath and Salmon Rivers."

He looked at us and smiled. "Up in that country, they call it 'the Rivers,'" he said. "They never talk of living in the mountains. You will find that they say they live 'on the Rivers,' and that is exactly where they do live. Our records show about seven hundred Indians in your field, but I am not sure how accurate the records are. It is wild country up there and it is hard to get any exact information.

"About your duties, it is a little difficult to say. I think the Government's idea in appointing field matrons is that women will have a civilizing influence. Of course, that is what we want to do—civilize the Indians. As much as possible you want to elevate them and introduce white standards. I think you will find conditions in your field that will strike you as rather deplorable.

"Actually"—he gave us a very friendly look—"I think we shall have to trust to your own good judgment. After you get up into that country, you will have a much better notion of what you ought to do."

It was understood that we should leave the following morning with the mailrider.

"He gets off about five o'clock," Mr. Kyselka told us. "It is about thirty miles to Orleans Bar, and, of course, that will mean a rather long day, but it isn't really a bad trail. I think you ought to be able to trot a good deal of the way," he added.

We thought of the sore places distributed over our persons and tried to hide our dismay.

Mr. Kyselka had told us to arrange with Mr. Mills about

horses for the trip. Mr. Mills tipped back his chair, stretched out his legs, and looked at us.

"First time you ever rode?" he asked, stroking his chin. "Well now, if I was you ladies, I tell you what I'd do. I'd take it just a little bit easy. Yes, just a lit-tle bit easy. You let the mailrider get up at five o'clock, if he feels that way. And you get up when you like and get you a good breakfast. I'll have the horses here waiting for you. Then we'll start out and I'll go along with you two-three miles until we get to the Witchpec trail. Once you're on that, you can't get lost. You keep right along and you'll get there, all right. And you'll find it a lot better than trying to keep up with that harum-scarum Pete Downey," said Mr. Mills decisively.

There are some kindnesses you never forget. After forty years, I remember the gratitude we felt that morning.

There was a little watery sunlight as we rode out of the reservation. Around us was a wide pleasant valley with cultivated fields. Hoopa had been an old army post. It was laid out with dignity and its live oaks were beautiful.

Mr. Mills set an easy pace and watched us critically.

"Now you ladies won't mind my saying you'd come out a bit fresher at the end of the day if you took things a mite easier," he said after we had ridden about a mile down the valley road.

"Sit back on your saddles and take it just as easy as you can. You don't need to sit all crunched up like that. It won't get you to Witchpec any sooner. Sit well back. That's it. Now take it kinda easy. You got all day. Just the tips of your toes in the stirrup. You don't want to get all messed up if that hoss was to roll with you. Now that's better. I guess you'll be all right now, and that's your trail. Just keep on it and take it easy like I told you. Good-by."

He wheeled his horse, waved his hat, and rode back.

For the first hour the trail led through the valley and, as Mr. Mills had advised, we took it as easy as we could.

Then the ground began to rise and we rode over beautiful, bald, grassy hills. Some of the stiffness began to wear away. We settled back in our saddles and had time to look around. Then the trail dropped suddenly and we were in thick woods. There were pines and spruces and madroña and manzanita. The underbrush was very thick. We could see the trail only for a short distance ahead. I was in the lead. The woods were very quiet. On the wet earth, the horses' hoofs made a soft, muffled sound. An hour passed. The trees opened up ahead and closed in behind us. Once I thought I saw a break in the thick bush, and thought we might be coming out, but around a little bend the trees closed in thicker than ever. We went on and on. I wished it had been possible for us to ride side by side but the trail was only a narrow trace, just wide enough for one person. Another hour went by. We met no one to assure us that we were on the right trail. In spite of what Mr. Mills had said, there did seem to be several places where you could turn off. Another hour went by. We slumped down in our saddles and let the horses take their heads.

Suddenly there was light ahead. Yes, it was really an honest-to-goodness break in the trees. We could see a rocky cliff. The woods fell away. We struggled up a little rise, and there, below us, was a great river, turbid and muddy and swift-flowing. The trail came to an end. We stood for a long time watching the water, not quite certain what we ought to do. There was no bridge, and no house in any direction where we could ask. We sat on our horses and looked down at the water. Then we heard a little sound behind us and we turned to see an Indian coming along the trail.

"You cross river?" he asked.

We nodded. He stepped to the edge of the bank and gave a long, musical cry. Then another. After that he stood quietly. The three of us watched the river. Then I noticed a dark spot near the opposite shore. Now it was in the center of the stream. We could see a paddle rise and fall.

The dark blur became a boat with two men in it. It landed just below us. We slid down the bank as one of the men came to meet us.

"You can leave your horses here," he said. "Gist will have 'em looked out for. There's two men will be going back to Hoopa in the morning. You ladies sit right there in the bottom of the dugout. Snow melting in the mountains and that makes the Klamath kinda high, but we'll get you over, all right."

Our first supper on the Rivers was not encouraging. We ate what we could. Several men were eating when we came into the dining room. They looked at their plates while we made the best we could of the meal, but there was a marked sense of relief when we got up and went out. The hotel was small and dingy. There were newspapers between the studs, torn and dirty, and our bed did not look inviting. We were glad that Witchpec was not in our field. There was another field matron at Witchpec. Mr. Kyselka had told us to look her up. Her name was Mrs. Mayhew.

Mrs. Mayhew was a small, stout, active woman. She looked out for the Indians, she said, and doctored them when they were sick. It gave her plenty to do. She tried to stop the drinking but you really couldn't do much with Indians. You had to be pretty firm with them to get along at all. And even then they did pretty much as they pleased. But she kept busy and that was the main thing. Of course, living the way she had, you got to know a lot about sickness. And you had to keep your wits about you. Last year, there was a half-breed going to have a baby. She did what she could but she knew something was wrong. When the baby started to come, it was breeches first. She knew that would never do, so she closed her eyes and prayed hard. Then she put her hands in and turned the baby around. Of course, she was scared, but it was the only thing to do.

That night in the sagging bed we clutched each other and tried to keep warm. The Government had evidently made a mistake when they appointed us as field matrons. If the sort of thing Mrs. Mayhew did was what they wanted, we were just not qualified.

Breakfast proved to be even less inviting than supper. Then the rain was beginning again. Mr. Gist had horses for us and we rode to the store and bought oilcloth. It was all right for us to get wet but our two flour sacks were going to have protection if we could get it for them.

The trail to Orleans Bar looked comfortingly well traveled. An hour out of Witchpec the rain stopped and the mists rolled back up the mountain. All day, the trail followed the Klamath. Sometimes we rode beside the river and then the trail would climb up and up and we would come out on a narrow ledge with the river far below, winding its way through the mountains. We got glimpses of snow caps in the distance. We forgot to feel sore and stiff. We had never seen such a beautiful world before in our lives.

Well before dark, we struck into a broad, smooth track and the valley widened out. The mountains drew back and there were wide stretches that looked like fruit trees and fields. We passed small cabins. Dark-faced women with children in their arms came out and looked at us. The track became a road. There were two stores and something that looked like a hotel. We were in Orleans Bar. That night we slept in a good bed and had food we could eat and were very thankful.

The next day we must again cross the Klamath. There was difficulty in arranging to have horses meet us on the other side, and it was late when we got into the dugout with the mailrider.

"Those are your horses tied to that tree," he told us. "I'll just get you started and then I'll go on. There's a dance up river this evening and I guess the folks would be surprised if I didn't come."

My horse put back his ears when I mounted. He looked uncertain in his temper. I hoped I would do nothing to annoy him. I rode ahead and Mabel followed. The mailrider was a little behind, cinching his horse and loading on mailbags.

"There's a strap dangling down between your horse's legs," called out Mabel, behind me. "I don't think it ought to be there."

The mailrider caught up with us.

"What's the matter?" he asked impatiently.

"Is that strap all right?" Mabel asked.

"Oh, that," said the mailrider. "Well, no. Damn that Indian! They're a shiftless lot. That's the cinch strap. Must have broken. Funny I didn't notice it. Just wait a minute or your saddle will turn with you. You must be careful." He looked at me reprovingly. "You don't want to let a thing like that happen to you on these trails. You never can tell."

We watched him ride off down the trail. I felt a little uncertain. He had fixed the cinch strap and I supposed it was all right. But as the mailrider had said, you never could tell. The trail led through woods and then over a slide. We did not at all like the looks of the slide and neither did our horses but there seemed nothing to do but go on. Part of the mountain had given way and rolled down to the river. There was a great, fresh scar of small stones and debris. The scar stretched from the top of the mountain, at a sharp angle, down to the river. Across it, at the same level as our trail, we could see the marks of hoofs. Evidently the mailrider had gone that way. We held our breath as the horses picked their way across. I never did like the notion of landslides. It seems to me a kind of unchancy way to end up. A few little pebbles rolled down and then I was on the other side. I held my breath while Mabel made it. It was all right; she was across. The trail went up a steep ascent and the woods closed around us.

It was a narrow trail and not well marked. Sometimes we were afraid it was not a trail at all. The dusk fell early, and we went on and on. The trees would crowd close around us and it would suddenly be very dark. Then we would come out on the side of the mountain and see that there still was a faint pink in the sky. As we watched the pink fade out, our hearts sank.

Were we on the right trail? What would happen if we were not? What did you do if you got lost in the mountains?

The last of the pink in the sky disappeared and a little, soft rain blew in our faces. It grew very dark and our horses stumbled a great deal. Horses in such country ought to know what they were about but these horses seemed extremely dumb. They were the kind that would take you off the trail and never know the difference. We went on and on.

Suddenly there was hard ground under the horses' feet. We could hear their hoofs strike on gravel. There was a building ahead of us. We could see its dim outline in the darkness. Another building loomed up, to our right. A door opened and a broad shaft of light lit up the trail. An old man with a white beard stood in a doorway. He held a lamp in his hand and peered out at us as we drew up.

"Can you tell us how far it is to Somesbar?" we asked.

The old man lowered his lamp.

"Why, folks, come right in," he said. "This is Somesbar."

CHAPTER II

Innocents Abroad in the Land of the White Man

We saw Mart Hamill yesterday. He will rent us his house in the Indian rancheria of Kot-e-meen for ten dollars a month. It is true that we hear very bad things about the Hamills. But then everybody here draws you aside and tells you quite scandalous things about everybody else. The Frames warn us against the Hildings. "Wait until you hear *that* story." Hilding drops his voice and says, "Did you hear about Sam? Pretty bad. That time he and Mart Hamill—" It is a long story, all about illicit whiskey, and no one seems to have come out of it with any credit. As we stood outside the house in Kot-e-meen, talking to Mart Hamill, he lowered his voice. Had we heard about Hilding? We hurriedly changed the subject. We had heard about Hilding.

Mart is three-quarters white. To look at him you would not think he had any Indian blood. He is big, blue-eyed, and fair-haired. He can swing an ax to beat anyone we ever saw. He is so very big and strong that everyone else looks small beside him. He has a very warm, engaging smile and he is gentle and a little shy. Sam is strongly against our renting Mart's house and going to live in Kot-e-meen. We can't make out whether it is because of the illicit-whiskey deal that he and Mart got mixed up in or because of the time they had the dance and Mart got thrown out of the hotel. Mr. Hilding told us about that. There was much he seemed to feel he couldn't talk about before ladies, but we were able to make out that Mart had no sooner been bounced out than he bounced in again and knocked out most of the guests, and they had some trouble getting him down and tying him so that he could sober up.

But we rather think the person that Sam is down on is Essie. Essie is Mart's wife.

"Of course, not exactly his wife," Sam said. "You know how Indians are. There is that Indian husband of hers. It ain't that she and Mart don't get along all right, but no one around here is going to stand for the way she treated Frank Offield right in the store before everybody. You can't kick a man, not where Offield got kicked, without his getting sore about it. There aren't many women do the kind of thing Essie does. You better keep clear of her."

"If you want the house," Mart was saying gently, "Essie'd be glad to fix it up for you. Les and Essie and Eddy and me are going to live right over there with Essie's grandma. You just let me know anything you want and I'll fix it."

But this was after we had been a month on the Rivers and were beginning to be less alarmed by what we found there.

At the end of our first week in Somesbar we found ourselves confused and a little frightened by what we had seen around us. We had come out on the porch after breakfast with Papa Frame, and were watching Anderson, the mailrider, cinch his horse before starting off on the trail back to Orleans Bar. Then Louis, the other mailrider, came out of the barn with his horse and made his way up the trail in the other direction. That trail goes to the Forks of Salmon, and then by stage, three days, to the railroad. Papa Frame stood watching them with us.

"They ain't such bad boys," said Papa Frame, "even if they are half-breeds. Riding trail steady like they do, you got to expect a man's going to drink some. Of course, they get accustomed to the trail getting pretty bad in the wintertime and they take it easy-like. Anderson got pretty mad about a month ago when a panther dropped off a limb onto his back and he had a kinda scuffle before he throwed him off and ended up by losing his hat. Funny about that hat.

He went back the next day and hunted over every scrap of trail and never found it. But, shucks, there ain't many panthers and you don't often have no trouble with them. Country round here is all right when you get used to it."

Except for the hotel and the store and the barn, there seems to be nothing in Somesbar but the river and the mountains. The mountains surround the narrow little valley on all four sides. Behind the hotel races the Salmon River and on the other side of the Salmon is East Mountain. It is a huge, rocky crag over which the sun peers for the first time a little after eleven o'clock. Even on bright days, there are only three hours of sunshine in Somesbar in the wintertime. No one can cross the Salmon by dugout; the current runs too swift and the rocks are too dangerous.

"Got to ford your hosses," said Papa Frame. "And people round here don't like to ford in wintertime lessen they have to. Like to lose your hoss even if you manage to get out all right. No, folks round here mostly take the bridge."

We had been looking at the bridge. It swung high above the river and its span must have been more than two hundred feet. Two steel cables were fastened into the cliff on East Mountain. Supports had been built for them on our side a little behind the hotel. Across these cables sleepers were laid, and on these sleepers there was a narrow, twelve-inch plank. These twelve-inch planks were laid end to end so as to make a narrow walk across the entire span. Some wires had been fastened into the cliff in an attempt to steady the bridge, but we could see it swing from side to side. Very far below was the river, racing through its narrow gorge.

Papa Frame saw our look.

"It ain't so bad," he said. "Not when you get used to it. You got to keep your balance, that's all. Just keep your balance. Used to be wire guides but they're kinda sagged. Wouldn't advise you to use 'em. Don't look down if the river bothers you. Put your foot down when the bridge goes down and keep a-going. That's the main thing," said Papa Frame firmly. "Keep a-going."

We watched the bridge rise and fall for a few minutes, with some discomposure. Then we turned our eyes away. "Aren't there any Indians in Somesbar?" we asked Papa Frame.

Papa Frame was not interested in our question.

"Well, I don't hold much with Indians," said Papa Frame. "Saw all the Indians I ever want to see in Arizony. Went there in 'forty-five along with about forty other fellows. Most of 'em didn't last long. Fifteen years later there was only two of us alive, me and another fellow. You got Apaches down there in Arizony—murdering devils. Only good Indian is a dead Indian, that's what I say. Apaches are bad *hombres* and they're bad medicine. I'd kill an Apache soon as I got a sight of him."

"Apaches torture people in a terrible way, don't they?" we asked.

Papa Frame looked thoughtful.

"Well, no," he said, "I never heard of Apaches torturing anybody. They ain't that kind. Kill you quicker than a wink. Always shoot to kill. Can't make friends with them. Don't want to. But I guess if there's any torturing, it's the whites who do it. Guess I ought to know. Most everyone I knew in Arizony got killed. I was 'bout the only man came out alive."

We were somewhat concerned about what we were going to do in Somesbar. After all, the Government was paying us each thirty dollars a month and traveling expenses to come to Somesbar and civilize the Indians, yet so far the only Indians we had seen were little twelve-year-old Bessie, who helped Mama Frame in the kitchen, and an Indian with his hat pulled down over his eyes who had stopped for dinner. He did not seem to want anyone to speak to him, and left as soon as he had eaten.

We had not seen much of Sam Frame since we had come to Somesbar. Sam Frame is the storekeeper here. We couldn't make out whether it was because he wanted to keep out of our way or because several men were staying at the hotel. The meals at the hotel had not been comfortable. While we were at the table everyone sat in silence, but as soon as we got up and left, the talk and laughter would begin almost before we closed the door. But one day when Sam was waiting to speak to Mama Frame, we plucked up enough courage to ask him about the Indians in Somesbar.

"Indians?" said Sam. "There ain't no Indians in Somesbar except Carrie. That's her cabin down along the river. You can't see it from the trail. Of course, you could do something about her if you want to. She would take it all right. She's accustomed to white people. Had a different white father for each of her children and she's got aplenty. If you want to start on her, I guess you can go ahead. Nobody here is going to make any objection."

Sam started to go out the door and then came back.

"Want to go over to the store with me?" he said. "I could show you some gold dust. We take in quite a lot over the counter. In the old days this was gold country," Sam went on as he opened the door to the store. "Pretty rich is what they say. Maybe five hundred to a thousand men here in 'fifty-two. You could see them everywhere, they tell me, panning along the rivers, or up in the mountains for quartz, or placer mining with giants. They took off all the easy gold and in a year or two there was hardly ten men left. Gone off to strike it rich somewhere else, I guess. Now there's only me and Papa and Hilding and Old Bob and Dutch Henry. 'Cept me and Papa, they're squaw men, of course. Maybe there's two or three more between here and Happy Camp, but that's not many in sixty miles and both sides of the river. Of course, there's plenty half-breeds. Those men didn't do nothing to the Indian squaws, I can tell you. High old times if all they say is true."

"Of course, there's plenty of whites in Orleans since Richards and that company of his came in and took over the mine. And there's whites and Indians at the Forks; some you could do without. They say the Bennetts make a lot more in the saloon than they lose in the mine, and between the two they are making a good thing of it."

We had been thinking we ought to go to the Forks of Salmon. It was a full day's trip across the mountains. We asked Sam whether he thought he could get us some horses. Sam said nothing and there was a closed look on his face, but when we came down the next morning there were two horses tied to the fence. They looked to be in very bad condition. They were thin and their bones stood out and their coats were starey.

"Sam must have thought these horses would get us to the Forks," Mabel said doubtfully. "If they were in too poor shape to make the trip, surely he would have said something."

But would he?

We were beginning to feel very much alone in this country. When people looked at us their faces were blank. They were not openly unfriendly and Mama Frame was kind, but if anything was really unsafe we had a feeling that no one would warn us. As the days went by we did not feel more at home; we felt more uncertain and not sure what we should do. And the trip to the Forks was not a success.

The men at the store at Somesbar, and at the hotel, had joked a good deal about the Forks and the drinking there, and how people got knifed or shot, and we had not thought much about it, but as we sat at the long dining table at the Forks we wished we had not come. We could not tell just what was wrong. As we ate, the men laughed and joked and said things we did not understand. No one looked at us or spoke to us. And nothing really unpleasant happened. But we were very thankful to leave the table and go into the parlor, where we found old lady Bennett. There had been no Indians at the table at the Forks. We asked old lady Bennett whether there were any Indians working in the mine.

"Indians?" she said. "Why, yes, of course, there are Indians. But they know their place and the men here see that they keep it."

"Oh, don't let's stay here," said Mabel, after we had crawled into bed that night. "Somes may be bad and there don't seems to be any Indians there but it isn't as bad as this."

We made pretty good time over the first mountain on the way home. The horses had been well fed and were not so logy. As we began the second climb, the sun went under a cloud and it grew very cold. We were glad to get off and walk. By the time we reached the top, the mountains on all sides of us were sprinkled with white, woolly balls of mist, which sparkled at the edges. It was so beautiful that we exclaimed with delight. Then we started downhill. Around a bend, my horse gave a little skid. He recovered himself on the edge of a hundred-foot drop. I jerked on the bit and he slithered down the trail and brought up in a stout bush. I did not like the view I got over the bush; there seemed to be no bottom to it. As I turned a corner, Mabel's horse swooped down on me, bringing a shower of stones.

"Look out where you're going!" I called. "You've got to be more careful on these curves." A moment later her horse gave mine a sharp push.

"I couldn't help it," Mabel said. "He slipped. Can't you see the trail is all covered with ice? I suppose it is all right," she went on. "I mean, riding when it is so slippery on the trail."

It was a relief to reach the little ravine at the bottom of the mountain. As we went into supper, the two mail-riders came into the room.

"How did you get down Butler?" asked Anderson. "Must have been icy."

"Me?" Louis replied. "I walked. Too far before you land, once you get going. Only a damned fool rides in weather like this."

The two damned fools made no comment and kept their

eyes modestly on their plates. But when everything looked
to us so very dangerous, how were we to know when it was
proper to be afraid?

It was after we had come back from the Forks that we
had a chance to get acquainted with Hilding.

"One of the cattlemen is out here," Mama Frame called
to us. "He says he wants to speak to you ladies." The cattle-
man was standing by the fence. He came forward and took
off his hat.

"I'm Hilding," he said. "I heard you ladies had come
here to teach the Indians." (I saw Mabel give a visible start.)
"And I thought—there's quite a few Indians round my place
—and I thought—you see, Lewis, my boy, hasn't had any
schooling since we left Orleans and he's awful good at his
books and my wife worries about it all the time and I
thought maybe you'd have time to help Lewis with his figur-
ing. You could have a room at our place and you wouldn't
have to pay anything, and my wife she'd be real pleased
to see you. She's lonesome, only Indians and all."

Hilding had horses waiting for us on the other side of
the bridge, tied to a madroña tree. We got across the bridge
with what credit we could. Hilding marched across ahead
of us, without looking to right or left, and Mabel followed
him. I held my breath. She swayed a little but she kept
going. I shut my eyes and prayed and then I stepped on.
The bridge moved up and down and swung a little. I did
not dare look down but I knew the river was there, very far
below me. I kept my eyes on the cliff ahead, put one foot
down, lifted it, tried to keep my balance, rested my weight
on it, and lifted the other foot. Every time I made a step
the bridge swayed a little. If it swayed too much, if I swayed
too much—better not think about it. Crossing a bridge like
this is nothing to make a fuss about, I told myself. If it wasn't
so far up in the air, and the bridge only kept still, it would
be nothing at all. Just keep going. That is what Papa Frame
said—just keep going. Heaven knows, I don't want to stop.

Don't look down. Don't look down. Watch the cliff. There, Hilding is over. Mabel is nearly across. Darn her, what makes her hesitate like that? Why doesn't she go on? She must be a plain, darn fool. Of course, she's bound to lose her balance if she doesn't keep going. There, she's across. Anyhow, she's across. It's after you reach the middle and have to climb up the bridge, instead of going down, that makes it so hard. If only I wouldn't lose my breath, I'd be all right. Now don't get nervous; you're almost across. Just keep going. I wonder how many feet there are in this bridge? It feels like three or four hundred. And how far above the river? Great heavens! Don't look down! Don't you know enough not to look down? Of course, you begin to sway as soon as you look down. Now just keep going. You are almost there. There is no sense in thinking you are losing your balance when you only have a dozen more steps to take. Don't lose your breath like that; you are perfectly all right. There, you're off; one foot is on good solid land. For goodness' sake, quit breathing like that. Can't you see that Hilding is looking at you?

It was not a hard trip. As we rode along the narrow trail, Hilding sat half turned around in his saddle and gestured as he talked with a washboard he was taking to his wife. His face seemed kindly enough for the most part, but occasionally it grew very hard. After we had seen that hard look on Hilding's face, we did not doubt the tales we were to hear later about Hilding and his saloon at Orleans.

We slept that night in Goodman's bed. Mrs. Hilding told us that Goodman is Hilding's partner and that he is a faultfinding man. It is hard, she says, to live with a faultfinding man, but what can they do with Jas needing help and all?

"If the Government thought Indians ought to come to the school, I wouldn't mind at all," Mrs. Hilding said. "Jas, he just worries awful about Lewis not getting any schooling." Maybe we would like to go up to T Bar the next day and see some of the Indians, she suggested. It wasn't a hard trail; we could find our way all right, she assured us.

It was growing dark the next day as we rode back along the same trail we had taken the day before with Hilding. As the light faded, we thought of Papa Frame's story of the panther that had dropped on the back of the mailrider. Whenever the branches hung low over our heads in an especially dark place on the trail, it bothered us to think of that panther. We were tired, and then we were also beginning to think that we were not the right people for this country. The Hildings had been kind, but Hilding was white and Mrs. Hilding was a very white-looking half-breed, with her fair hair. We had gotten nowhere with the Indians.

When we stopped at a cabin, sometimes the Indian woman would nod her head but more often she would look at us and then go in and shut the door without saying a word. It was the same everywhere we stopped. Well, they didn't like us and they didn't want us and that was all there was to it. Maybe we might try going to live in an Indian rancheria like Kot-e-meen, two miles from Somesbar, but we didn't know. Perhaps, after all, we should not have come.

The trail grew darker. We couldn't remember whether we should have crossed that little bridge. Mrs. Hilding said that if you lost the trail you could travel for days in the mountains without getting anywhere. She said a man had come up here and been lost and never heard from again. We listened for the sound of the river. The main trail, Mrs. Hilding said, always runs near the river. We were thankful when we came within sight of a cabin. At the sound of the horses' hoofs, an Indian woman came out of the door and looked at us.

"Schoolmarms?" she asked.

We turned in our saddles and shook our heads. She went back into the house and shut the door. We kicked our tired animals along the trail.

Suddenly Mabel drew up and waited for me. "Did you hear what that woman said?" Mabel called to me. "She said 'Schoolmarms' and she meant us. I've been thinking it over. Schoolmarms! A nice familiar occupation that everyone understands. It's bad enough for us to be women. No one thinks much of women in this country. And no one likes them. And missionaries are worse. We simply can't be missionaries. And government agents are worst of all. No wonder people won't look at us or speak to us.

"But schoolmarms are safe. And everybody knows about them. They may not particularly like schoolmarms but at least they think they are harmless. As long as we stay in this country, we are going to be schoolmarms. And if the Lord didn't cut us out to be schoolmarms, it is just too bad for us, for that is what we are going to be."

It was our last night in Somesbar. The next day we would cross the Salmon and go to live in the Indian rancheria of Kot-e-meen. It was all arranged with the Hamills and we had paid down the ten dollars in advance. Mama Frame followed us upstairs.

"I'm sorry you girls are going," she said. "It has been kinda company having you around." She came into our room and fussed a bit, setting things to rights, as we packed our things and got ready for bed.

"Papa's pretty old now," she said, "but Sam's a good boy. I wouldn't ask for no better. I've had a pretty hard life but Sam's always been good to me. I wasn't no more than sixteen when my folks came across the plains. We come from Texas to Gila Bend, Arizona, by prairie schooner. It took five months from April to September. The first three months was all right, nice and easy and pleasant. We had plenty to eat and in the evenings all we young folks used to sit around and sing after the stock had been looked out for and things fixed for the night. There were seventy-five of us—men, women and children.

"The last two months everybody was wore out. All the men was so cranky it kept you worried all the time for fear of what might happen. And they had awful fights. I'd just git in the wagon so I wouldn't have to see the kind of things they did. Just for nothing at all, all the men would come rushing out with their guns. We started with a lot of wagons so it would be safe when we come to the Indian country. But before we got there we were all split up. When we got to the places where the Indians were real mean, there wouldn't be more than four-five wagons together.

"At Gila Bend we stopped at a roadhouse. It was on the stage route from New Orleans to the coast. The stage route carried a lot of people; they had as many as a hundred horses. It made 'em awful busy at the roadhouse. They couldn't get no rest for days at a time just feeding the passengers as the stages brought them in. The roadhouse was run by Papa Frame. He was some older'n me but he was spry enough when it come to work.

"We camped there for three days, resting up our stock. Mama, she come to me and said how Mr. Frame wanted to marry me. I didn't take to him much. Not in those days. But Mama says to me, 'You know how it is with your stepfather, ugly all the time and getting worse.' I knew that was so. He wasn't a good man. He got drunk most of the time and beat Mama and me pretty bad. Mama and me drove the oxen most all day and took care of them when it was time to unhitch. He'd just lie and sleep in the back of the wagon.

" 'You'd better marry Frame,' Mama says to me. 'You see how it is. I can't do nothing for you and he may get worse.'

"So we were married and Mama and my stepfather they got in the wagon and drove on and I never saw Mama again. I worked hard, the passengers coming in and all, but I got along all right.

"Then after a while I got to feel not so good. Papa Frame, he said to me he was going off to get some horses. He said maybe he'd be gone a week. Then he went out and our hired man went after him and said maybe he better not go. But Papa Frame said he'd got to go and he went along. One day I got to feel pretty bad. I couldn't seem to get about good and the hired man come in and looked at me and asked how was I getting along. When I said I felt bad, he looked scared and he says to me, 'There's some wagons camped down the road a piece. Maybe there's a woman with them.'

"So he got on his horse and rode off. After that I didn't seem to know much for a while and the hired man come back and brought a woman with him. He shoved her in and shut the door. The woman come over to the bed and looked at me and she says, 'My God, you're going to have a baby! He never told me.' And she begun to run up and down the room and scream.

"Then Sam was born."

We Cross the River into Indian Country

We slept well the first night in the Indian rancheria of Kot-e-meen. We made up a bed of sorts on the floor, and we put a little billet of wood under our window to hold it up about three inches from the bottom. Personally I did not want to open the window any more than three inches because I had an uncomfortable feeling that a panther might push his way in. No one had told us any stories of panthers that came in through half-opened windows but then they do not tell you all they know in this country.

We find that we have moved into a very, very large house, according to Indian standards, and that it was built for a white man. It has a large room all across the front and space back of this room that can be used as a kitchen. Then there is a loft upstairs where you can stand upright in the middle of the floor. The ten-dollars-a-month rent we pay for the house apparently includes a chair, a stool and a frying pan. Mabel is especially pleased by the discovery of the frying pan.

Quite a little distance behind the house is a little grove of pepper trees, and hidden among the pepper trees is a delightful little spring. And, added to everything else, we are very much set up to find that we have a privy. From what we hear, it is the only privy between Somesbar and Happy Camp, a distance of sixty miles. We found it lurking in an unexpected place in front of the house. It discreetly turns its back on the Hamill cabin, concealing the fact that it has no door.

But the really important thing in our young lives is our little stove, because there were some bad moments when we doubted whether it would ever get here.

It was soon after dinner on our last day at Somesbar, on the main trail between Yreka on the railroad and Eureka on the Pacific Ocean, that Sam brought out his two animals and put the pack saddles on them. Anderson, the mailrider, rode in from the Forks of Salmon, and when he saw what was going on he began helping Sam with the roping. As there were two of them, they used the diamond hitch. Sam is an old hand at packing, and the two men worked quickly and with precision.

The first pack animal was mean and they feared he would buck off the load. Sam quickly got on Anderson's horse and, taking the lead of the mean horse, started down toward the river. Bart, Sam's own horse, followed with a load on his back. We ran down to the river's edge to watch them take the water. The Salmon is not only swift but dangerous because of hidden rocks. The ford is on a sandbar, some two to four feet below the surface of the water. With the eddying, gleaming ripples and the swift current, it was difficult to keep the animals on the sandbar. Sam was in the lead. We watched his horse give a little plunge and then go in. The water rose above his feet and then to his knees. The loaded animals followed him. The noise of the river was so loud that, although we could see the splash of the fording animals, we could hear nothing but the roar of the water as it whirled by us, flinging up brush and tree trunks and grinding them against the stones.

The horses went steadily forward until they were almost in the center of the stream. Then Bart made a misstep. He went down to his middle and the load tottered. It was the load with the little stove. We held our breath. Then Bart scrambled back on the bar and went on.

As they neared the other bank, the water deepened. It came up to the loads. Then Sam's horse took a step and the water was only to his knees. Another step and he was struggling up the bank, with the loaded animals following him. We raced back to the store, gathered up a small mirror, a kerosene oil can, a package of crackers, and a flour sack of odds and ends. Then, with prayers that our loads would not shift, we pattered across the swing bridge. We have now been over the swing bridge several times but we still pray hard whenever we have to cross it.

Sam took the loaded animals up over the mountain in order to avoid the thick brush on the trail. It seems that he missed the trail he should have taken and we came down the mountain back of the house in Kot-e-meen, through gullies and across ledges and down slides that seemed to us poor going for a goat. The loads stuck in the deeper gullies and once even the sure-footed Bart went down on his knees. Our precious little stove wavered on its side of the load, got stuck on rocks, and was nearly wrenched off in the bushes. We began to think the chance of its coming to rest, upright and secure, in its new lodging was very slim indeed.

Mart Hamill was waiting for us at the front door. We could see him, a tiny speck, far, far below as we crept and slid, loads and all, down the mountain. Mart and Sam competently put up the stove and Mart made a hole for a stovepipe through the roof. Then we bade Sam good-by. At last we were at home in our own house in Indian country, in the Coast Range of California.

At first, as we unpacked our things, we were set back because we had no cloths to scrub with. It took us quite a while to learn all the things you can't buy in this country. But Mabel has pioneer ancestors. It is true they flourished about 1700, but the strain is there and can be relied on in an emergency. For an hour, Mabel went about looking inward, and then she went out and dug up an old pair of overalls that had been buried behind a pepper bush. They took a bit of cleaning but are now serving nicely.

Mart was the first member of the Essie family to come to call. He stood in the doorway, looking shyly into the room, and asked whether we "fellows needed anything." Then he came in and sat on the woodpile. There isn't any place we can ask our guests to sit but the woodpile. The following day he came over again with lumber in his arms. It was the lumber for our bedstead. Now what do you know about that? That night we slept like ladies. Sam had already packed over some excelsior for us. Mama Frame said it was nice, clean excelsior, and we hope so. Over at Somesbar Mabel seemed to scratch a good deal, but Sam said it was probably fleas and recommended persian powder. He said old Andy Merrill just poured it down his pants and it worked real well. Sam also said to buy blue-mercury ointment. You just touch yourself with blue-mercury ointment and you don't have to worry about lice.

"Everybody's got lice," said Sam. "You know, the Indians and all, and you just can't keep 'em out of the beds, so just stock up with blue ointment."

We did and are hoping for the best.

When we go back home, we may cause a ripple among our treasured relatives, but from what Sam tells us it will be nothing compared to the splash we are making on the Rivers. I would prefer to be modest about it, but it seems that we are the most talked-of individuals in two hundred miles. A chance meeting with anyone on the trail will set that man up for life because afterward he can tell everyone: "Well, I met the schoolmarms."

There is no longer any need for us to introduce ourselves. Apparently there is no one this side of Hoopa, two days over the mountains to the west of us, to Etna Mountain, at least ninety miles in the other direction, who does not know every single fact in regard to our private history. In fact, we cannot even tell our friends what we have done or what we plan to do. They always say, "Why, I heard that in the store yesterday."

A few days after Mart's visit, Essie came over to call with the second husband. It was the first time we had a chance to see much of Essie. She is a full-blood Indian, small and dark, with a soft, low voice and very pretty manners.

She is one of the few Indians we have met who speaks English.

The second husband is a full-blood Indian named Les. For the most part he is a bit withdrawn but at times he giggles engagingly. We all sat around the fire and made conversation, and it was a very pleasant affair. But we were a little doubtful, as we discussed bears and rattlesnakes and river crossings, whether we were upholding the standards Mr. Kyselka, the Indian agent at Hoopa, had talked about when he sent us up into the Indian country.

Of course, if Mart and Essie and Les are all satisfied, it really does seem as though it were their own personal concern. On the other hand, two husbands at the same time would scarcely be tolerated in most white communities. We were not sure as things warmed up to an account of Pic-i-ow-ish, which is the Indian New Year's and Essie says comes sometime in September, whether we were exercising the civilizing influence for which the Government is paying us thirty dollars a month and traveling expenses. But we couldn't help being impressed by the way Essie carried off the situation. Socially, she put her two husbands on the map. It is plain that her abilities are not confined to downing Frank Offield before a scandalized audience.

The thing that really does worry us, however, is that we are hungry all the time. Of course, when Mrs. Hilding can spare us a few eggs we rise to the height of little cupcakes, which are tremendously popular with the Indians. But for the most part you can't get much to eat in this country in February. Of course, we expected to be hungry at Somesbar and at the Forks of Salmon and at the Hildings. Meals are all off the same piece when you go anywhere to spend the night. Only at some places they are worse than at others.

The standard practice is to put bacon in cold water, then put it on the stove. When the water comes to a boil, the bacon is considered cooked. It is then a pulpy, gelatinous affair and generally a little rancid. As a finishing touch, you pour the greasy bacon water over the beans and the fried potatoes. Tea and coffee making also have pecularities. You put a pinch of coffee or tea into your pot. Then you put it on the stove and boil it up. Each day you keep adding more pinches, and boiling them, until the pot is full of grounds. Then you dig out your grounds and start fresh. So far, we have never had the luck to be anywhere when they started fresh. Generally there will be frying-pan bread (soda biscuit) and dried-apple pie. Neither very good. And that is all. At best you eat sparingly, unless driven by hunger.

We had hoped for better things in our own house, but living in the Indian country is a costly affair. When an Indian paddles you across the Klamath, you pay him four bits (fifty cents). When Eddy goes to Somes for your mail, you pay him two bits (twenty-five cents). If you offer Eddy ten cents for any small chore, he politely refuses it because ten cents will not buy anything in this country. The morning before we moved to Kot-e-meen, there was simply no restraining Mabel. She bought a dishpan and a broom and a handbasin and a lamp. Then she cast her eyes around for food. She bought three pounds of cheese and some coffee, which seems to have been a bad buy as there is something awful the matter with the taste. Then she bought rice and flour and lard and baking powder and beans and prunes and potatoes. The total purchase came to fifty dollars. Just as we were ready to leave, she remembered sugar.

"Give me a couple of pounds," she told Sam.

"Better take twelve," said Sam.

We thought of the load we already had to pack over the swing bridge. "Why should we take twelve?" we asked.

"Because," said Sam, "twelve is all the sugar I have and there won't be any more sugar until the pack train comes in July."

We felt very rich in the Essie house as we went over all our possessions, although we had rather hoped for some plates. We noticed five when we were in the store, but Mama Frame said we didn't need them. If we would only buy breakfast food, we would find a piece of china in every package.

"Of course," said Mama Frame, "sometimes you get a cup when what you want is a plate, but Carrie and I exchange and I'm getting a real nice set."

The lumber Mr. Hilding packed down for us on mule back cost us ten dollars and fifty cents. We were certainly glad to get it, for we should have a table and two chairs, but I couldn't help feeling a little worried as there are now only a few silver dollars left in my little buckskin bag.

But Mabel says she doesn't care. She has mixed all the griddle cakes she is going to mix without a table. Moreover, she doesn't think the floor is the best place on which to mix griddle cakes or wash dishes. And if we have any more guests, they simply cannot all sit on the woodpile.

Meantime our social life is looking up. Essie and Les are going to take us on a round of calls at Pich-pichi, across the Klamath. Mart told us about the Schenck-Pepper feud. He says Dumphrey Pepper is a near neighbor of ours and lives just above Kot-e-meen on this side of the river.

We found Essie and Les waiting for us on the tall bluff above the Klamath, with Eddy gamboling about like a young fawn. As we stood on the high bank, with the river below us, Les gave the beautiful, singing call of the Indians, and a dugout with an old Indian in it nosed its way out of the bushes on the other side. At Kot-e-meen, the current is very fierce and strong. The river races between the two high bluffs of Pich-pichi and Kot-e-meen. At the fork of the river, just above its junction with the Salmon, is the mountain we call the Sugar Loaf. Below are the Great Falls. If you miss the landing place at Pich-pichi, the tremendous force of the current carries you over the Great Falls, an ordeal virtually certain to smash a boat and one that few men have survived.

Essie and Eddy went across in the first load, with Les at the stern and the old Indian at the bow. Dugouts on the Rivers are long and narrow, and are hollowed out of a single tree. The two men poled with all their strength, forcing the boat upstream along the bank, farther and farther, until we almost lost sight of it in the bushes that grew along the river's edge. Then with a mighty shove they were in the center of the river, rushing down with the current. We could see the flash of Essie's bright pink sleeves and the men standing, dipping their paddles deep in the water. The paddles rose and fell, gleaming in the sunlight. The boat swept down until it was directly opposite us, and we could see how fast the paddles moved and how the men strained to make the landing on the other shore. As they landed, Essie waved, and the two men turned the boat and came back for us.

Calls at Pich-pichi were not very different from calls at home. Some of the Indians had a few words of English, and we tried out our few words of Indian, which were well received. On the way back, as we passed an empty house, Eddy, who is only twelve, glanced in at the window. Essie put her hand on her son's arm.

"We do not do that," she said. "It is not polite. You do not look in a house when there is no one there."

We felt uncomfortable. When we had passed the house we also had looked in the window. If we were to be friends of Essie's, it was plain that we should have to mend our manners. However, it looks as if the trip was a success, because both Essie and Les said on the way back that next week they would take us on a series of calls all up and down river. But as we went up the trail to our own house we felt doubtful.

Ought we to go to village after village introduced by Essie? Ought we to sanction Les as husband number two by going in his company? How would the Indian Department and the Northern Indian Association look upon our chosen companions, not to mention Bishop Moreland, who evidently considers us members of his flock and has sent us forty Bibles.

On the other hand, why exclude Essie, who sports two
husbands, and include Sam, who regularly breaks the law
by selling illicit whiskey to the Indians? Or Hilding, who
kept a notorious saloon in Orleans Bar and, they say, had to
be run out of town. Or Luther Hickox, who, according to
everybody, is a desperate character and quietly does away
with people when they annoy him? Or Frank Offield, who
seems to have a very doubtful history?

Maybe it is just as well to go ahead and not ask too
many questions.

But to come back to the feud that Mart was telling us
about, which, he says, is the only feud now on the Rivers
that is still going strong. One afternoon about two years
ago, Barney Schenck and one of the Pepper boys, both
Indians who lived on this side of the river, went to the Hildings' to sharpen their tools. On the way home, Barney cut
the Pepper boy's throat. Of course, the Peppers got after
Barney and told him he would have to pay one hundred
dollars. But Barney refused to pay a cent, and took to the
mountains with his young brother. They led a hard life of it,
and finally the young brother caught cold and died. Shortly
after this, Barney's wife and baby and his old grandmother
died also.

By this time, others had tried to adjust the quarrel. Both
sides were willing, but there was a violent argument over
how much should be taken off for the four deaths in the
Schenck family. Of course, everyone knew the Schencks
must have been deviled by the Peppers, and the Peppers did
not deny it. Then a Pepper died. That complicated things
still more, and negotiations were broken off.

Since then the Peppers had tried to hire Swanny Pete,
who is one of Barney's best friends, to go to Scott's Valley
and kill Barney. But Swanny Pete took one hundred and
fifty dollars for the job and then went to Scott's Valley and
warned Barney against what the Peppers were trying to do
to him. Finally Barney consulted Mr. Hilding, and, on his
advice, gave himself up to the sheriff in Etna, saying that

life in the woods wasn't worth living and he would rather be in the white man's jail. He lay in prison ninety days while the sheriff sent word to the Peppers to come and appear against him. But the Peppers were most unwilling to do this because they had an unexpiated killing of their own to account for. So Barney said firmly that if he was going to hang so should the Peppers.

When the ninety days were up, and no Peppers had appeared, the sheriff pronounced Barney a free man. He is now working in Scott's Valley. However, the Peppers are still trying to hire someone to kill him, and that makes Barney distrustful of his friends. Mrs. Hilding says she thinks that both Barney and the Peppers would now like to see the feud settled.

From what they tell us, killing people in this country is very expensive. You have to pay twenty-five dollars just for shooting at someone. If you hit him, it costs you fifty dollars. And if you are unfortunate enough to kill him, his relatives demand one hundred dollars.

It seems that a regrettable incident took place a year or so ago. An up-river Indian made a trip to Scott's Valley and got a bit too free with his gun. As a result, he had to make a settlement of four hundred dollars to quiet the relatives of the deceased. On the whole, Mart tells us, regardless of expense, most Indians here on the Rivers feel it is better to settle up at once and pay down your money like a man.

CHAPTER IV

The Course of True Love, Indian Way

We are beginning to feel very much at home in the Indian village of Kot-e-meen. Although the thick chaparral
(the abode, I am sorry to say, of endless wood ticks) closes
in around us on all sides, we live in a continual social
whirl. And we find we like very much being members of
the Essie family.

As we are eating breakfast or supper, or sitting before
our wood fire in the evening, the door opens (only white
men knock in this country) and one of our Indian neighbors stands in the doorway. It may be Jim Tom or Hackett
or one of the Tintins or Mamie from Pich-pichi or a quite
new up-river Indian. Or, more likely, it is one of the Essie
family. It now seems simpler for Mart to leave his hat
permanently in our living room. Les does all his drumming
with his back against the outside wall of our house, while
Eddy seems to live on our drinking water.

And then there is always something doing in an Indian
rancheria. Yesterday, Essie came in to tell us that all the
Indians on both sides of the river are talking about the
salmon smoke and they say it will come off in the dark
of the moon. No one is allowed to fish in either the Klamath
or the Salmon before the salmon smoke. When the night
of the salmon smoke is due to arrive, an old salmon is
caught and brought up to the flat above the river. All the
next day it burns over a slow fire. One of the old Indians
tends the fire and guards the salmon. He must have fasted
five days before the ceremonies commence. While the fire

burns and the salmon smoke rises in the air, the Kot-e-meen and Pich-pichi Indians go into a large tent and sit there all day. That is, all the men. I think no women are allowed in the tent. The flap of the tent is carefully closed, for if anyone sees the smoke or catches a salmon in the river before the old salmon is entirely consumed, that person will not survive the year.

His horse will slip on the trail and he and his horse will fall down the mountain and be crushed on the rocks below, or his boat will miss the landing and he will go over the Great Falls and be drowned, or a rattlesnake will get him, or he will be shot by an irate neighbor. Anyhow, something unpleasant will happen to him.

It is true that last year Mart caught a glimpse of the smoke and nothing happened to him, but then Mart is nearly white so that may be the reason. But the year before, Little Ike saw the smoke and only two weeks later got into trouble at the Forks of Salmon and was badly knifed. So it is well to be careful.

The Indians are now saying that the salmon smoke will come off next week. We are to shut ourselves carefully in our house and neither of us is to look out the window. Even Mart is going to stay home and has asked for some magazines to look at. Evidently he doesn't think it would be wise to take a chance two years in succession. Essie has just been over to say please be very careful. She knows how afraid Mabel is of rattlesnakes and she is worried for fear Mabel might get just one glimpse of the salmon smoke because, if she should, a rattlesnake would be sure to get her.

To keep ourselves occupied, Mabel and I have been practicing the Indian love song that Essie has been teaching us. I would have you know that this is not a plain, ordinary love song but a true love charm, and it is warranted to bring down any gentleman we have set our hearts on, no matter how great his disinclination. All either of us has to do is sing him this song and drop a few grains of dirt from a special ant hill in his coffee, and the deed is done.

Very valuable knowledge, Essie considers it, for unprovided-
for young ladies like ourselves. She says it is an heirloom in
her family and very few Indians know about it. Any young
lady would gladly pay a large sum of money for it. We get
it as a gift. Essie says her aunt, old Graham's squaw, taught
it to her.

"I got a white man with it," her aunt said, "and a fine
gentleman. And what is more, I kept him."

Essie said she could not have gotten Mart without the
love song.

"It was when I come back here to live," Essie said, "and
my aunt, she'd paid back the money to Rube Morse, and
Mart, he'd come in and see old Graham and he'd sit down
and eat his dinner. And I think about Mart all the time,
and Mart, he don't pay no attention to me. And I don't
know what to do. So I talk to Mart and Mart, he says, 'It
ain't no use, Essie. I ain't never going to marry an Indian.'
And he keeps coming to the house and he won't look at
me nor nothing.

"So I think I don't want to live no more if I can't be
married to Mart. And my aunt says, 'You can get him, Essie,
if you want to.' So I done everything my aunt told me.

And after Mart had drunk up his coffee he come round
where I was and he stood round for a while and then he
said, 'How about you and me going to a dance, Essie?'

"So everything was all right and we got married."

"And was everything all right?" we asked.

"Yes, everything was all right," said Essie. "After we
got married, Mart, he'd drink an awful lot and he'd treat
everybody and he wouldn't bring no money home. But the
Indians didn't get mean with him and he didn't have no
fights except with Frank Offield. And that was the white
men's fault. The white mens wanted Mart to box but Mart
didn't know nothing about how to box but the white mens
kept at him. So Frank come along and come right at Mart,
and Mart, he caught hold of Frank and threw him in a

corner and sat on him. He hit him and hit him and Frank just lay on his face and put his arm over his head.

"Then Frank Merrill he run in and said, 'Don't you know nothing to go on hitting a man when he's said enough?'

"So Frank Merrill, he hit Mart straight in the jaw and knocked him to the other side of the room. Then they carried Frank Offield across the road into the house and Mart ran after them, but they locked the door, and though he beat and beat on the door he couldn't get in."

"What happened then?" we asked. "Did anyone get killed?"

"No," said Essie, "there wasn't no trouble that time. But old Graham, he wouldn't give me no money because Mart, he just got drunk all the time. Old Graham, he said to me, 'You know, Essie, how it will go. Mart, he don't think about nothing but whiskey.'

"So I went and panned gold in the river but I didn't buy nothing to eat. I just bought whiskey. And Mart, he'd come in and say, 'Essie, you ain't eat nothing.' And I'd say, 'I don't want nothing to eat, Mart, only whiskey.'

"And when Mart come in I'd put the bottle on the table and say, 'Here's your dinner, Mart.' And Mart, he'd put his head on the table and cry and he'd say, 'You look awful bad, Essie. Ain't you going to eat nothing?' And I'd say, 'I don't want nothing but whiskey, Mart.'

"So one night he come home and there was the bottle of whiskey on the table and he sat and looked at it and then he pushed it away and he said, 'I don't want it, Essie. I ain't going to drink no more.' "

"And did he never drink any more?" we asked.

"No," said Essie. "He didn't drink no more. Only a little now and then."

She sat a long time staring into the fire. Her face was troubled. Then she sighed and looked up.

"You don't sing that love song right," she said. "You got to sing it this way."

We are finding Indian music very difficult. In fact, we are finding all music a little difficult on the Rivers. When Mart comes over to play his fiddle, all his selections sound to us very much alike. When he was over here last night and had played for quite a long time, we told him how much we liked the pieces he played and asked him to play "Buffalo Gals."

"Why, that's the one I just played," said Mart sadly.

As for Indian music, at first, when Les drummed and sang for us, we could make nothing out of it. It seemed no more than a jumble of discordant sounds. Then slowly we began to recognize that it was music and that some of the songs were delightful. But when we tried to sing them ourselves we broke down completely. The intervals were different from ours and the placing of the voice was different.

The Essie love song is really lovely and very moving. But no matter how hard we tried, it was plain that Essie was far from pleased with our performance. We were not sorry when Mart came in with his fiddle and the lesson was interrupted.

Ever since we came to the Rivers, we have been wondering why this part of the country is not more like the westerns you read in books and magazines. Mr. Kelsey said he was sending us to the roughest place in the United States, and people certainly do get killed here. There is the Barney Schenck-Pepper feud. And the Indian from I-ees who came to the Hilding class. They say he has killed quite a lot of people and nearly got killed himself at the last deerskin dance. Then there is Luther Hickox, who lives on the other side of the river, a few miles above Pich-pichi. He seems to be quite unduly handy with his gun, and it is said he has several killings to account for. And we hear some pretty lurid stories about a young fellow in Orleans Bar called Willy Salstrom.

Of course, there are quite a good many people who nearly get killed, like the man who was coming down the mountain above the Grants and had two panthers attack him, and last year Mr. Hilding nearly got snowed in coming over Marble Mountain, and then there is the bridge at Somes. I lost my balance and nearly went over the last time we went to Somes for supplies. And last year Swanny Tomer actually did fall off and was drowned.

But when people write westerns, although the things they write about may actually have happened, the pace they set is terrific. On nearly every page, someone gets killed or murdered or abducted, and so on through the entire book, generally with a big mass murder to end up on.

But here on the Rivers we take things much more leisurely. Of course, everybody packs a gun and has probably used it on occasion. But most of the shootings or knifings we hear about are a long way off, at the Forks of Salmon, for instance, or up river where we only have a slight speaking acquaintance with the Indians. For that matter, not many people seemed to get killed in any one year, and most killings occur in a fight or at some kind of festivity like a deerskin dance, and the next deerskin dance doesn't come until a year from next August.

On the other hand, what really does concern us at Kot-e-meen—the things we talk about most—are river crossings and what happened the last *ti postheree* (high water) and salmon smokes and bears and eels and Indian gambles and, of course, *apruan* (Indian devils), and things like Indian marriage.

Before the white men came to the Rivers, Essie tells us, the Indians were very strict about marriage. If a man so much as asked a married woman for a drink of water, he had to pay her husband or there would be trouble. A man had to pay for his wife or it couldn't be a marriage. He paid the money to the old woman. If he paid no more than thirty dollars, he had to support his wife's family. But if he paid sixty dollars it was all right and he didn't have to support anyone but his wife. If he didn't want to be married any longer, then the old woman had to pay him back his money. That was the way things were when Essie got married to Rube Morse. Then it was all right. The man could go off and get married to some else, and the woman got married to someone else, just as Essie had done.

According to Essie, "If a man didn't pay no money for his wife and they just lived together then his childrens got a bad name. It made a man ashamed when his childrens got a bad name." Essie said Eddy's name was all right; she had paid Mart thirty dollars for it.

"If I'd kept the sixty dollars Rube paid me for Eddy," Essie said, "Eddy he'd have belonged to Rube. Some childrens are cheap and some childrens are expensive. A man he's got to pay sixty dollars if he wants expensive childrens. Some womens would treat cheap childrens and expensive childrens different way. But I never would," concluded Essie piously.

"Eddy was awful sick when he was a baby," Essie went on, after a pause. "He was all swelled up and nobody couldn't do nothing. So an Indian doctor came and she said Eddy was going to die. And she said, 'Essie, you went and took something off a grave.' And I said, 'No, I ain't.' And she said, 'Yes, you did, Essie, and that's why Eddy is going to die.'

"So I didn't know what to do. And Eddy, he got worse. So I didn't sleep, just thinking about Eddy. Then I wake up in the night and I think about when I was a little girl and I was playing house and there was a little blue shell on a grave and I wanted it so I could play house and I took it and hid it. And it was down to Sandy Bar. So I went down to Sandy Bar and told them I would pay for the shell, and so we got it fixed and I come home and there was Eddy all well and I didn't have no trouble no more.

"Eddy, he thinks a lot of Mart," said Essie. "He thinks more of Mart than he does of Rube. Seems as though Eddy was afraid of Rube. Mart, he's awful good to Eddy. When I get mad at Mart, I say to Eddy, 'Which will you stay with, me or Rube?' And Eddy says, 'I won't stay with you and

I won't stay with Rube. I'll stay with Mart. If I don't stay
with Mart, I'll just die. That's what I'll do.'
    "I'm awful fond of childrens," Mart said once when he
was talking to us.
    It was growing dark. We didn't light the lamp but we
built up the fire. As the flames grew brighter, Essie and
Eddy sang deer songs. They sang for a long time, and then
Eddy stopped singing and Essie sang a love song. It caught
hold of you and did something to you. Essie's voice went
on until she had sung the song twice, and then she stopped
and everything was quiet. Watching Essie as she sat there
singing in the firelight, we thought it was no wonder that
Essie had had three husbands.
    It was only a few days later when we had our first sight
of husband number one. We had been sitting by ourselves
over the fire when a knock came on the door and Mart entered followed by a white man.
    "I want to make you acquainted," gasped Mart,—"ac-
quainted with— This is Rube Morse."
    From Mart's uneasiness, when the two men came in,
we judged that Rube had turned up unexpectedly, and
though the social and marital situation didn't seem to worry
anybody, we thought there might be quite a different kind of
problem. There had been a small run of eels a few days before. Essie had been able to dry over a hundred. The beds
were canopied with eels. Eels hung from every inch of the
ceiling. Grandma occupied a scanty couch. Mart and Essie
had a bed. Les had a bunk and Eddy another over it. All the
rest of the space was filled with eels. Where Rube was going
to dispose of his expansive person we couldn't imagine.
    Rube was as tall as Mart but a good deal heavier, and
he looked soft. Although a half-breed, anyone would take
him for a white man. There was nothing menacing about
Rube, nothing that makes one catch one's breath, as with
Luther Hickox. As for Essie, she took three husbands at
the same time quite calmly, when she ran over for a minute to say supper was ready. Rube went back with her but

Mart still lingered. He stood on the porch with a hoe in his hand, and we watched the sun go down.

"How long have you been married to Essie, Mart?" we asked. Mart was silent a long time. He ran his finger up and down the handle of the hoe and then tested the blade.

"I ain't married to Essie," he said. "Over to a white dance I done something and Essie, she got mad. I told her it didn't mean nothing. Everybody does at a dance. But Essie said she didn't want to be married to me no more. And she kept at me and kept at me and I got drunk and so I took the money. And next day I tried to give the money back, and Essie, she wouldn't take it. So we ain't married no more. And now Essie, she don't belong to nobody because she paid the money. And the Indians don't like it because a woman ought to belong to somebody like they always have. But Essie, she says, 'You took the money, Mart. So I don't belong to you and I don't belong to nobody. So what you going to do?' "

Mart turned to go. He stood for a minute, looking out into the gathering darkness. His shoulders drooped.

"I guess I better be going," he said. "Essie she's got supper ready, so I guess I better go."

We sat on the porch in the darkness for a long time after he had gone. We kept thinking about Mart, who was white, for all his Indian grandmother. Mart had the white way of doing things. You couldn't think of Mart as an Indian. He was white, with his blue eyes and his fair hair and his magnificent broad shoulders and the way he felt about Essie, even if he had been unfaithful to her. It was true that that didn't mean much on the Rivers.

And we thought about Essie. Essie, who was small and dark and very Indian. Or was she? No other Indian woman was quite like Essie. And how Essie cared very much for Mart, and couldn't forgive him for what he had done.

And then we thought about Les. Where did Les come into this? Sometimes it seemed to us that Les cared more about Essie than Mart did. Then, too, Les was an Indian and Essie was an Indian and that made a difference. When Essie was with Les, they felt the same way about things. Personally we liked being with Essie and Les much better than we liked being with Mart. Essie and Les were gay. It was always an adventure to be with Essie and Les. If we crossed the river with them or made garden with them, it was the same. Life was gay and full of adventure, and we were glad we were alive.

We liked Mart very much. We grew to like Mart more all the time. We were fond of Mart. But Mart was white. Working in the garden wasn't an adventure to Mart. It was a chore. Crossing the river in the dugout wasn't an adventure to Mart, as it was to Essie and Les and ourselves. It was a chore. Of course we were fond of Mart, but when you came right down to it we would much rather go off for the day with Essie and Les. With them we always felt glad we were alive and were living in the Indian village of Kot-e-meen. And our spirits went up as we thought of crossing the river or riding the trail.

White people were all very well. We were white ourselves. But white people were dull, after you had lived with Indians.

Essie cared about Mart. Essie was in love with Mart. But would Essie rather play around with Les? It was all very confusing.

It was very still on the porch. And it was very dark. We could just see the darker blue of the mountain against the sky. Over at the cabin there was a light. We watched it for a long time before we got up and went to bed.

CHAPTER V

Indians at Home, When There Ain't No Growl, nor No Trouble

With the coming of spring, the really important event all up and down river is the big eel run. Indians who live as far away as Orleans Bar or I-ees-i-rum come to Kot-e-meen, and Essie's cousin Hattie and her husband, from the Forks of Salmon, are staying with the Essie family. We are rather glad of all this company because we have a notion that all has not been well at the Essie cabin, but, whatever it was, peace now reigns, and as usual it is Essie who has brought it about. Essie is an Indian. Eddy has an Indian mother and a father who is three quarters white. Mart is three quarters white. Les is an Indian. Grandma is an Indian. And in a cabin that can't measure more than fifteen by seventeen feet they all live together in reasonable harmony.

Moreover, in this country, Sam Frame tells us, the man rides ahead on his horse and his woman walks behind with the load. But when the Essie family went over to the Forks, we noticed that it was Essie who rode and Les who walked. Sam says it is always the squaw who packs the bag of flour across the swing bridge. But the day we went to Somesbar, Les staggered home under an enormous load while Essie walked beside him carrying only one small basket. Of course, Mart is almost white, so it is not surprising that he should take up the white man's burden. But Les is Indian and Essie is Indian. Yet she rides and he walks.

It seems, however, that the harmony in the Essie family does not stand up under the pressure of visitors. Last night the whole family went eel fishing, and this morning it appears that things are far from pleasant. We learn that, coming home, Les packed a bag inshore filled with about a hundred and fifty eels, the entire evening's catch. Going over some very wet rocks, he slipped and nearly went over into the Great Falls. Worse, according to both Essie and Hattie, he lost the bag of eels.

This morning, Les is sulky because he wrenched his knee, and Essie and Hattie have been at each other since before breakfast, Essie sitting on a box outside the door and Hattie standing over by the fence, about two hundred feet away. Between them sat Nero, scratching for fleas, while Mart and Les wandered to and fro, not wanting to get into the growl and not sure just how to keep out of it. Finally Mart seated himself on a rock by the side of the garden, and when Mabel called over to him said dismally, "Three melons is planted all wrong and I don't know what they are going to put in here, but Essie, she's having a growl with Hattie, and I guess I'll just have to wait until she gets through before I ask her."

We have made no effort to conceal our interest in eels and have been hoping for an invitation to go with the Essie family down to the Great Falls, but it was not until Abner and Hattie had disappeared in the bush, on their way back to the Forks, that Eddy ran over to tell us that the big run was on and that the whole family were going down to the river to get their winter supply.

The place where the Indians catch their eels is directly beside the Great Falls of Kot-e-meen. We skirted the base of Ah-o-wich (Sugar Loaf Mountain) and then headed toward the river, over great masses of tumbled stone and rock. The roar of the river grew nearer and nearer as we leaped chasms of foaming water and jumped from stone to stone, until at length we could see the Great Falls themselves, boiling down from far above us in an enormous expanse of spray and foam.

Under circumstances like these, there is marked advantage in our being considered the most feminine sort of young ladies. The soles of our shoes were as slippery as glass. We minced from rock to rock, hesitating before we took the required leap. Yet we only acquired merit for our performance. On the other hand, if we had worn trousers instead of skirts, our shoes might have been quite as slippery and it would have been wise for us to display an equal amount of caution. But would we have acquired merit? We would not. We should have been considered tenderfeet and treated with the contempt we deserved. No, if you want to go into a strange country, by all means go as women. You take it easy and acquire merit at the same time.

Close to the Falls, with the spray dashing over us and the roar of the water in our ears, we looked up the plunging rapids to the crossing at Kot-e-meen and Pich-pichi, far, far above us. The water plunged down in a series of great waterfalls. It dashed itself against the rocks and through whirlpools and, gathering itself together, plunged down again and again. Everywhere was tumbling water. The force and pressure and roar, the great expanse of foaming, tumbling water, and far, far above us the bluffs of Kot-e-meen and Pich-pichi made us feel no bigger than eels ourselves.

A fair-sized stream of water had left the main body of the Falls and taken a roundabout course through the rocks. This, in its turn, became a smaller waterfall, pouring down onto the rocks below us, As we stood watching it, we could see a slimy tail wave for a minute and then disappear. Sometimes we could see the entire eel as it hung for a minute above the water. Then it would wave its tail, slide under the water, and reappear in the whirlpool above.

Essie and ourselves sat on a rock a few feet from the water while Les, stripped to the waist, took off his shoes. Then, cautiously, he began to make his way out over the rocks and down by the side of the plunging water. Finally he took his stand just below the pool. Steadying himself to be sure of his footing, he held his bag in his left hand, leaned down, and with his right hauled out a squirming eel. Sometimes he managed quite easily to get it into his bag, and sometimes he had to try several times before it dropped out of sight. At other times, no matter how firm his grip, an eel would slide from his grasp and fling itself back into the pool.

As Les stood far out from the shore, with the tumbling water of the Great Falls all around him, his lithe, dark figure was sharply outlined against the white water of the cascade. The spray from the Falls made his dark shoulders glisten. His body swayed with a quick rhythm as he leaned forward, caught up a twisting, squirming eel, and thrust it into his bag. As we watched him, he did not seem like our Les, who was bashful and giggled if you spoke to him, and who adored Essie. He was an Indian, with dark glistening body and black hair, who was very beautiful as he stood poised at the very edge of the Falls. We thought he might very well be one of the First People who, Essie told us, had come down out of Ah-o-wich to fish in the thunder and spray of the Great Falls, as they may well have done long before the Indians came to the Rivers.

Then Les would shake his hair out of his eyes and look up at us and wave his hand and laugh, and he would no longer seem to us one of the First People but only our Les, and we would wave back at him. He was not more than twenty feet away from us but, although he shouted once or twice, not a sound of his voice could we catch above the crash and thunder of the water.

We watched him for a long time, and then Essie gave a little cry and pointed to his bag. It seemed surprisingly flat, considering how many eels Les had put in it. Then I saw what Essie was pointing at. Les leaned over, snatched an eel, and thrust it into his bag. A moment later we saw the flick of a black tail at the bottom of the bag. The tail grew longer and became an eel. It wiggled out of the bottom of the bag and was lost in the pool. Another eel followed it, and then another.

"Les!" screamed Essie. "Les! Look at your eels! Stop!

There's a hole in your bag. You're losing them." She screamed again and again.

Les was not looking at us. He leaned over and snatched up another eel, quite unaware of what was happening.

"Les!" screamed Essie again. She stood up on the rock and waved. Les saw her and waved back. He was evidently pleased by her attention. Essie almost lost her footing. It was useless to scream, she discovered, but she continued to make excited gestures. Finally Les looked down at his bag. He seemed startled. He weighed his bag in his hand. He looked more startled. He opened up his bag and looked into it. Then he looked at Essie. She began to laugh. We laughed. Les threw back his head. We could not hear his laughter but we could see it.

"We'll go home to dinner," said Essie. "Les, he'll just have to get more eels this afternoon."

Well, to each his own particular brand of trouble. Eels for the Essie family, and for us our perennial difficulty about horses. Summer is hard upon us and there has been no pasture for weeks. All the horses in Kot-e-meen have been sent up into the high mountains. We have word that Sam Stenshaw, a half-breed who lives up beyond the Hildings, has a little horse that he may not be using and Les is going to see about it. There is also a possibility that Jim Tom has a horse. On his way up river, Les will see if he can get that horse for us.

We are beginning to wake up to the advantages that come from friendship with the men in this community, that is, the men here on the Rivers. In the East, things are different. But on the Rivers, masculine qualifications certainly do sing out, and, there is no doubt about it, men are valuable. Essie, with the brains that distinguish her, perceives this and attaches three—Mart, Les, and Eddy. We, with the brains that distinguish us, attach Essie, and so enjoy the blessings of all three with no embarrassment and none of the problems. Essie could also have Willis Conrad if she wanted him, but there appears to have been a slight disagreement. Essie said they had a little fight, but Eddy interrupted and said it was a big one. Essie had beaten Willis and Willis had pulled Essie's hair.

Willis seems to be born to trouble as certainly as sparks fly upward, for when his father, Jerome Conrad, learned that Essie had beaten Willis, he was so annoyed that he beat him very thoroughly himself. That annoyed Willis, so he left home and went to live in Happy Camp. It seems that that was all right with Jerome until the hogs began to come through the Conrads' fence, and it was up to someone to make new pickets. Jerome couldn't do it, so he had to pay Willis two dollars and a half for his feelings before he could persuade him to come back from Happy Camp and undertake the job.

It was late afternoon and the sun was well down behind the mountain when Les came in to say that all was well with the horse question. Jim Tom's horse was back from Orleans and the mailrider would bring Sam Stenshaw's little pony down to Pich-pichi tomorrow. That means that everything is set for the long-delayed trip to Hoopa.

It is heavenly to have horses, even temporary ones, and to be again on the trail, after having been cooped up so long in Kot-e-meen. Outside of Witchpec, we stayed at the Moonharts' and had a really good dinner. At Hoopa, Mr. Kyselka received us with something that almost amounted to enthusiasm. And to ensure that nothing should interfere with this wave of good fortune, we stopped at a place just above the trail to Sandy Bar to gather some Indian medicine. Indian medicine is called *op-si-e-kan-e-wan-ich* (black leg) and it grows among the rocks. We had to climb up a very steep place to get it. *Op-si-e-kan-e-wan-ich* are the First People. When they died, this fern grew up where they were buried. When you are sick or in trouble you hold some in your hands. You ask the First People to help you. Then they will take care of you and nothing will happen. If an *apruan* comes after you, you must put some *op-si-e-kan-e-wan-ich* on the trail. Then, as *apruan* cannot pass it, you will be safe.

I think Essie felt we should have gotten the *op-si-e-kan-e-wan-ich* on our way down to Hoopa because everyone knows the Hoopa Indians are *apruan.* Therefore we were in a very dangerous part of the country. But by the time we were back in Orleans we were again in our own country, and reasonably safe.

Fritz put us across the Klamath at Pich-pichi. Tintin waved to us as we went up the trail through Kot-e-meen. We pushed our way through the heavy brush and chaparral and walked up the path to our own house. It was with a sense of homecoming that we opened our door. But our house was not as we had left it. It was in a curious disorder. While we had been away, the Essie family had decided to move in and start housekeeping. Their goods were scattered in every direction and our living room did not look inviting. Les showed a simple, childlike pleasure at the sight of us, but Essie was quite aware of what we were thinking and lacked her usual poise.

Living with Indians is going to spoil us for living with white people. Indians know what you are thinking, and they know you know what they are thinking, and that simplifies things very much. We were very civil to Essie and said everything was all right. But Essie is an Indian. She knew exactly what we were thinking. And how we felt. She knew everything was not all right. We knew exactly what Essie was thinking, and she knew that we knew it, so everything was perfectly clear.

After all of Essie's things had been taken out of the house, Essie sent us over a big dish of strawberries. If we hadn't taken the big dish of strawberries, Essie would have known that we had decided to stay mad, and there would have been a feud. But we took the strawberries. That meant we thought that Essie had made adequate compensation for living in our house and leaving it all dirty, that the slight unpleasantness was forgotten so far as we were concerned, and that we and Essie were friends again.

To cement this happy state of affairs, the whole Essie

family came over in the evening and we discussed *apruan*. Essie and Mart had seen a devil fire the year before we came to the Rivers. They were both up on the mountain back of our house, after dark, when they saw a fire directly below them on the small flat between our house and the Offields'. They knew it must be a devil fire because it was blue, burned round like a bonfire, at first, and then spread out long, so it looked as though the whole flat was on fire. As they watched it, the fire gathered itself together and lifted itself off the ground, and they could see the face of a man in the air above it. Essie had caught hold of Mart's arm. "Oh, Mart," she had cried out, "I'm afraid. That's a devil fire." Mart wanted to go down close to it, but Essie was afraid to go with him and afraid to stay alone. She began to cry, so Mart couldn't go.

If you want to go deviling, you must have a peculiar, round, pinkish stone. With that you can do a good deal. You devil a man, and after a few weeks he gets sick and sometimes he dies. Penny Tom's wife gave the two little Pepper boys a piece of gum she had been chewing and deviled them both. Three weeks after they had chewed the gum, they began to feel bad. Then they got sicker and sicker until they died, both of them.

One night as Essie was closing the shutter a stone hit it. She called out to Mart, "Mart, what are you doing? You might have hit me." And Mart said, "I didn't do nothing." So they knew it must have been a devil stone. And two days after that Essie took sick and was sick for four or five months.

The best way to devil a man is to dig up a skeleton and take some of the grease out of the backbone. If you put some of the grease into the man's food, it is all up with him, that is, if he is an Indian. You can't devil a white man that way.

"But if you have just a little Indian blood in you, you can be deviled easy," Mart said sadly, and Eddy looked sympathetic.

Hackett was caught deviling once and had to pay a white

deerskin and twenty-five woodpecker heads before they would let him go. If he hadn't paid, Essie said, they would have killed him.

Mart said there are a lot of *apruan* all along this side of the Klamath and he wishes he were out of it.

"I try to keep friends with everybody," Mart said morosely.

But here Eddy chipped in. "Yes," said Eddy, "but Essie, she fights with everybody." To which Mart rather heavily agreed.

"Dogs are pretty good to have around," Mart said, after a long pause. "A dog ain't going to stand for a *apruan* coming clost to him."

Les had started to go. He had drifted over to see what was going on. Now we saw that he had stopped and was listening.

" 'Bout this time last year," Mart went on, "when Essie and me were living in this house, it was a moon just like this, and I went to the spring to get some water. The dogs seen it first. It come after me but the dogs got it down, and I come inside the fence. I got the gate shut just in time. It was big and black. I got me a good, thick pole and went after it. I hit it pretty hard and the pole snapped off and the thing came at me. Then it got on its hind legs and I saw it was a man. '*Apruan!*' Essie yelled. 'Mart, you come right into the house.'

"It was a devil, all right. I could see it plain. The dogs were after it and I could see it in the moonlight, right there back of those bushes. Then Essie and I went into the house and I shut the door and I didn't see it no more."

"That's what people do who are mad at you," Essie said. "They change into an *apruan*. *Apruan* always go home. They can't change back until they are at home in their own house. Mac-i-arum Joe, he shot at one that got after him and the next morning there was an up-river Indian in his cabin with a bullet in him."

That is all very well for Mac-i-arum Joe with his gun.

And for Mart, who is six feet two and can throw all his neighbors into corners if he wants to. But the spring they were talking about is our spring. It is right behind our house, and we often have to go there after dark for water. We hope very much that one of our neighbors, whose feelings have been hurt quite unintentionally on our part, won't take it upon himself to meet us there by the spring in the form of something very big and black and disagreeable the next time we have to go for drinking water after nightfall.

CHAPTER VI

Indians at Home: the Essie Growl and the Water Growl

It all started with Frank Offield, when he came in with the milk. Milk is hard come by in the Indian country and we were very much set up when we heard the Offields would let us have some. Frank is a half-breed but he looks like a white man. He is the sheriff, Sam tells us, and therefore a very important person.

When we came in, we found Frank looking at the lumber Mr. Hilding had packed down for us. We were planning for a dining table and at least one extra chair, but evidently Frank had other ideas.

"Oh," said Frank, "I see you ladies have gotten the lumber for your Sunday-school benches."

We looked startled and said we had not.

"Who told you there was going to be a Sunday school?" we asked Frank.

"Why," said Frank, "over to the store everyone is talking about it, and the mailrider said he heard about it in Orleans. They think it will be a big affair."

We were trying to adjust our minds to Sunday schools when we noticed that Frank was looking gloomily into the fire. Finally he said that he felt pretty bad about the Sunday school but he guessed he had better not come. He and Luther Hickox had been looking forward to it all week, but if anything happened and someone got killed it meant a hundred dollars, and that was a good deal of money, and his wife said he had better not come and that we would understand.

Maybe we didn't know about Essie, he went on. Why, he had to give her a beating before a whole roomful of men. (Sam's account had certainly been different.) For that matter, they were betting on it up river, how long it would take before Essie got after the schoolmarms and pulled out all their hair. And over to the store they were saying, if Essie was going to run the Sunday school, people wouldn't come. It just wouldn't be safe.

About this stage of Frank's recital, we had gotten around to accepting the idea of the Sunday school and we gently deplored Frank's staying away.

"Well," said Frank, "if you make a point of it, maybe me and Luther Hickox could arrange to come." Of course, he and Luther ought to come to Sunday school, he continued, because if someone got shot it would save time. If you were a sheriff, you ought to be right on hand when people get killed. But he wasn't sure about Essie. In fact, he had to go over now and arrest Les, and he was afraid it would only make more trouble. But Essie had set Les on to kill his hogs and he wasn't going to stand for that. He sort of hated to arrest Les. Sometimes he thought he'd resign being a sheriff. Just nothing but trouble. It was very disagreeable, and his wife didn't like it.

We stood at the window and watched him go slowly over to the cabin. From our front window we could follow the path down to the fence and then beyond the fence through the stretch of grass and low bushes to Grandma's cabin, where the Essie family were living. Frank walked very, very slowly. As sheriff, he was evidently dressed for the occasion. He had on a cutaway coat that was too small for him. He was not impressive. We thought of Les and his broad shoulders and wondered how things would turn out.

"These Indians, they don't know nothing about law," Frank Offield had said as he went out. "I guess maybe it's going to be hard to explain, Essie taking things the way she does."

We thought he was probably right, and our hearts sank as he reached the cabin door. He went in and the door closed. There was a long silence. Nothing happened. We didn't pretend to go about our business. We stood with our faces pressed tight against the glass, watching the cabin door. With Essie, anything might be possible. We were scared. It was no use pretending we were not.

Suddenly Frank Offield came out of the cabin door as though he had been shot from a gun. With incredible swiftness he leaped in again, and the door slammed. We could hear shouts and Essie's shrill voice. There was another long wait and then Frank came out, followed by Les. Essie stood in the doorway, and from the sound of her voice we were glad we didn't hear what she was saying. The sound of her voice was quite enough. It sent chills through us. Les stood by in silence, looking at the ground.

Frank was waving one arm toward the hills. We could positively see the hogs, wandering at ease, before Les had done them in. Then Essie's hand, the forefinger pointing accusingly, shook furiously under Frank's nose. We gulped as she moved closer to him, but Les was too quick for her. He stepped in front of Frank and held her off. Secure in Les's protection, Frank's voice rose high and strong. Then Frank turned, a rather insignificant figure beside Les, with his quiet poise and dignity, and the two of them walked away. We stood watching them until their figures were lost in the chaparral, and then we saw that Essie was making her way over to our house. We wondered whether the time had come for Essie to pull out the schoolmarms' hair.

Mabel sat on the settle with as leisurely an air as she could command. I did my best to look equally at ease. The door opened and Essie came in. She was composed and serene. She sat down quite unperturbed, with Indian repose and dignity.

She had come over, she said, to ask whether we would

like to see some pictures of Indian dances. She had found some snapshots last night and had saved them for us. If we liked, she would go and get them. We did like. We drew a long breath and tried to adjust ourselves.

It was a long time before Essie brought the conversation round to the late unpleasantness. She started in by saying that Grandma had a basket for us.

"It's a *muruk* and it's *tach-i-oori* (a present)," said Essie in her soft, low Indian voice. "Grandma hopes you'll like it."

We said casually that Mr. Offield had been down to see us. We had asked him to play his fiddle at the Sunday school. We hoped that both he and Essie would give us some help with the singing.

Essie said guardedly that Frank had been at their house.

"Was he?" we said.

"Yes," said Essie. "In fact, he came to arrest Les. He said Les killed his hogs. But nobody saw Les, and anyway Les had paid one hundred dollars for the hogs. But Frank is mean. He wanted forty dollars more and he said I had kept Les from paying the money. And I'd like to know what I have to do with it, anyway.

"Frank, he's Mart's uncle," went on Essie. "And he talks awful mean about me. Why, down at Somes—"

"Yes," we said hastily, "we heard about that."

"And as to that," continued Essie, "maybe he better not come to Sunday school. Just going around and making trouble for everybody."

It was time to speak plainly. We did our duty as field matrons, representatives of the Government, and recipients of forty Bibles from Bishop Moreland.

"Besides, we think both Frank Offield and Luther Hickox ought to come to Sunday school," we ended up firmly. "And we don't want any trouble at the Sunday school. It will only cost you money, Essie, and it really isn't worth it."

Essie agreed with us. She leaned back in her chair and looked at the fire.

"You know, I used to live here when I was a little girl," she said. "Old Graham, he was kind to me. He was a white man. That's why I speak English so good. There's pictures of his folks in a book he used to keep on the table. They was white folks where he came from. But he didn't never go back to them, just stayed here with my aunt and me. My aunt she wanted me to get married. Rube Morse, he came and give her the money, and my aunt said I was to go along with him. She used to beat me awful when I wouldn't go. Old Graham, he was sorry for me. But my aunt said it wasn't right and I ought to get married, and she kept at me and kept at me.

"So then I got so I didn't care, and I got married to Rube Morse, and Eddy come, and he was three months old and I said, 'I don't want to live with you no more, Rube.' And Rube said, 'Maybe you better go, Essie.'

"So I come home. And my aunt said I could, because Rube he didn't give her all the money, so I stayed with her and old Graham. And then Mart came along. I'll tell you about that sometime. But I've got the book of pictures that old Graham had, right up under the eaves. I'll go and get it for you."

It was an old-fashioned album. In it were pictures of old Graham, a courtly-looking old man with a good deal of presence. There was a picture of Essie's aunt, a stout Indian woman. In the back of the album were photographs of old Graham's people. Gentlefolk. Ladies with crinoline and gentlemen with high stocks.

"That one's his brother," Essie said. "Old Graham used to talk about him. And that one's his aunt. He used to say she was an awful fine woman."

When Essie got up to go we had forgotten all about Frank Offield. But Essie remembered about the Sunday school.

"There won't be no trouble," Essie said.

And then she went out.

We were having a leisurely breakfast the next morning

when Essie came in and sat down by the fire. A little later, Eddy came in, followed by Mart. We had hoped when Essie left the day before that we could go ahead with the plans for a Sunday school without trouble or the probability of someone getting killed, but from Mart's expression it looked as though we had reckoned without the Rivers.

For a while Mart sat without saying anything. Then he looked at Eddy and said maybe they had better go and look at the irrigation ditch. But instead of going he continued to sit looking at the floor, and then he burst out. It appeared that the Essie-Offield growl was not the only trouble in the Hamill family. Jerome was trying to take the ditch away from him, and he was going to law. And then Jerome would see who would come out ahead.

This warmed Essie up. She said that Frank Offield "had tooken" one of Hilding's steers and she hadn't said anything about it. And then he took the pig she had brought up after she had washed it and marked it. And he put it in his corral, and, of course, it got out. So it came back to her. And when they wanted some meat they went and killed it. And now Frank says they kill his hogs. But nobody can prove that Les did it. However, poor Les got scared and paid Frank forty dollars, which was too much for a hog, anyway. She wouldn't have minded if Frank had just come in and arrested Les. But she wouldn't stand for the kind of things he said. So she just started to tell him some things, and he slapped her. So, of course, she kicked him. And he said he was going to take the ladies right away and her to prison. But she didn't care, she said defiantly.

By this time she was out of breath. And it looked as though it were high time for us to take the floor.

We said we did not doubt that Mart would win his lawsuit. If things had happened as he said they had, he might have a clear case. Of course, it sometimes took years before a lawsuit got settled. And the court might not allow anyone to use the water during that time. And also a lawsuit might cost Mart five hundred or six hundred dollars. Lawsuits were expensive. And the case might go against him, no matter how just his claim might be.

We were sorry for Essie because it was an awful thing to kick an officer of the law. Probably she didn't understand about it. Had she ever talked to anyone who had been in prison? Well, prisons were pretty bad.

There was a long silence. The Hamills were plainly depressed. We felt we were making an impression. We hoped we were. It was our first "trouble" on the Rivers, and we hoped, we very much hoped, that no one would get killed.

We did not like to think of Essie going to prison, we went on. Essie was a friend of ours. Suppose we talked to Frank Offield? That is, if Essie felt it was the right thing for us to do.

It appeared that Essie did. She and Mart were looking at the fire.

"I guess you can if you want to," said Essie.

And should we mention the lawsuit? Maybe it could be arranged without going to law and spending all that money. What did Mart think about it?

Mart was silent a long time and then he indicated that it might be wise.

Did we know, he volunteered, that he had seen Frank that morning? Well, he had, and there had been a kind of a tussle. We knew, didn't we, that he had licked Frank once, licked him good?

Essie said something in an undertone.

"No," said Mart, "that wasn't the time my nose got broke. Frank kinda got me licked that time. But the time I was telling you about I got him licked real good." He looked gloomily at the fire again, and then added, "If you want to see Frank, I ain't got no objection."

It was fortunate we had gotten the loan of some horses the day before. They now stood outside, tied to the porch. We left the dishes unwashed. We left the plates and cups on the table. We made the best speed we could to Somesbar.

What happened when you were faced with a trouble on

the Rivers? It seemed so very easy in this country for someone to get killed. Were we doing the right thing? Essie and Mart were our friends. Suppose we did not handle this the right way?

From behind, Mabel gave my horse a savage poke. My horse was the slow one.

"Why don't you use your spurs?" said Mabel crossly. "I should think you'd want to get to Somes and have this settled."

I dug in my spurs. I did want to get it settled.

We had crossed the swing bridge and had nearly reached the store when we saw Frank Offield coming out of the hotel. When he saw us, he increased his pace, as though he was trying to get to the store as fast as possible, but we headed him off.

"We hear there has been a little trouble," we said. "Would you like to tell us about it?"

Frank said that it had nothing to do with the trouble over the water rights. Of course he had said he would back Jerome up, and Johnny Pepper, too. He wasn't going back on his word. He wasn't that kind of man. As for Essie, she could pay that five-hundred-dollar fine or get three months' imprisonment. He didn't care if it took his last cent. He'd pay out everything he had. Yes, if necessary he'd sell his wife. But he'd have the law on Essie. And he didn't care what Mart had said. He never stole anything from his grandfather. For that matter, Mart owed him one hundred dollars at the store and had never paid four dollars he had owed him for three months.

We looked sympathetic. We said that Essie should not have kicked him. It was a bad business. Very bad. But he must remember that Indians knew very little about the law. They did not know how bad it was to kick a sheriff. He had a perfect right to have Essie arrested. Of course, it was a pity he had to do it though, because it would only make more trouble. If Mart retaliated by killing off all his hogs, it was the least he might expect. It did seem too bad that

such near neighbors should quarrel, especially when they
had stock. It was hard to prove who killed one's hogs. Then,
too, Mart was a good shot. In this country, you never
could tell when there would be trouble, and it was easy
to get a man at close range. Even if the Hamills did pay
the money, if Frank were dead, it wouldn't do him much
good.

Frank looked impressed.

As to that, he said, it really wasn't worth while going on
living the way things were. People killed your hogs all the
time, and he'd just as soon move away and let the whole
thing go. Only he'd promised Jerome that he'd stick by
him, and he was sure we weren't the kind of ladies who
would expect him to go back on his word.

We assured him that he had always struck us as a man
of the nicest honor. But suppose Jerome withdrew on his
own account? That would be all right, would it not? We
could see Jerome and find out how he felt.

We were standing a little way from the store as we
talked. An Indian with a sack of flour on his back came
out of the store and passed us.

"Hello, Dumphrey," said Frank.

The Indian was the redoubtable Dumphrey Pepper, who
was carrying on the death feud with Barney Schenck. We
had never seen Dumphrey before, although we had heard
of him often enough. We looked at him and he looked at us.
It struck us unpleasantly that our own past was not entirely
clear. Someone who was not a friend might take the position that we had deviled a baby at T Bar. We had been up
to T Bar to call on the family, and the next day the baby
had come down with grippe. On the face of it, the baby
could have been deviled.

It might be just as well to make friends. We asked
Dumphrey to come over to see us. We said we had heard
that he was the best drummer on the Rivers. Dumphrey
gave us a wintry smile and went on toward the swing bridge.

When we turned back to Frank Offield, he was looking less ruffled.

Frank said that Essie was a pretty mean woman. Maybe we thought he liked being ordered off the place, and all the other folks going to have a nice time at Sunday school. And his wife said she was coming, anyway. And he said she shouldn't. He guessed husbands and wives ought to go to Sunday school together. And Luther Hickox was pretty sore because his wife had said she was going to come. Of course, maybe it might be fixed up with Essie. He'd think it over. And if the Hamills wanted to make it up, he guessed he'd be willing.

We recrossed the swing bridge and took the trail home. As we rode into Kot-e-meen, at the first house in the rancheria we saw a familiar back. It was Jerome. On being questioned, Jerome said mildly that he didn't want to fight Mart. Mart was a pretty big man, and he, Jerome, hadn't felt so good since he got kicked by his horse about two weeks ago. He guessed it could be fixed. It was all right with him. Only Essie, she got mad, and Frank, he got mad, and there you were.

It had grown dark as we rode home up the trail. We have never grown to like night on the trail. It had turned cold and there were gusts of wind. It looked as though there would be storm. We wondered if Essie would approve what we had done. You never could tell with Essie.

The next day we went in for an elaborate housecleaning. It served to take our minds off what might be going on. In the evening, we made only a small fire and let it die down. A rather dampened fire was in line with our feelings.

But at nine there were steps on the porch, and soon the room was full of Indians. The Essie-Frank-Mart-Jerome growl was over. They had come over to sign a paper. Jerome was to have the water three days, and Mart was to have it the rest of the week. Everything was all settled. When they left in the morning they had gone over to the Conrads, and it wasn't so good. Frank was there and Frank was mean. Essie and Jinny Conrad had growled some, but after a while they got it fixed.

"Essie told Jinny all she had done for her," said Mart, who told the story. "Jerome, he used to gamble an awful lot, so he didn't bring no money home. And there wasn't no food in the house, and no fire, and the childrens ain't got nothing to eat. And every day Essie, she'd go and pack them some dinner. Essie, she reminded them of this, and Jinny, she cried some more, and Jerome, he said, 'That's so, Jinny. And if I get the water three days, I ain't going to fight.' "

So it was all right, and they asked everyone to come to Sunday school, and nobody would have to pay for the hogs, and Frank said he wouldn't get out a warrant for Essie, and so they all came home.

After Mart and Essie had signed the paper, they handed the pen to Jerome. Jerome shook his head and mumbled that he would go get Willis. Willis would sign for him. But we would have none of it. We wrote a large, clear JEROME CONRAD on a piece of paper and then closed Jerome's flaccid fingers around the pen.

"You copy this," we said firmly.

Jerome giggled wildly and everybody joked in Indian, but when he was finished and sat wiping the sweat from his face, there clear on the agreement was his signature, quite good enough for anyone to read.

After everything was over and the Conrads had gone home, Mart brought in a great armful of wood from his own woodpile and we sat around while the flames leaped up and the room grew bright. We were all in high spirits.

"We used to have lots of dances over to this house," Essie said. "Dances cost an awful lot of money. There's always fights at dances. Last time we had a dance here, Mart, he had an awful fight with Billy Oscar, and I told him he got to stop and help me in the kitchen. And Mart, he pitched me right across the table. It made me feel bad," went on Essie conversationally, "Mart hitting me like that right before all those people. It got me ashamed. Mart, he had to pay me ten dollars. Then Mart, he come along to the kitchen, and Anderson Grant, he finished up Billy Oscar for him.

"But that wasn't as bad as Les. Mart, he didn't do nothing but pitch me across the table. But Les, he mussed things all up. I got awful mad at Les right here in this room. He and Anderson Grant, they jumped clean through that window over there, and broke all the glass, and took the frame right out with them."

"But why did they jump through the window?" we asked. "Were they drunk?"

"No," said Essie, "they wasn't drunk. At least not much. Willie Tom, he was shooting at them."

The fire died down. It was getting late.

"*Jora* (let's go)," said Essie. She smiled at Mart and then she smiled at us.

"*Jimmi co-yap* (goodby)," said Essie, and they went out.

CHAPTER VII

Innocents Abroad on the Professional Trail

At long last we are to have horses. Frank Offield has rented us two of his and has sent Ernest up into the mountains to get them. You cannot be properly equipped schoolmarms in this country without horses, and you certainly can't get anywhere without them.

The first week on horseback has definitely set us up in our own estimation. My horse is to be called Sally, so named because she is "the darling of my heart." It is true, as Frank put it, that she is "a good one to buck you off," and when we start out in the morning she hunches her back in a very disagreeable way, so I mount very, very gently and try to get her going without hurting her feelings. But as soon as we get to the mountain above the Offields', where the slope is extremely steep and any nonsense on her part will take Sally off into the view, I stick in my spurs and show my real disposition.

Meantime, Mabel is some distance behind me, on Jane. Mabel calls her Jane because her "temper is so very odd to-day." I judge from the language Mabel uses that Jane's temper is a little odd most days. But here on the Rivers your affection for the animals does not depend on the sweetness of their dispositions but upon the number of miles they can travel. My devotion to Sally is based on the way she cheerfully trots up the little hills (that is, after the slight unpleasantness of the start), and the way she comes in fresh after a twenty-mile jaunt up river.

You may think we mount in an ordinary, everyday

fashion. Not at all. When we got up on our horses at Bair's for our first ride into the Indian country, we did not consider form but just hopped and hopped, and hoped that sometime we would land safely in the saddle. So when it came to mounting at Hoopa, we hopped our way up with childlike confidence.

Mr. Mills watched us with marked disapproval.

"Do you always get on that way?" he asked coldly.

We said that we did.

"Don't you know," said Mr. Mills impressively, "that at any time you might get dragged and killed?"

We were silent.

"Always mount this way," said Mr. Mills, and he showed us.

The method on the Rivers, the swell method, in fact, the only method is this: You stand by your horse's head, facing his tail. You seize the stirrup, twisting it around toward you. You insert the tip of your toe, never the ball of your foot, in the stirrup. (Remember about being dragged and killed.) You hop in the air and the stirrup swings around, carrying you with it. The horse, naturally of a stylish habit, immediately starts off at a trot. You throw your leg over the saddle, and there you are—trotting along as peacefully as you could ask. And talk about style! Of course, if you light on your horse's neck, or on his tail, it is not so good. But when it works it is really impressive.

But the real excitement of riding horseback on the Rivers is due to the things we pack with us. (Back east you would say "carry.") First, there is the burden of the eggs. They are my concern. Eggs are very rare on the Rivers and the Hildings seem to be the only people who have them. The hunting coat my brother gave me when we left home has the most marvelous pockets. In one pocket I pack a tomato can with layers of eggs in it, each egg wrapped in newspaper. The crackle of the newspaper as the eggs thump against the can makes a pleasant accompaniment to the trot as Sally pounds along. In my other pocket is a box stamped

in heavy black letters: BAGSTER BIBLE. This is filled to overflowing with eggs so that the top will not fit down, and you
have to be very wary when you slide it out of your pocket.

Directly in my middle is the precious buckskin bag
that Papa Frame made me, and which is belted round my
waist with a deerskin thong. It has fringe along the bottom
and fastens with a little wooden button. It packs a kodak
and all the money we possess, which in this country of five-
dollar gold pieces and big silver dollars is no light matter.
The little buckskin bag beats me cruelly upon the abdomen
even when *mani gishi* (my horse) progresses at a walk, and
when she trots the castigation is severe.

After all the excitement of the water growl, the first
Sunday school at Kot-e-meen was a very peaceful affair. Only
thirteen people came, most of them Indians from Kot-e-
meen and Pich-pichi. Nobody got killed and "there wasn't
even no row," as Mart commented sadly on leaving.

It was after our part of the Sunday school was over and
we were wondering what to do next that Essie came into
the picture. She said there was a drum "over to their house"
and that Les should go and get it. The drum was made of
skin, stretched tight over what looked like the frame of a
cracker box. The skin was painted with an Indian design
and the drum had a very clear, rich tone. We learned later
that the drum belonged to the Pepper family. As there is
a feud between Essie and the Peppers, how she came by the
drum is not quite clear. It seems that a drum is a very
personal affair. You beat on your own drum and sing your
own song, and only as a special favor is anyone else allowed
to beat on it.

However, with no Peppers present, the drum was received with marked favor by all the drummers present at
the Sunday school. The rhythm was very quick, and the
men sang "ai-ai, ai-ai," placing their voices differently from
the way we do. As song followed song, the beat became
more pronounced and the men swung in time to the music.
Everybody talked and laughed, and it was evident, even

though there were only thirteen present, that the first Sunday school at Kot-e-meen was a success.

But that was only our first attempt at a Sunday school in the Indian country, before we had really gotten our hands in. Now things are different. With horses to ride and a steady pressure of demand from both Indians and whites, we opened a second Sunday School at Somesbar. I regret to say, however, that on the opening day the trip to Somes was attended by a slight misadventure. At least from my standpoint. It was an especially nice day, and in honor of Sunday I had on a spotlessly clean shirtwaist and a high, clean, starched collar, very hard to come by in the Indian country.

As we ambled peacefully along the trail to Somes at an easy trot, my mind properly occupied with memorizing the appropriate prayers for the day in the Episcopal prayer book, we suddenly came upon old Henry, stretched out at full length on the trail and quite indifferent to our approach. My first awareness of the situation was when I found Sally's tail where her head had been a second before. Sally was annoyed at finding old Henry stretched out on her particular trail, and she didn't care who knew it.

The next minute I found myself and the prayer book in a bush and Sally a short distance away, nibbling the top leaves of another bush and keeping an eye on old Henry. I picked myself up, very mad. But, praise be, my clean shirtwaist was quite unmussed and my high, white collar unblemished—no doubt the reward of virtue. But thereafter it made me regard Sally more respectfully.

But to come back to our Sunday schools.

Now, on every Sunday morning at nine, you may observe what were once considered the somewhat heathen members of the Episcopal Church of Somerville, New Jersey, in specklessly clean shirtwaists, mounted on their steeds. On this particular Sunday I am in the lead and have in my hand my prayer book. It has just occurred to me that "Lighten our darkness" is not the appropriate prayer for

Sunday morning and I am memorizing a collect while Sally, with a clear trail ahead, moves at a sedate trot. We are on our way to Sunday school number one.

We tie our horses to a bush and cross the swing bridge, having been very careful to dismount so as not to dirty our nice clean shirtwaists. At the store, Mama Frame is waiting for us. She says she is feeling better, for which we are thankful, and together we walk over to Carrie's, having, as we go, a heart-to-heart talk about funerals and marriages and anything else about which we find we are sympathetic. Sunday school is held in Carrie's house because her room is good-sized and all the benches and boxes, ordinarily reserved for a white dance, are around the walls. There are also two beds, which are very large and will hold quite a number of the congregation. In all, twenty people are present, the most important being Frank Offield and Mrs. Wilder.

Les has also come over with two bashful youths. When you go to two Sunday schools on the same Sunday, as Les does, I call that doing pretty well. Mabel, of course, leads the singing but I supply the volume of sound, which, although you may not think so, is a very important part. We sing "Onward, Christian Soldiers" and "Little Children, Can You tell" until the walls shake and the dust rises from the floor in clouds. We have a masterful hand these days and Sunday school goes with a snap.

After the last hymn has been sung, everyone comes back with us to the swing bridge, we recross it, mount our *gishis*, and ride pell-mell for Sunday school number two.

"I rather hesitated to come," Mrs. Wilder told us, "because, you see, Carrie and I don't speak. But I felt I really couldn't miss a Sunday school."

Sunday school number two is in our own living room. It is a fairly large room but the pressure of Sunday school tries it to its farthermost limits. Of course, there are the large bench and the small bench and the three chairs and the two woodpiles. But these we have always with us. In addition, for Sunday school, we have the special supports that Mart made us out of the lumber he got from someone's mine. We hesitated to ask whose. Planks are laid on these supports and they cover all the available space in the room. We have just seated Dora, Martha, and the Essie family from Kot-e-meen when there is a sound outside and all of Pich-pichi boils in—two men, four women, three children, and a baby. They are followed by Pete Henry and Hackett and the two strange Indians who were here last week.

I gather myself together and begin with a collect and a reading from the Bible. I love the collects and enjoy the freedom to choose the ones I like best. We have just gone on to "Greenland's Icy Mountains," which is in Mabel's province, when I see two shy Indians youths lingering by the fence. I go out and gently urge them in. They sit on the woodpile. We have gotten as far as the "sunny fountains and the golden sands" when Essie nods at the door and I get there just in time to see three men escaping through the fence. We hold parley at the top of our lungs, and they come in and find seats to the accompaniment of "Waft, Waft, Ye Winds, His Story." The latest members of the congregation are the Brizzard storekeeper from Orleans and two Orleans Indians. The Indians are able to squeeze themselves onto one of the benches, but the storekeeper and myself have to stand.

We have a prayer and have just embarked on "While Shepherds Watched Their Flocks" when the members of the congregation rush to the window. Something uncommon is coming along the trail. White dresses. Chiffon hats. The door opens and a lady holds out her hand to me.

"I am Mrs. Hickox," she says.

The last barrier is down. The Hickoxes are half-breeds and stand very high on the Rivers. Luther Hickox is accounted the most dangerous man with a gun within a hundred miles. With Frank Offield at the Carrie Sunday school and the Hickoxes at Kot-e-meen we are made men. Backed by the Hickoxes, the singing goes with a will. Only the gathering dusk rouses the congregation to the dangers of the trail, and then Sunday school number two is over.

We have our own infallible rule for discovering the church affiliations of the members of the congregation. "Come, Ye Disconsolate" brings out the Roman Catholics. "Rock of Ages" goes strong with the Evangelicals. "Lead, Kindly Light" is sure-fire with the Episcopalians. When the Richardses from Orleans turned up, one Sunday, and we started "Lead, Kindly Light," the unrestrained volume of Mr. Hale's voice was unmistakable.

Mrs. Richards is the wife of the manager of the Orleans Bar Gold Mine and Mr. Hale is the mine's superintendent. We were in full swing in "Abide With Me," when they arrived. Mrs. Richards proved quite competent to meet the situation. She sat on a bench between two young Indians and found their places for them in one of the twenty hymnals sent us by the bishop, while Mr. Hale modestly found a seat for himself on the table. When an Orleans Indian arrived, Mr. Hale courteously gave up his seat on the table and joined Mrs. Tuxbury, another member of their party, on what space remained vacant on the woodpile.

After Sunday school was over, we were startled to see Mr. Hale scrambling out with the planks and the saw horses. Men sit while women work in this country. As they had left their horses in Pich-pichi, Les put them back across the Klamath. We went down with them to the Kot-e-meen crossing and stood on the high bluff, watching the long paddles gleaming in the afterglow, with Les at the stern and Mr. Hale at the bow, until they made the other side in safety.

But Sunday schools are only one of the activities that have opened up for us since we have obtained horses to ride.

In four weeks, the school at the Hildings has climbed to twenty-three scholars. At first, we had only children, but in a relatively short time all our pupils were grown

men and women. We thought it must be the songs we sang
with the children and the dangerous attraction of "Drop
the Handkerchief," played Indian fashion, that brought out
so many grown Indians. Young men and maidens, old men
and children would line the trail as we rode in and would
join in the games at the mere hint of an invitation. But
it was slowly borne in on us that the fascinations of arithmetic surpassed even the attractions of the games. As for
the alphabet (interpreted by Mabel), it was enough to make
any squaw walk ten miles and cross the Klamath for even a
half hour of attention.

Indian women on the Klamath are skilled basket makers
and have a feeling for design. Mabel would write a big
A on the blackboard. A squaw would come up to the blackboard and slowly and carefully produce an excellent copy.
Indian children in this country learn to read and write at
Hoopa, but the older men and women have never had a
chance to learn anywhere. When the children come back
from school, there is a barrier between them and their
parents. In short order, the pressure on us was so great
that the children were allowed to play out-of-doors while
their mothers sat entranced, learning to write their own
names and those of their children.

Then came the big event. After a trip to Hoopa, kind
Mr. Kyselka sent us a bagful of primers that had been
discarded for a later edition. The excitement in Mabel's
corner grew with every class day. The number of squaws
who came to school increased so fast that Mabel had to
divide her work into grades. For the more advanced scholars,
those who had weathered the alphabet, she presented the
picture of a large Newfoundland, identified below as THIS
IS A DOG.

"Dog," a squaw would murmur, and dig her elbow
into her neighbor. On the next page, in equally large letters,
you would find THIS IS NED. HOW DO YOU DO, NED.

"Tisss isss Net," Mamie and Nettie and Mrs. Johnson
would murmur. "Ow to you to, Net."

But while the gentle buzz of talk and laughter went on in Mabel's end of the room, it was nothing to the excitement in mine.

In my corner of the room were all the Indian men. Mabel completely monopolized the blackboard (except on very special occasions). Most of my young Indians had already had a year at Hoopa and were not interested in primers. I had no arithmetic. So one day I collected a group of young fellows who had been leaning against the door and tried them out with a few questions in mental arithmetic. We are getting to be very much at home with Indians these days, so I ragged my group in a very approved Indian way.

"When Luther Tom goes to Orleans, they say it takes him three hours to get there. Maybe Luther Tom, he goes to sleep on the trail." (Stifled laughter.) "But Shan Davis is big man." (Loud laughter. Shan is a bit undersized.) "He walks maybe four miles an hour. They start from Pichpichi at eight o'clock. What time does Luther get to Orleans, and what time does Shan get there?"

There would be one steady roar of laughter while each man in the crowd strove to be first with the answer.

In a couple of class days, like Mabel, I had to divide my group into grades. The number of Indian men who came to school doubled and then trebled. A wonderful time was had by all, that is, with one exception. While the class shouted with laughter and yelled and stamped as they competed for the answers, the unfortunate instructor, who has always been extremely poor at mental arithmetic, strove in mental anguish to arrive at the correct amount before anyone else could get there. It is true that I seem to lack for nothing in the popularity of the questions. But heaven help me with the answers! I generally make it. At least, up to the present time I have made it. But at a frightful mental cost. I have ridden back from the Hildings' so spent I have had to cling to the saddle.

It was on a particularly large class day that I found

Bernard Jerry at my elbow. I had just been working with a young fellow who seemed to have an appalling facility in arithmetic. He moved through the shoals of 289 tons of hay at $18.75 a ton with a sureness that was staggering. But he was nothing compared with Bernard Jerry. We had noticed Bernard standing outside the Hildings' gate for a couple of class days. The third class day he came inside. He shook his head when I asked him if he had ever been to school. I wrote "1-2-3-4-5-6-7-8-9" on the blackboard and we counted on our fingers until Bernard got the idea. Then I left him with a pencil and some paper I had managed to dig up to copy off the figures for himself.

While I worked with a hilarious group of young bucks, I could feel Bernard's eyes boring into my back, so as soon as I could I took a look to see what he was doing. All the numerals were copied correctly and neatly and Bernard was evidently quite conversant with them. I started in afresh with the blackboard and showed Bernard how to count up to one hundred. Bernard's face was impassive. I went over everything with him a second time, and then the demand from the mental-arithmetic class became so insistent that I had to leave Bernard to his fate. As I turned away his gentle murmur followed me: ". . . twenty-two, twenty-three, twenty-four, twenty-five . . ."

There was only a half hour of school left when I got back to Bernard. Without hesitation he counted from one to nine, and then went on without a miss to one hundred.

"I am sure that is all you will want today," I said, thinking of Lewis Hilding, who had had only a half hour on his fractions.

Bernard looked wistful.

"Would you like to learn some more?" I asked dubiously.

"*Ha* (yes)" said Bernard.

Well, it really did not matter so much if we got home late. It was about time we quit being so afraid at night on the trail. We buckled down, and Bernard and I went over the whole theory of addition. I demonstrated with little

sticks what carrying one meant. Then I wrote out an example in addition and showed it to him. He nodded. After I
had finished with Lewis and his fractions, Bernard showed
me his example, added correctly.

"Have you never done any arithmetic before?" I asked
him.

Bernard shook his head.

"No, he ain't never been to school," said Luther Tom.
"He don't know nothing. And he don't talk English so
good," Luther added.

The Hilding class broke up.

When we got to the Hildings' the following Friday, Bernard was not there, but he was the first to arrive the next
school day. He counted to one hundred correctly. He wrote
all the numerals on the blackboard with skill and finish.
He did the most difficult example in addition I could devise
for him without a single mistake.

I drew a long breath and taught him to subtract in the
interval that remained, while I was keeping ten young
bucks going with a complicated purchase at the Orleans
store, and ordering the lumber for a one-story house. When
I could give Bernard a minute, I found all his examples
correctly worked out. When we saddled up for the ride
back to Kot-e-meen, I regarded Bernard with considerable
apprehension. It began to look as though I had turned up a
mathematical genius, and I did not feel that the Lord had
qualified me to deal with one.

Two weeks later, Bernard came to school and learned to
multiply in one lesson. A month later, he cleaned up long
division in another lesson, proving all his examples correctly
by multiplication. I rode back to Kot-e-meen in a state of
collapse. I was convinced that Bernard *was* a mathematical
genius. What if the Karoks were only bow-and-arrow Indians? What if they had not arrived at the stage of textiles
and pottery? I could see Bernard Jerry rising higher and
higher in the mathematical scale until finally he reached
heights where I could never follow him.

But after his complete mastery of long division, Bernard Jerry never came back to school. Whether he was satisfied with what he had achieved or whether something interfered with his return, we never knew.

With an elementary treatise sent us by Mr. Kyselka, my classes are now studying geography. When you are teaching geography, something to guide your own footsteps is a great comfort. It also gives wide range to the imagination. I hold up a map and put my finger on a spot. Then I ride high, wide, and handsome. Geography, history, and legend all flow from my lips. The only difficulty is that the more I tell of the history and traditions of the whites, the more I question whether they are fit subjects on which in instruct the Indians. The Kot-e-meen class was so shocked by what I told them of ancient Rome that I was very much discomforted. Lewis Hilding, aged twelve, wept over the story of Little Red Riding Hood and kept saying in a trembling voice, "But the old woman. The wolf got the old woman."

After the quiet, peaceful life we lead here on the Rivers, with only an occasional panther and a few shootings and knifings at the Forks of Salmon, conventional history is really too bloody. It looks as though we should have to suppress a large part of it.

CHAPTER VIII

The Ford at Siwillup

Essie was over to tell us that they are planning a hunting trip on Baldy, the high mountain on the other side of the river that we can see from Kot-e-meen, and urged us to come along. The more we think about it, the more we want to go. It is true that it is the policy of the Indian Department to uphold the game laws, and that the hunting season is still several weeks away, but we find we are not much in sympathy with the game laws as they affect the Indian. To our mind, the Indian's hunting code is much better than the white man's. No Indian kills for sport or can understand such a point of view. He kills only for food, and he safeguards the game in his district much more effectively than does the white man's law.

Then, too, there is the highly expedient attitude of Mr. Hunter of the Forestry Department. He said with a sigh when Sam Frame had venison in season that it was a great relief to be able to ask what kind of meat he was eating.

Moreover, we have had it in mind for some time that it would be a good thing if we knew more about the up-river country, and that if we should go on the hunting trip we could ride up to Siwillup and see Old Bob Elliot. Anyhow, hunting season or no hunting season, we have decided to go.

As Fitzy Offield was not going to bring the horses until the afternoon, as soon as we had finished breakwast we panted up our mountain and helped Mart roll down cuts for their winter supply of wood. It was a most inspiring

job. We would both tug at an enormous cut and shove it
to the edge of the decline. Then, in a moment, it would
be thundering down, leaping and bounding sometimes three
or four feet in the air, like a thing possessed. We were never
tired of watching Mart handle his enormous double-bitted
ax. It might be a carving knife for the accuracy with which
he can touch any piece of wood at a given spot and make
it fall apart.

What with one thing and another in the Essie household, it was mid-afternoon before we were ready to make
the start from Pich-pichi. It was a long, slow climb. Mart
and Les were in the lead, then came the loaded animals,
and last, Essie and ourselves. Past Prospect Hill we struck
along the ridge, and the sky became a bright pink behind
the blue mountains. Mart came back to tell us that this
was the place he had caught two little bears, and Les jumped
off the trail, saying he wanted to see the bear's den. We
went on without him for a half mile and then we heard
a shot. Mart caught up his gun and crashed down the mountain while Essie and Mabel and I sat on little tufts of grass
by the trail and watched the mountains grow more and
more dusky, until the moon came up. Then Les panted up
with a radiant face and told us he had shot a four-point
buck that must weigh at least three hundred pounds and
they were going to take Baby down after it. We helped
shift the loads, and in a few minutes the men were back
with a beautiful deer thrown across the saddle.

It went hard with our feelings to think we were going
to eat that beautiful thing for supper, but then, of course,
a panther might have gotten Les and eaten him. It seems
that all is fair on the Rivers when it comes to the hunting
season.

It was bright moonlight when we took the trail again.
We walked in Indian file, the two men, Baby with the deer,
the loaded animals, Essie and ourselves. Around us were
tall pines through which the moonlight came in bright
patches. The clip-clop of the horses' hoofs and the scrape

of the packs against the saddles made a soft, subdued sound. Mart told us later that it was an old trail and hard to find.

The next morning, Les had difficulty in finding it in the morning light, although he had just been over it the night before. But Mart never hesitated. He twisted and weaved, in and out, but we were always on the trail, although he had only been over it once before, several years ago.

It was just after daylight when we left the hunting party and started up river for Siwillup. It was a beautiful morning and would have been pleasant enough anywhere; but here in the high mountains it was so cool and so fresh that we felt as though we were walking on air. For a long time we followed the ridge. Then, at length, we came out on the side of the mountain, and far, far away below us we saw the Klamath.

It was after six in the evening when we pulled in at Siwillup, the ranch of Old Bob Elliott. Long before we drew up at the gate, we had gotten glimpses of the wide expanse of clearing, and the barns and corral. The house was painted, which was very unusual in this country. There were wide stretches of cultivated fields. We rode up and asked two half-breed boys, who were sitting on the porch, whether we could spend the night. They grunted and said nothing. The door opened and a half-breed girl looked out. She said she guessed we could stay, and went in and shut the door. We dismounted and stood by our animals, not knowing quite what to do. An old white man came around from the back of the house, looked at us a minute, and then went up onto the porch. He was very old and bent. He walked with difficulty, and when he looked at us we were not sure whether he really saw us or knew what we were doing there.

We guessed this must be Old Bob Elliott, known all up and down the Rivers as a just man in his dealings with the Indians. Old Bob had crossed the plains in a covered wagon, settled down on the Rivers, married an Indian woman, and had never left the Indian country, seen a

railroad train, or been out of the mountains since the day
he rode in, nearly sixty years before.

As Old Bob seemed to have forgotten us, we went out
to the barn, unsaddled our horses, and then came back and
sat on the porch. The two half-breed boys got up and went
away. Old Bob sat on a chair near us, bent over and talking
to himself. He kept pulling at his fingers and looking at
the floor. An hour went by. It grew dark. We could hear
sounds in the kitchen but the arrival of two "white womens"
had evidently spread consternation. It had been dark for
some time before we were bidden to come in, and we found
supper on the table.

From the porch, we went first into a little room with
an airtight stove in it. As we came to know the Elliotts
better, we found that summer and winter Old Bob sat
crouched over the airtight stove, pulling his fingers and
talking to himself. When white men spent the night at
the Elliotts', they sat in the little room with Old Bob and
ate with him in the dining room. But when half-breeds
or Indians came, they ate in the kitchen with Mrs. Elliott and Eliza and Bill. Everyone on the Rivers spoke
well of Old Bob.

"Old Bob will treat you right," they say.

But Indians did not eat with old Bob in the dining room
or sit with him over the airtight stove. Old Bob married
a squaw. She bore him a son and a daughter. But his wife
and his son and his daughter did not eat at the table with
Old Bob. Old Bob was white. He never forgot that he was
white, and he did not let his wife and his children forget
that he was white and that they were Indian. His wife and
his children came into the dining room and put the food
on the table. But only white people ate with Old Bob Elliott.

As we sat beside the airtight stove with Old Bob, after
supper, he told us about the days when Happy Camp was
booming. He sat pulling his fingers, and he did not look
at us, but his quiet old voice droned on and on. He knew

more about the Rivers and the Indians and the white men in the old days than any man we had seen, and it was plain he liked to talk about the things he knew. But he never looked at us, and sometimes we were not sure whether he knew we were there. Once we had asked Sam Frame about Old Bob Elliott and Sam had said, "Oh, well, you know that's the way old Elliott does things. He never would eat with his wife nor let his children come to the table. He believes that Indians should keep their place."

When Eliza Elliott came in to take things off the table, we asked her whether we might go to bed. She guessed we could go, she said, but she was afraid we wouldn't like the bedbugs. Then she brought a lamp and showed us the way upstairs. The stairs were between walls and very steep. We stumbled up with our saddle bags and found ourselves in a large attic room. In one part of the attic, near the stairs, a partition came a little way out from the wall. It partly screened a bed from the rest of the room. Eliza pointed to the bed and said that was where we could sleep.

We were very thankful to find clean sheets on the bed. Clean sheets are not at all common on the Rivers. We modestly undressed in the dark and crawled into bed. We had just pulled up the covers when there was a heavy thump on the stairs, and Old Bob, with a lamp in his hand, came slowly up. The light from the lamp fell full on our bed and Old Bob peered down at us, but we were not sure whether he was looking at us. He and the light passed on and we saw him getting ready for bed. Later, the other members of the family came up and stowed themselves away. Everything grew quiet and we went to sleep.

No wicked bedbug so much as looked at us. Life on the Rivers had taught us to be prepared. Neatly wrapped in a sheet, in our saddle bags, was about a pint of insect powder. We shook some of it over our sheet and lay down in the midst of it. As always, it proved quite effective, and in the morning we got up unblemished.

We had heard that there was a Klamath ford from the Elliotts' to T Bar, across the river. The Indians did not speak any too well of the ford, but we wanted to see some of the Indians at T Bar, and since we were going to live on the Rivers it was time we quit being so afraid of things like panthers and rattlesnakes and fords and after dark on the trail. We certainly ought to know enough to find our way around.

As we got up from the breakfast table, we asked Eliza Elliott about the ford, but she only shook her head and went out to the kitchen with the dishes she had in her hands. While we were saddling our animals, we looked around for anyone who might give us a few directions, but there was no one, so we went back to the house and asked Old Bob. We had to shout to make him hear us but he finally looked up.

Was the ford all right? Had people crossed it this summer?

Old Bob nodded. Yes, he guessed they had.

He looked straight before him at the little stove. We were not sure he understood what we had said.

Where was the ford?

Down the trail a piece. We couldn't miss it.

Was he sure that someone had been across this summer?

Old Bob nodded. He guessed so.

We stood hesitating. We ought to know more about the ford. The ford at the Elliotts' had a bad name. But Old Bob did not look up, so we left.

Our breath was coming a little fast as we rode down the trail. I hoped we would meet someone. We had never taken a new ford all by ourselves, without any directions. At Somesbar, we had watched men take the ford several times, before we attempted the Salmon crossing. But there were no Indian cabins along the trail and the only person we met was a little Indian boy.

"Where is the ford?" we asked.

He pointed to a faint track off the main trail. We turned

our horses toward the faint track and rode down to the river. Before us stretched the Klamath. It lay smooth and quiet after the long drought of the summer. But the river was very wide between the Elliotts' and T Bar. The Salmon was only a small stream in comparison. And no man on the Rivers, Indian or white, spoke lightly of fording the Klamath. There were plenty of tracks on the sandy bar at our feet. Horses might have forded at this place or cattle might have come down to drink. On the other side of the river, directly across from us, was a steep bank. We could see no sign of any tracks indicating a crossing, but we thought, still farther down the river, we saw something that might be a trail. It was very faint and distant, however, and we could not be sure.

We stood for a long time searching with our eyes for the little ripple of water that would mark the ford. It was hard to find anything like a ripple on the smooth surface of the river. Then we thought we saw it, a faint, faint ripple, across from where we stood, then down, then diagonal, then straight across to the other side. This must mark the ford.

"No one cares what happens to a fellow in this country," Mr. Hunter, the forester, had once said to us. No one cared whether or not we took that ford, and no one cared whether or not we made the other side. We were full of a hot rage at the Elliotts. There was a lump in my throat. I saw Mabel tighten her lines and her horse took the water. I followed. At first, the ripple was very clear and the water was only up to my horse's knees. We were out and away from the bank, moving steadily toward the center of the stream. The Klamath seemed very, very wide.

Step by step, the horses splashed along. I tried to fix my eyes on a tree, far, far away on the other side of the river, but I could not see very well. No one in the Indian country might care what became of us, but I cared a great deal. I winked my eyes hard but they blurred again and again with tears, and it was hard to see. Then I became sharply aware that we were definitely farther downstream and that the water was becoming very deep. Mabel must have seen it also. I saw her stop and try to spur her horse back to safety and the sandbar. The water was now up to the horses' bellies. With our feet out of the stirrups and hooked up on the saddles, we had very little control of our animals, but they must have sensed the danger of the deeper water. They answered to the lines and presently the water was not so deep. We were safe again on the sandbar.

The opposite bank was still very far away. I glanced back. The place where we had taken the ford was also very far away. We were two tiny dots slowly splashing our way along the great expanse of the river. Then we began to feel the sharp pull of the current. The lump in my throat was very big. I wondered whether there was any chance that we could make the other shore. It was hard to watch the ripple. I grew dizzy with the glancing motion of the water. We were now going directly downstream. Would Mabel know when to make the turn that would take her to the opposite bank? Or would her horse go on? If he went on . . . I swallowed and then held my breath. In the current, as we were now, one plunge from the safety of the sandbar and even a good swimmer had little chance in the swift-flowing and treacherous Klamath.

It seemed as though I could not breath at all. Then I saw that Mabel had made the turn. Her horse was moving steadily toward the opposite bank. Slowly, very slowly, the bank came nearer. The water was no longer up to the horses' knees. It barely washed their hoofs.

We were across.

It was months later when we saw the Elliotts again. But Old Bob remembered that we had taken the ford.

"Get across all right?" said Old Bob. His face broke into a smile and he chuckled softly to himself. "Last man who went across that ford, he was drowned."

CHAPTER IX

Indian Gambling, and Other Topics of the
Day in Indian Country

The pack train came in this Sunday. Yes, it did. It was hard to believe, but there it was, for anyone to see. It is the first pack train to arrive since we came to the Rivers in January, and it is now July. We saw it straggling up the trail as we stopped at the Somes store for a minute, after the Carrie Sunday school—fifty mules loaded with all the things we didn't have during the winter and couldn't buy for love or money.

Everyone was a bit abstracted at the Kot-e-meen Sunday school, and of course, we thought it was because of the arrival of the pack train, but when Sunday school was over, after we had sung all the now familiar white hymns, nobody stayed for the Indian singing; the crowd drifted over to the Essie cabin. There had been an unusual number of men and boys among the congregation and we were keeping an eye on what was going on, because, as Mart would say, we didn't want "no row" as a finishing attraction to Sunday school. Then Essie came over.

"They are gambling Indian way," Essie told us. "They've got the drums and everything. You come over and we'll watch."

Jimmy Johnson and Willis Conrad were squatting down facing each other and a large circle of Indian men and boys were crowded around them. As we made our way through the chapparal we could hear the sound of drumming. As we came into the circle, Willis was facing us but Jimmy had his back to us and we could only catch a glimpse of him when he moved. The crowd was plainly excited, and the drumming and singing was very loud.

When they saw us the crowd opened up a little and we stood quite close to Willis, with the circle of Indians pressing up against us from behind and on both sides. We could see Shan Davis just behind Willis, sitting on Essie's upturned washtub. He was drumming and singing, "Ey-yah, ey-yah. Han-o-way."

All the Indians swayed to the beat of the drum.

Then we saw that directly in front of Willis was a square of calico, held to the ground by little stones at the corners. Willis was squatting and swaying to and fro before the calico, with his hands held behind his back. Suddenly Les, who was just in front of me, stepped forward and flung out his arm. He pointed to Willis's right. In response, Willis brought his right arm from behind his back. He flung out his hand with a wide sweep and threw upon the calico in front of him a handful of carefully fashioned little sticks. They were all white except one and that one had a little black band at its center.

There was a roar from the crowd of Indians. Les's face broke into a smile and he gave a little giggle. Everyone else shouted. Shan abruptly stopped drumming. The crowd drew back and we saw Jimmy Johnson. Jimmy was facing Willis and he also had a little square of calico in front of him. He leaned forward and picked up the handful of sticks that Willis had thrown down. As Jimmy picked up the sticks, Willy Jones, who was sitting behind him on a box, began to drum and sing. But it was a different song from the one Shan Davis had sung.

"Han-o-way-yah. Han-o-way-yah," sang Willy.

Les leaned forward and placed a little twig on the calico before Jimmy.

"Les, he's awful pleased he won," said Essie.

But we had no time to watch Les. Jimmy was beginning to sway back and forth as Willis had done. His hands were hidden behind his back. The beat of Willy's drum grew more insistent. A young up-river Indian stepped out and flung out his arm, just as Les had done. In response to the gesture, Jimmy brought his left arm from behind his back and flung the handful of sticks onto the calico. The stick with the black band was not among them.

"Ah-h-h-h-h-h," said the crowd, and then was silent.

The young up-river Indian had lost. Willy continued his drumming. Jimmy again put his hands behind his back. Every dark face in the crowd was intense. There was a pause, and the sound of the singing and drumming was very loud.

"Han-o-way-yah. Han-o-way-yah."

Pete Henry stepped forward and flung out his arm. Again the sticks were thrown on the calico.

"Ah-h-h-h-h-h," breathed the crowd.

Pete Henry had lost. As our eyes examined the sticks, the stick with the black band was not among them.

Again Jimmy swayed to the sound of Willy's drum. Several young Indians stepped forward but an older Indian pushed them aside. He flung out his arm. The sticks fell on the calico. There was a roar. Some of the young Indians leaped in the air. The roar grew in volume, but strong and clear above the noise of the shouting Indians was the beating of Shan's drum.

"Ey-yah. Ey-yah. Han-o-way," sang Shan, and there was no mistaking the triumph in his voice.

It was growing dark when we came away. The sun had gone down behind the mountain but we had not seen it go. If we had not been field matrons and representatives of the Government, not to mention our somewhat tenuous relations with the bishop and his forty Bibles, we would have bet the bottom dollar in our little buckskin bag.

"Let's back the Indian gambling," said Mabel. "Down with the white dances and their influence on the Rivers. They are just an excuse for everything that is bad. Drinking and cheating and losing all your money and worse.

Think of Mart and Essie and how they have never gotten over what happened.

"And then just look at this Indian game. Why they have gambled all afternoon and all that Les has lost is two dollars and fifty cents. That's cheap enough the way things cost on the Rivers. And just consider the thrill. I wish I could have bet some money this afternoon. I know we haven't much, the way the Government never sends us any salary. Of course, we might have lost our last cent, but I should have liked the chance to try."

The next Sunday, in spite of the fact that there should have been no rain until November, a nice heavy shower fell and there was no chance of an Indian gamble. After the congregation had gone home from Sunday school, we thought there might be a chance of our settling down before a little fire with a *McClure's* and an *Ainslie's*. We snatched a bit to eat and had just seated ourselves when we heard a step on the porch. Big Steve stood in the doorway. We were very much gratified. In the opinion of everyone, Big Steve was one of the outstanding Indians on the Rivers. But those days we were a bit outstanding ourselves. We couldn't go calling on people in the perfectly careless way we did when we first came to the Rivers. It was proper that Big Steve should call on us.

One day, a couple of months before, Big Steve had come to the Hilding class. We had just given Lewis Hilding his scanty half hour in fractions when I looked up and saw a powerfully built Indian standing in the doorway. He had unusually broad shoulders and carried himself with great presence and dignity.

"That is Big Steve," someone near me had murmured. "That is Big Steve from I-ees-i-rum."

While we went on with the lesson, Big Steve stood by the window watching us. In a quiet interval I asked him whether there was anything he wanted to learn. Big Steve's face was impassive.

"No," said Big Steve.

Well, there were plenty of Indians clamoring for attention. I guided one class through some problems in multiplication and then went over the same ground with a second class. It was Big Steve's opportunity. He leaned carelessly again the window frame, but when anyone in the class hesitated Big Steve would drawl the answer. Every answer was correct.

When school was over, he let me give him a paper with the figures one through nine written on it.

"Maybe I come to school for old men," Big Steve drawled. "How long I come to school here so I can count?"

"I grinned and said, "Oh, maybe two or three years."

Big Steve's face relaxed into a grin.

"I think I come maybe two-three weeks," he said, and still grinning he joined the other Indians on the porch.

But after that one day up river, Steve had never come back to the school at the Hildings'. It would seem that we had not made a good impression. Now he stood in our doorway.

Conversation with Big Steve was very formal and quite in accord with Indian custom. When we had first come to Kot-e-meen, our manners were very bad. We talked too much. We lacked reserve and dignity. We were much too polite. Now we knew how to behave.

Big Steve sat on the settle and we occupied the two barroom chairs that we had finally persuaded Sam Frame to sell us. There was a long pause. We all three sat in silence until Big Steve opened the conversation.

"At I-ees-i-rum the water is not so high now. I come across ford."

"*Ha* (yes), we replied.

As was proper, there was another long pause.

"The trail is good now," we observed in our turn. "We have been *urok* (down river). It is good traveling."

"*Ha,*" said Steve.

There was another long pause, and then, as was proper, we relaxed a little. Big Steve permitted himself to look around the room.

"You got baskets," he said. "*Karok* (up river) we got good baskets. My woman make good baskets." (This was true. Later, we found that Big Steve's wife made some of the best baskets on the Rivers.)

By this time the preliminaries had been observed as prescribed by Indian etiquette, and Big Steve settled back on his seat. We then conducted the conversation much as we would at home.

"When white mens come to River," Big Steve began, "all Indians very sick. Indians up river die. Indians at Kot-e-meen and Pich-pichi die. Very big sickness. Very bad for Indians."

(The sickness Big Steve referred to was an epidemic of measles. It struck the Klamath country in 1852 just before the big gold rush and wiped out half the Indian population. The disease itself must have been severe, but the number of deaths were probably due to the Klamath Indians' method of treating any kind of ailment. This was to sweat out the disease in the sweat house and then jump in the icy Klamath.)

"Many Indians are sick now," we said. We gave a brief talk on TB and syphilis and the causes of infection.

"Mebbyso," said Big Steve.

He thought a minute and then began to describe the days before the white men came to the Rivers. Steve had been a boy when he saw his first white man. He could remember it very well. White men wore clothes. "In old days, Indians don't wear clothes. In old days, Indians don't get sick. Everybody go in sweat house. All Indian men go in house. Light fire. Put stones on fire. Pour water on stones. Very much steam. Very much hot. Indian, he sweat and sweat. Drum in sweat house. Sing in sweat house. Stay two days in sweat house. Come out and jump in Klamath.

Klamath, he very cold. Very good for Indians. Nobody sick before white mens come to Rivers."

Steve leaned back against the settle. We said nothing.

"You know Old Man Elliott?" he asked. "Good man. Treat Indians very good." Steve implied this was not common. He waved aside his own hunting exploits although the interest we expressed would have brought out a full personal history from any other man on the Rivers, Indian, half-breed, or white. But Big Steve preferred to talk about forestry regulations, the status of the Indian, and the moral code of Indians and half-breeds.

"Indian has a trouble," said Big Steve, "Pay one hundred dollars. Never think of it no more. Half-breed has a trouble. Much talk. Take one hundred dollars for trouble. Every time he get drunk, come back and talk about trouble just the same. Half-breed, he no good."

The only Indian Steve seemed to think ill of was Jim Ike. Jim wears the skin of a king snake for a hatband, and we secretly admire it very much and wish we had one. But Big Steve is unmoved by the hatband and strongly dislikes Jim Ike. He refers to him as "tam little Chim."

"That tam little Chim," said Steve, "he want trouble. Trouble. All time want trouble."

This hardly seemed fair to us. Jim Ike is one of our most faithful scholars. He appears to have a quite peaceful disposition and we have never heard of his killing anybody.

Before he left, Steve sat for a few minutes looking thoughtful.

"Half-breed he no good," said Steve slowly. "White man, he got God. Indian, he got God. Half-breed, he no got God. He no good."

Then he stood up, straight and impassive. His face was expressionless and a little sad. "*Jimmi-co-yap* (good-by)," said Big Steve, and he went out.

The next day we rode over to Somesbar for our mail and found Mama Frame and Sam on the porch consulting about a coffin for Papa Frame. After the long months in an Indian village it gave us a start to find ourselves again in the familiar atmosphere of the white man.

"Sam doesn't see how Papa can last the winter," said Mama Frame "and he'd like to have something nice."

"Of course," said Sam, "it does seem a long time ahead to be thinking about it, now in July, when we ought to have three or four more pack trains, but it takes an awful long time to get an order through and it ain't safe to leave the coffin for the last pack train because something might happen and it could get left behind. So we've sent for a catalogue to see what we can get."

"We don't want nothing fancy," explained Mama Frame, "but I think Papa would be real pleased to have us send down below for one that's made up nice, the way they do things down there. Sam, he's seen a picture of one he thought Papa would like and it didn't cost as much as you would expect. I tell Sam both Papa and me would feel easier in our minds once the coffin was ordered and we had cause to think it would be here in time.

"Sam's a good boy, taking so much trouble and all," said Mama Frame as we turned and went into the hotel. "I wisht you'd stay to dinner. I don't never have a chance to talk to you girls these days. I do hope you'll be around when Papa goes. I'd like to have some reading from the Bible and a prayer said over him. It makes me so easy in my mind about that coffin. I ain't never got over the time my baby died in Arizona. I wake up in the night and think about my baby and it don't seem as though I could get resigned.

"My baby was sick and I done all I could but there wasn't no doctor nowhere in the country, and everything I did, she just got worse. And I pretty near went crazy with the worry and the work going on all the time, and then a man rode in and said how the Indians were up and we would have to run for it. Seems like I couldn't stand it. Always living there and never having nothing and the baby looking so bad. So I said, 'You men folks go along.

I ain't going nowhere with a sick child.' And Papa Frame, he kept saying, 'You got to wrap her up and come along. This feller says the Indians are awful near.'

"And the baby was awful bad. I held her in my lap and it seemed as if she couldn't get her breath. Most every minute I'd think she was going to die. 'I ain't going to move this child,' I said. 'I don't care if the Indians is coming. You go along, all of you, and let me be. If this baby's got to die, it's going to die in peace.'

"So the men folks leaned their guns against the wall and they stood around, and Papa Frame and another feller, they stood by the window, and they'd look out and then they'd kind of whisper together. Every so often Papa Frame, he'd come over and ask me how the baby was, and then he'd go back and stand by the window some more. Then one of the men got up and he went out and come back with a spade.

"Let's us fellows get busy on the grave," he said. "Better'n waiting until those murdering varmints get her." And they all went out.

"By-and-by the baby didn't gasp so bad and then it straightened out. I didn't need to look. I knew it was dead. Papa Frame, he'd been standing right there beside me. He gave a look at the baby and then he reached down and took the baby right out of my lap, and before I could say nothing he was out-of-doors. I didn't try to stop him. Seems as if I felt so bad I just didn't care. I sat there, and then all the men came in. Papa Frame came back and put a shawl around me. Then all the men took hold of me and shoved me out of the door. The horses were saddled, standing tied to the fence. They drug me up and put me on a horse. One of the men was shoveling dirt into the grave. When he saw us come out, he let go his shovel and come over and jumped on his horse. Papa Frame took hold of the bridle of my horse.

" 'You hold on,' he said. 'We got to ride.'

"The last thing I saw was the shovel, lying on the ground where it fell."

CHAPTER X

We Make the World Over and Leave Out Something

Ever since we came to the Rivers, the Kot-e-meen Indians have been talking about the Indian New Year's. They call their New Year's Day Pic-i-ow-ish, and every New Year's Day the world has to be made over. Charlie Offield tells us that Santa Claus will have to come past the peach tree just outside our gate. We can't make out whether the Indians really call him Santa Claus or whether it is an Indian word that sounds like Santa Claus. In any case, he will have to go up the mountain past our peach tree, and it seems the world would suffer if he went up another way.

It is very improper for anyone to see Santa Claus, so we hid behind the curtain in our living room and were careful that no one should see us. He proved to be an old Indian, naked to the waist, who carried a black basket in his hand. Charlie Offield told us that he had already been in the sweat house for twenty-four hours without anything to eat or drink, and that tomorrow, still with nothing to eat, he must climb the mountain on the other side of the river. At the top of each of the two mountains, in a particular place, he will find a twig, which he must bring back to the sweat house in his basket. Neither Charlie nor Essie seemed to know what he did when he got back to the sweat house, but it seems to be something very important.

While Santa Claus is climbing the two mountains, six of the younger Indian men must shoot with bows and arrows. Yesterday, the shooting was on the other side of the river but today it comes directly past our house. We hung over the fence with Essie and exchanged some lively com-

ments with Grandma, who called out to us that she was "going to be white woman" now and come out and see the
shooting.

First, Hackett appeared with a green bough in his hand,
followed by all the old men and boys carrying green boughs.
He stopped in front of our peach tree, planted his bough
in the ground, placed a little stick in the center of the
bough, and shouted. The shout was repeated by all the
young Indian men, who had collected in a group by the
stile. They had bows and arrows in their hands and stood
about a hundred yards away from the bough with the stick
in the center. While the shooting was going on, the old
men and boys kept up a sharp, staccato yelp. First, Jimmy
Johnson shot and then George Leary and then other Indians, until finally Penny Tom's arrow struck the stick in
the center of the bough. Everyone shouted and the whole
crowd moved forward to another stand, farther up the mountain and out of our sight.

By the time we got back to the house, we found the
entire Tom family waiting to be fed doughnuts. It is proper
to feed people at Pic-i-ow-ish. Then Charlie Offield came
in and told us there had been "big trouble."

It seems that in spite of everything that they said in
the sweat house, Fritz from Pich-pichi is going to set up
a table at the dance and sell refreshments for two bits
(twenty-five cents) a head. This is entirely contrary to
Indian custom as everything should be free at Pic-i-ow-ish,
and all the Indians are very much upset. They argued
all yesterday with Fritz, and they got so excited that they
forgot to carry on the proper ceremonials for that day, so
that some of the world has not been made. Nobody knows
just how bad this is or what will happen. Even Essie is
very much disturbed.

The dances are held on a grassy flat on the bluff above
the river. We walked down with Luther Tom, who told
us there are two trails to heaven. One is a good trail and
all the virtuous go that way. After a long time you come

to a very deep, swift-flowing river. You stand on the bank and call until some of your friends on the other side come over in a dugout and put you across. There are always dances going on in heaven, and plenty of hunting and fishing, with no game laws or canneries down river to interfere with you. It seems well to know as little of the bad trail as possible, but at one place you have to pass through a burning forest, and Luther says the hot stones burn your feet terribly.

It was nearly dark as we came out through the thick bush onto the flat above the river. On all sides tiny campfires were springing up until the entire flat was covered with them. The supper was to be very orthodox, smoked salmon and acorn soup. In the soft half-light around the twinkling fires we could see the dim forms of Indian men and women. Close to each little fire Indian women were spreading Indian baskets on the ground before their guests. The *ossips,* or Indian cooking baskets, are quite large. These are filled with acorn soup, about the consistency of thin porridge. Then hot stones from the fire are put in the cooking baskets and left there until the acorn soup is cooked and ready to eat. Everyone was eating, each with his own little *ossip* before him. First, before the fires, where everything was free, and then ending up with a regular gorge at Fritz's fire to the tune of two bits.

Whenever there was a lull in the soft Indian talk, we could hear the roar of the Great Falls of Kot-e-meen, very clear and very close. Dark figures would appear, distinct in the firelight, and then become only moving shadows in the distance. Then the firelight would light up a shadow quite close, and it would be Martha or Les come to ask us if we were having a good time and how we liked acorn soup.

The dance was held at the lower end of the flat. We could just see the men standing in two long rows facing each other, each man holding a piece of brush in his hand. At both ends of the double row a man was crouching. While the Indians in a row sang a low chant and waved their pieces of brush, the crouching end men, with enormous pieces of flint in their outstretched hands, would spring out and dance to and fro, crossing and recrossing back and forth. It was something on the idea of the Virginia Reel. As we watched, Essie came out of the night and stood by us. She told us that the war dance would be further up the bank, and that the dancing would go on all night. But there would be no Indian dress. The Indians in Kot-e-meen and Pich-pichi had sold all their ceremonial things. "But next year, down to Orleans," Essie said, "when they have deerskin dance, everybody will come and they will dress Indian way."

We had watched dance after dance and it was getting late when Mart came up with a lantern and said that if we liked he would see us home. Next day, Pic-i-ow-ish was over, and though there had been a lot of drinking Essie said it was the first time that there hadn't been "no shooting or trouble," and that nobody had got knifed or killed.

In spite of no trouble at Pic-i-ow-ish and an attendance of forty-one at Sunday school, from our standpoint the year is beginning badly. There is a sudden marked increase in our medical practice. We are not born medicine men and we can acquire painfully little from our small store of written material. Yet the practice of medicine is being thrust upon us. Cuts and bumps and bruises we can take in our stride, but Mamie Tom and Short Annie are quite another matter.

Of course, there is Dr. Kyselka at Sawyer's Bar. He is retained on an annual basis by all the whites in his community, and a proportional amount of his salary is levied against every white man in the district. He then treats every dues-paying member free, and if he can keep them well and satisfied, with little trouble to himself, so much the better for everybody. But when Dr. Kyselka leaves Sawyer's Bar and crosses two mountains into our country, he charges one hundred dollars a visit. That is all right if you have struck it rich, but as most of the population in our area have not struck it rich, Dr. Kyselka's calls in this neighborhood are strictly limited.

Naturally, there are Indian doctors. And when an Indian doctor does take you on, they are wonderful. Big Nancy cured Mart of something that had all the earmarks of appendicitis when he had just about given up hope, and the next day he was able to get up and go to work in the mine.

The disadvantage with Indian doctors lies in the fact that they can only cure you when the auspices are favorable. When the mists flow down river, your cure is assured, because all the Witchpec devils who have been causing trouble flow down with the mists. But when the mists are coming up river, naturally the Witchpec devils come with them, and no self-respecting Indian doctor is going to take a chance with a Witchpec devil. However, the honest thing about Indian doctors is no cure, no pay. All the Klamath Indians look upon the white practice of payment down, kill or cure, as a straight steal.

So when the mists are blowing up river, that is the place where we come in. For Indians on either side of the river, Dr. Kyselka at one hundred dollars per is out of the question, and most of the Indians seem to be of the opinion that we are competent to deal singlehanded with any Witchpec devil.

Last week, Essie told us that Short Annie had a new baby. It appears that is very bad for Short Annie to have a baby.

"Indians say," said Essie, " 'long time no baby; woman, he die.' "

"But didn't Annie get through her confinement all right?" we asked.

"Yes," said Essie, "baby, he come all right, but Indians say Short Annie he die and Grandma says so too."

We went to see Grandma. "No good. Woman, he die," said Grandma.

We went to see Short Annie as soon as we had finished breakfast. Short Annie was washing the baby with Cuticura soap and powdering it with Mennen's talcum powder. Then she laid it in its tiny basket. The advantage of being an Indian is that you have an endless supply of baskets, so you can fit one to any baby no matter what its age or size. Annie held the baby's hands close to its little naked sides while she wrapped pink outing flannel around it until only its nose was showing. Then she put the baby in the basket, lacing a piece of thong from side to side until the baby was completely bound in from chin to hips. When it was all dressed and ready, Short Annie handed the basket and baby to William, who dandled it very competently. Short Annie appeared perfectly well but she said she had a "peen" in her chest, so we gave her an elaborate rubbing with oil and turpentine and came away.

The next day, when we went to see her, Short Annie was worse. She breathed with difficulty, and when Mabel asked her where the pain was she gasped and said, "All over."

Short Annie is not a friend of ours. She wanted to rent us her house when we came to Kot-e-meen. We tried to explain that we were going to rent Essie's house because Essie's house was larger, but Short Annie was not satisfied. We ought to have given Short Annie a present when we refused to rent her house, but at that time we knew little of Indian customs. Since we did not give Short Annie a present, now she is no friend of ours. She does not believe we can help her, so there is nothing we can do.

Mamie Tom has also been very ill. We think it is pneumonia. But every day, after we rubbed Mamie Tom with oil and turpentine, there was a look of hope in her eyes. There were days when Mamie Tom could hardly breathe at all but she always looked at us with hope. Now she is getting well.

However, Short Annie is now very ill indeed. She has fever and her breathing is difficult. We brought her a mustard plaster but she pushed it away. She turned her face from us, and her breathing was very bad.

We went over to Essie's and asked if there was anything

we could do. "Grandma says Short Annie he die," said Essie. "Grandma says there ain't nothing you can do."

The next day, when we went to see Short Annie, she was very weak. She followed us with her eyes but she would not let us help her. We went over to Somes to see Mama Frame.

"Poor Annie," said Mama Frame. "Poor thing. Carrie and Alice say she will die. All the Indians thought she would die when the baby was born. I don't think there is anything you can do."

Back in Kot-e-meen, we were not yet unsaddled when Tintin came to say that Short Annie had sent for us. The room was full of Indians when we opened the door. The air was stifling. William was holding Annie in his arms.

"She wants you to give her water," said William. We heated water and put a little whiskey in it from the tiny bottle with its basket covering that Essie had made for us. Annie tried hard to swallow it. Then she shook her head. An Indian doctor came in. The room was so filled with Indians that we could not see what she was doing. But the mists were coming up river and she went away. The filling up of the lungs is a terrible thing. It took all our resolution to sit there watching Annie die.

Each of the Indians, in turn, came to the bed and said, "*Jimmi-co-yap* (good-by), and then went back and wept. There were so many in the room that it took a long time. Then, at last, the terrible sounds stopped. Annie was dead. We crept out and went away.

The funeral is to be tomorrow. "Indians say you better come," Tintin told us.

The men worked all day digging the grave. We had not far to go. The house is just above the Great Falls. with a beautiful view of the river and the mountains. As we came up, the men were putting the last nails into a large box. They then covered it with a black cloth so that it might look like a bought coffin. They lowered the box into the grave, and then William set fire to some straw to light Annie on her way to the other world. The women stood around crying softly but the sound was drowned by the roar of the Falls. Then the men filled in the grave and the crowd melted away. All the work was done by half-breeds because they do not have to purify themselves as Indians must if they touch a dead body.

When we passed the grave the next day there was a picket fence about it to protect it from the hogs. All of Annie's dresses were hung on the pickets. An alarm clock and some dishes were placed on top of the grave. A little distance off was a pair of shoes. When an Indian dies, no one may use any of his personal possessions; they are all placed on the grave. This does not apply to ceremonial dress like white deerskins, or woodpecker heads, or flints. These are family belongings and pass from father to son. But personal possessions must go with the dead so they may use them in the other world.

Tintin walked home with us. He says that Daisy James's mother is dead and that all the Indians have bad colds. Bad sickness like this is because the world was made wrong at Pic-i-ow-ish.

Tintin's face was troubled and a little sad. We stood for a minute looking down from the bluff at the Great Falls of Kot-e-meen. The roar of the Falls was very close. Then we turned back into the chaparral.

"Very bad to have world made wrong at Pic-i-ow-ish," said Tintin slowly. "Very bad for Indians. Everybody got trouble when world was made wrong. Indians and everybody. Just wait and see."

CHAPTER XI

Everybody Got Trouble When the World Is Made Wrong, Indians and Everybody

For some weeks now we have been having a taste of really warm weather on the Rivers. The sun shines clear and hot from a cloudless sky. They tell us that at the Brizzard store in Orleans the thermometer holds steadily at one hundred degrees. All the little showers are gone away, and the Indians say that not even a few drops will fall until the rainy season in November. All the flowers have gone and the grass is dry and brown. It is true we still sleep at night under one blanket, but the wool comfortable we made for ourselves, and the traveling rug, have been rolled up and put out of sight.

About ten days ago we had a call from Mr. Hunter, who is one of the foresters, and we had a long heart-to-heart talk about vacations. It seems that everyone who works in either the Forestry or the Indian Service gets two days' vacation for every month that he has been on the job. The idea has gone completely to our heads. We have now been seven months on the Rivers and that would mean fourteen days' vacation. It also means we could go east. Mr. Hunter tells us that technically our field extends to Yreka, which is on the railroad. It is true that no Indians live in that part of the country, but from the standpoint of a vacation, until we reach Yreka, we are still in our own field, and therefore on the job. At Yreka, we could board the Southern Pacific, see our families, call on the Indian Department in Washington, talk Forestry regulations, traveling animals, and all the things we need so much here on the Rivers, and be back in Yreka again, like Cinderella, before the clock strikes the hour of midnight on the fourteenth day.

I want iced tea, with lots of ice tinkling in the glass, and fried chicken, but Mabel says ice cream for her, plate after plate of it. We can hardly bear to think of it. Without a moment's delay we sat down and wrote Washington for permission to leave our field.

There is another question we want to talk over with Washington. We have just been confronted with our first serious problem in regard to water rights. Mac-i-a-rum Joe came to see us yesterday with another Indian who lives near him. It is Old Man Nelson who is causing the trouble. Old Man Nelson has turned the course of the stream that runs through his property so that all the water is carried through his own property, and the little garden of Mac-i-a-rum Joe, his nearest neighbor, is dying for lack of moisture. We have thought for some time that we ought to cross the river and make a call on Old Man Nelson. Now there is trouble.

The sun shone hot when Mac-i-a-rum Joe put us across the river. Mart tells us that yesterday the thermometer stood at one hundred and three, in Orleans. The trail to the Nelson place led straight up the mountain, a pretty stiff climb. Mac-i-a-rum Joe would wait courteously for us, as all the Indians do, when he realized that we were completely winded. We did not feel the heat as much as we had expected, but we were thirsty all the time and gladly stopped to drink, at every tiny creek, from the little silver cup that we always carry with us.

Joe's cabin was on a little flat about two miles back from the river. Beside the cabin was a tiny wisp of garden, in which all the plants were dying or dead from lack of water. The bed of the little stream was dry. Mac-i-a-rum Joe stood leaning against a tree.

"It ain't no good," he said. "It just ain't no good."

We were very doubtful whether there was anything we could do, but we left Joe looking sadly at what had once been his garden and went over to see the Nelsons. In California, proprietary water rights give a man unquestioned right to turn the course of a stream so that it benefits his own property. We felt hot and tired after the climb, and a good deal bothered. It was a bad situation and it looked as though the law was on the side of Old Man Nelson.

Old Man Nelson's house was about a half mile down the trail. The ground was fairly level. It was well wooded and cool in the shade. We saw a dead rattlesnake hanging from a tree, but the trail was so obscure that twice we lost our way and had to retrace our steps. Then the trees fell back and there was a large clearing, in the center of which was the Nelsons' house. Mrs. Nelson was Old Man Perch's daughter but she looked very Indian, even more so than most half-breed women. She had been to school and there were marks of education in her speech. Old Man Nelson was twice her age, and tall and lean. He had agitated white hair, and he came from Illinois. The Nelsons were friendly and we sat down and had a long talk, but we got nowhere so far as the water was concerned.

Old Man Nelson had his wrongs. The "Injins" killed his hogs and once his house "got burned down." He'd done a lot for all the "Injins" around there. Mac-i-a-rum Joe "wasn't no good."

"I'd have given him the water," said Old Man Nelson, "but first thing I knew I was in a lawsuit and I got to take my witnesses to Yreka because there ain't no proper law in Orleans. You know that," said Old Man Nelson belligerently. "And whose going to pay me back all that money? That's what I want to know."

We tried everything we could think of, but Nelson grimly refused to consider every suggestion we made. We got up and went outside and stood on the porch.

"Just have a talk with Joe," we pleaded.

"No," said Nelson, "no. It won't do no good. He'll get mad and I'll get mad and it'll be worse than it is now."

There seemed nothing for it. We were licked. We turned

around for one last try. Old Man Nelson leaned over his fence and shook a bony finger at us.

"You want your own way," he screamed. "You want your own way. And you won't get it. But I glory in your spunk."

Mac-i-a-rum Joe walked back to Pich-pichi with us. We told him we didn't think it would do any good but we would be glad to go to Orleans and find out whether anything could be done. Joe wanted to fight it out, but personally we thought Old Man Nelson had the law on his side and that Joe wouldn't stand a chance. Not in Orleans, anyway, and not with the way white men felt about Indians in the gold country. Joe thought he could find horses for us and after a long wait he came back leading two. The horses had saddles but no bridles. Of course, we are getting accustomed to riding anything that turns up, but a ten-mile ride with nothing but a halter did seem to be carrying things pretty far.

We hunted up the foresters and saw everyone we thought might have any influence in Orleans but everyone was of the same mind. Mac-i-a-rum Joe didn't stand a chance in the world. It was no use. Nothing could be done. We came away thinking of that tiny garden, parched and dying for lack of water.

The night was very beautiful as we sat crouched down in the dugout, watching the flash of the paddle as we re-crossed the river to Kot-e-meen. The moon was just coming up behind our mountain. It was the harvest moon. Each night it rises big and round in the same place.

"When moon comes up same time three nights," the Indians say, "moon, he eat supper with his wife."

As we stood on our porch, the moon had just cleared the trees at the top of the mountain. There was a light in the Essie cabin and two people came out and stood for some time talking in its shadow. Mac-i-a-rum Joe's garden was not the only trouble that night in the Klamath country.

Early the next morning, Les came over to say that Essie was bringing us an *articken* (Indian basket). It was a present. The words were hardly out of his mouth before Essie stood at the gate. We went inside and put the *articken* on a stool to admire it properly, but it was plain that Essie was not listening when we thanked her. She stood with her eyes fixed on the basket, and then without looking at us she went over and sat on the settle.

"There has been trouble," she said, "over to the cabin." She didn't know what to do.

Before we had left in the morning, we thought there might be trouble. Essie's aunt from Witchpec had been staying at the cabin. While we were eating breakfast, we saw the horses saddled, tied to the fence. Then Les came out and unsaddled them. After that, Mart and Essie leaned against the fence and talked for nearly an hour.

It had been about Les, Essie told us. Her aunt didn't like it that Les lived there. Her aunt was mean. She wanted to take the place away from Essie. The aunt and Willis, the aunt's husband, had talked it over with Mart, and Mart didn't say nothing to nobody. The three of them would go into partnership and farm the place, and Les would be put out. And nobody was to tell Essie till it was fixed up. But they talked while Grandma was there because they thought that Grandma, she don't know no English. But Grandma talks English all right, only she won't tell nobody she can talk it. So she told Essie all her aunt had said. So Essie went to her aunt and said she was mean. And her aunt said Essie was bad because she lived with Mart and she lived with Les. And Essie said anyone who had got married seven times, like her aunt, better not call people names. So then Mart and Willis had come in and there was a growl. So Essie had come over to tell us, and Mart, he was coming too.

It was a bitter business. At first, it had seemed no more than any other Indian growl. But it was more than that. It started with Mart, who came over looking very black. Whatever happened, it seemed advisable to have Mart in a more amenable frame of mind. We opened up by saying that we understood the question was how much Les should be paid for the work he had done on the place. Of course, Mart understood that, as he was not married to Essie, she owned the place and could turn either Mart or Les off whenever it seemed to her best.

At this, Mart appeared completely taken aback. It was plain that he had thought nothing of the kind, and the purely legal aspects had never occurred to him. While he was muttering that he had put an awful lot of time and money in the place, Les came in, followed by Willis.

Mart's argument was that he and Willis were going into partnership and he didn't have no money nohow.

Willis argued that as far as he could see Les had never done any work on the place so he shouldn't be paid. That brought up the whole question of the hog. It was the one that Les was arrested for and had to do thirty dollars' worth of work for Frank Offield in order to settle the debt. As he had only killed the hog for Mart, of course the money ought to be refunded to him. Here we came into the conversation and said that we thought Les would be satisfied with the thirty dollars plus the fifty dollars that Mart felt was due him for work on the place.

From here on it was smooth going, as all agreed that Willis should pay the seventy dollars, and the combination of Mart and Les and Essie and ourselves proved so strong that Willis was just sitting down to sign a note for Les when we glanced through the windows and saw the aunt coming through the fence to our house.

The aunt came in quite placidly and seated herself on the settle. The trouble with her, she said, was that she was only a poor Indian and didn't know anything. We should have to begin at the beginning and tell her just what we wanted her to do.

We gathered our forces. It was plain that the old woman was no mean opponent.

We started the ball rolling by saying we understood that

she thought it was a bad thing for Les to continue to stay there.

The old woman said she did think so, and went into details.

Here Mabel came into the conversation, saying gently that Essie was a good niece and wanted to do anything that her aunt thought was right.

At this both Essie and the aunt looked surprised.

If the aunt felt that Les should be sent away, Mabel went on, they naturally would want to pay him for the work he had put in on the place. Just before the aunt came in, it had been agreed he should be paid seventy dollars. We had been told there was some question of going into partnership. Of course, if Willis was to have the use of the place, he should put money into it. He was therefore making out a note to Les for seventy dollars.

At this point, the door opened and Mr. Hunter, one of the foresters, came into the room. They had been saying at the store, he said, that when we came back from our trip east we would probably be looking for another location. He had in mind something that he thought would interest us.

While he talked, the Indians sat with expressionless faces. Mart looked at the floor. Mr. Hunter might just as well not have been there, for no one acknowledged his presence in the room. There was a silence, and then Mabel threw herself into the breach. She got Mr. Hunter out onto the porch and poured a stream of talk into his slightly unwilling ear.

Finally the old woman said that she was not going into partnership because the place was hers anyway. As she spoke she looked thoughtfully around the room. It looked as though she was planning to live in that room and was considering what she would do with it.

I murmured politely that, of course, if it was a question of legal ownership, it might take some time to arrive at a settlement. When was she coming back to Kot-e-meen?

I got up. Everybody got up and we started toward the

door. But here the aunt laid a restraining hand on the door latch.

It was true, she told us, that she knew very little about Les. She had never seen him until she came down yesterday and found him with his hair parted in the middle like a woman's.

Everybody laughed, and Les, though he winced, tried to laugh too. Still they lingered. In desperation I brought out a little bag that Mabel had intended for Grandma. I formally presented it to the aunt, saying I was afraid that she had not had a good time in our house and I wanted her to remember us pleasantly. She thanked me and went off in excellent humor, the others following her. It was just in time as, in spite of all that Mabel could do, Mr. Hunter had broken away and was coming back into the room.

While we were discussing the question of location, we saw the Essie family coming back again. They had gotten rid of the aunt and Willis, who had saddled their horses and taken the trail for Witchpec. Now they had to face their own domestic situation. This time it was Mr. Hunter whom we edged out the door. Then Essie and ourselves sat on the three best chairs, with Mart on the settle, while Les took the stool by the window.

It was a very bitter business.

Mart turned red, gulped, and then said that he wished he was dead, that he would just go away and never come back. Then he picked up a magazine and began to turn over the pages.

Essie looked completely washed out. All the life had gone out of her face. Mart could leave the place, she said, for all she cared. She didn't ever want to see Mart or Les no more. Anyway, she'd just like to die.

Les, with his eyes full of tears, said that he didn't want no money nohow. It didn't make no difference what became of him. He'd go away right now if they wanted him to.

Finally, we made out a note to Les for seventy dollars. Both Essie and Mart signed it, and then they all went away.

We saw nothing of the Hamills until nearly sundown, when we had to call Mart to help us chase out a hog that had gotten under their fence and was rooting about in their garden. Mart came over with a very red face. He looked as if he had been crying.

When night came, it was very still and hot. We sat on the grass in front of the house and watched the moon rise over the mountain. We did not hear his step, but when we looked up Les was standing by the gate. He had been across the river, he said. He had his drum. Maybe we would like to hear him drum.

He sat against the house in the bright moonlight with his legs straight out in front of him. We could see the bald mountain back of the house quite clearly. For a time there was no sound but the beat of the drum, and then we heard the bark of a fox. The house and the fence and the garden and beyond them the dark outline of the chaparral stood out very sharp and clear in the moonlight, while above us towered the mountain. It grew toward ten o'clock and we were getting a little sleepy, when we noticed that Les had stopped drumming and was sitting very still, looking straight ahead of him.

"What is it, Les?" asked Mabel.

Les was silent a long time. Then he said very softly, "*Apruan.*"

Essie and Mart have been encouraging us to take *apruan* rather lightly and have giggled when we made fun of them, so Mabel laughed and said, "*Apruan*, Les? Is he after us?"

Les sat very still and made no reply. Then he got up and took his drum. "No, ma'am," he said. "After me."

Then he went very quietly away.

We were troubled because we knew that Mabel had not said the right thing. And, of course, if an *apruan* is really after you, you probably get drowned or bitten by a rattlesnake before the month is out. Then, too, poor old Les was in enough trouble without our adding to it. I awoke several times in the night, wondering if we had really hurt Les by laughing at *apruan,* but when he came over in the morning he seemed to have forgotten it.

He said maybe he would go down to Orleans. He didn't have no money but he didn't want to stay around here no more. A man down to Orleans owed him some money, so he guessed he better go.

Poor lad, we gave him a red silk handkerchief we had been saving for months for a very special occasion and he couldn't help smiling when he took it. He said Penny Tom would come and pack his things down river tomorrow.

Then he went away.

CHAPTER XII

We Hit the Trail for Points East, with all the Glories of Iced Tea, Iced Coffee, Fried Chicken, and Ice Cream in the Offing

It was very quiet as we sat on our little porch with the dark ring of chaparral around the outer edge of the clearing. There was no light or sound in the Essie cabin. We could barely make out its dim outline in the darkness. We were deeply disquieted by the troubles of our friends on the Rivers. The trip east, going home, all the glories of the Southern Pacific and our own Royal Blue Pullman cars, all the things we had been looking forward to, seemed of very little consequence after all.

Mart, Essie, and Les. Mac-i-a-rum Joe and his tiny, dying garden. Little Eddy Owl and his horrible leg that wouldn't yield to any treatment we could give it. Eddy, who stood aloof while the other Indian children played, and had something in his face that ought not to be in the face of a child. Eddy's leg was far beyond any skill of ours. For that matter, the troubles of all our friends were far beyond any skill of ours. Confronted with them we were helpless.

But at least there might be a chance for Eddy Owl. They told us at the store that the following day Dr. Kyselka would ride through Somes on his way back to Sawyer's Bar. Everyone speaks of Dr. Kyselka and his kindness to the Indians. If only we could talk to him about Eddy Owl.

It was early in the evening when we rode into Somesbar. We had put Eddy up behind Mabel on our latest horse, which is to be called Mr. Slopey Tanner. As we rode in, the trail was lined with Indians. They called to us as we rode by. No one knew how late the doctor might be, but, like ourselves, no one was going to take the chance of missing him. Two buyers of Indian baskets were in the hotel, but everyone went to bed early except Sam Frame, who was working late on his accounts.

It was nearly midnight when we heard the sound of a horse's shoe strike against a stone. We jumped up and ran to the window. The door of the store opened and Sam came out with a lantern. We saw a dark figure on a horse. It turned toward the barn, with Sam leading the way and the light from the lantern shining on the doctor's stout person. I went to wake Eddy Owl and had a moment of misgiving as I shook him for fear I had gotten hold of one of the buyers by mistake, but it was Eddy's voice that answered.

Sam and Mabel and the doctor were all in the lighted sitting room when Eddy and I came in. Dr. Kyselka is both tall and very stout. From a distance he looks a little like a huge baby. But there is nothing infantile either about Dr. Kyselka's approach to medicine or to his patients. He made a thorough examination of Eddy's leg.

"When you two girls ride through to Yreka, bring this little fellow with you," said Dr. Kyselka. "I'll arrange it so that he can get into the hospital there."

We nodded.

"You'll like it there," he said, smiling at Eddy. Eddy smiled back.

After he had finished with some of the Indians outside and had had something to eat, Dr. Kyselka leaned back in his chair very much at ease. At between one and two in the morning, he appeared not at all tired, after goodness knows how many days in the saddle and doctoring in the evening thrown in. He took in very good part our excursions into the field of medicine. Mabel explained that her brother was a physician and she was sure would look with great disfavor on our amateur efforts. We were afraid that Dr. Kyselka would feel the same way.

"Now that comes from not knowing the country," said Dr. Kyselka placidly. "All right back east where he comes from, but he doesn't know that a fellow like me has to saddle his mule and ride fifty miles. You just keep on with what you're doing, and if you'll stop at Sawyer's on your way to the railroad I'll give you some medicines and tell you how to use them."

He then settled himself comfortably in his chair and plunged into an intimate account of arteries, ruptures, fractures, and fevers until after three in the morning, and we could see a weary Sam squirming in his chair and trying to stifle his yawns. By this time the doctor was well launched on the lenses of the eye and the whole principle of fitting glasses. We were just going on to some of his really favorite germ diseases when Sam's patience gave way and he herded us to bed.

We slept so late that the doctor was well on his way to the Forks of Salmon and all the mail that came the night before had been distributed before we had finished breakfast. When we went over to the store, there in its little pigeon hole, sticking out for everyone to see, was a long, official envelope. Washington had written us that our application to leave our field for two weeks had been approved.

Well, the two gingham dresses mailed us from home, are pressed and ready. We hope to connect with our trunk in Sacramento. Then the California limited for all points east, ending up at Plainfield, New Jersey. And coffee with cream for breakfast. We haven't tasted cream since we left San Francisco. We can hardly bear to think of it.

Even before we got back to Kot-e-meen the news of our going east had gone up and down the Rivers. When we arrived at the Hildings' the next day, the room was packed to overflowing and the porch crowded with Indians. I did my best with questions in mental arithmetic, and I will say that the shining lights among my Indian men are driving me hard.

On the other side of the room I heard Mabel putting her whole soul into "Tisss isss Net." But it was a lovely day, our last at the Hilding school before going east, and we decided to cut lessons short in favor of the games.

There were about thirty in the ring. Herman and Mrs. Albers, who were on the porch, cast wistful glances at us, but the entire yard was full of equally wistful Indians, and, with the limited space, we did not see how even one more person could possibly get in, let alone two.

"Now all the men bow this way and all the women this way," sang Mabel, and her directions were received with wild enthusiasm. Swanny Pete, who can pack two hundred pounds on his back for ten miles, gingerly pulled his feet under him and gave a little squat for his bow. Everyone sowed oats, peas, beans, and barley, and then we came to the real event of the afternoon.

Back home you call it "Drop the Handkerchief." But you have never seen it played Indian way. The children are always enchanted by "Drop the Handkerchief," but they are slow little monkeys and it takes them some time to catch the idea. But there were no children in the ring this particular Thursday. Six of the most outstanding young Indian men on the Rivers were in the ring, as well as a large number of older men and squaws. The circle was so large that it made us feel as if something like a hundred-yard dash was necessary. The women play very prettily on the days we have only women and children, but this Thursday most of the running fell to Mabel and me.

We couldn't make out whether it was too pointed for one of the young bucks to choose one of the squaws or whether the fact that the squaws only trotted quietly around the ring was a deterrent. But Mabel and I would no sooner get rid of the handkerchief then back it would be behind one of us again. I tore around and around the ring until my hair came down twice. I made but poor speed on the sharp turn, but on the long stretch my foot was on my native heath and I pressed many an agitated young buck so hard that the spectators yelled and roared with delight.

But you should have seen Mabel. She runs bent over like an Indian and could easily beat anyone on the sharp turn. As she would gain on a flying Albers, her long arm within a few inches of his back, his eyes would start from his head and there was no doubt that his one idea in life was to pant into his place in the fewest possible seconds. While the race was on, young and old Indians roared and screamed and beat upon the ground and leaped in the air. The ground was slippery and the men fell continually amid shouts of joy from the bystanders. Fortunately Mabel and I kept our feet.

Today was the last Sunday school at Kot-e-meen before we go east. And everyone on both sides of the river was out in force. Not even all the small boxes from the Essie house, together with her washtub, could seat the congregation. Mrs. Tintin and Grandma sat on the floor, but for many of our most intimate friends there was standing room only.

As a final celebration, we brought out all the old Christmas cards that had been sent us for the Indians, and, scattering them out on the table, bade each of the congregation choose the one he liked best. For a moment no one moved, and then the rush was terrific. Macy's bargain counter could not touch it. I snatched a handful of cards and spread them out on the settle, and instantly the Indians in front of them were so thick you could not have gotten a knife between them.

Essie's presence of mind, as usual, was to the fore. She triumphantly displayed a sort of paper screen and a card that opened out into numberless little dogs' heads. Poor Les told us bitterly later that when he got a card someone would ask to see it, and he never got it back again. Pete from I-ees-i-rum sadly went off with a picture of Bishop Moreland in black and white as his only share of the spoils.

But I think on the whole it was a great success.

Tomorrow we take the trail. It is true that from what we hear Sawyer's Bar is both drunk and disorderly, but we go among friends. There is Dr. Kyselka, and Mr. Halvorsen, who is Mrs. Hilding's father, and the soup bone man we met at Somes last Friday. At the Forks of Salmon, Rube Morse is eagerly awaiting us. And beyond Sawyer's Bar is the unknown Etna, Yreka, and the railroad.

We are writing our last batch of letters. Sam asked us with a grin what we wanted him to do with our mail while we were away. He had a good-sized room, he said, that he would rent us for five dollars and fifty cents a month. Our saddle bags are already packed. We plan to spend the night at Somes with Mama Frame, and then, in the early morning, we take the trail, with only four days between us and the railroad.

CHAPTER XIII

Return to the Rivers: Everybody Got Trouble, White People and Everybody

The trip east has retreated into a faraway haze and we feel as though we had never left the Rivers. We certainly did not impress the porter as Easterners when we boarded the train for Chicago, in Yreka. As we flew down the platform with our conspicuously discolored saddle bags and our spurs clanking, the Pullman porter gave us one horrified glance and sternly waved us toward the day coach. He was hardly more resigned when we appeared later from the ladies' room in neat gingham dresses, which did their best to conceal the riding boots we still wore. We never did connect with our trunk, so east we went in riding boots and sombreros, with the gingham dresses modestly disposed between.

California looked at us askance, but as we drew nearer and nearer to the Atlantic coast, our social status went up. By the time we reached Chicago, the porter humbly took our saddle bags, and the two enormous baskets that had been a good-by present from Essie, with an expression of marked respect. And when we dropped off the B and O at Plainfield, New Jersey, we created a most pleasurable sensation.

But it was on the trip back that we showed our true colors. We were Westerners going west. We spent our money freely. At the faintest excuse, or with no excuse at all, we had ice cream. We tipped in a big way. There was only one thing we economized on and that was water. We could hardly bear to drink the alkali water, and mineral water cost fifty cents a bottle. We refused to buy it.

"It is just plain extravagant to spend our money on that little bottle," said Mabel firmly. "We may not have anything else on the Rivers, but we have water—rivers and creeks and springs, and plenty of them. Don't let's waste money on water. Let's have some more ice cream."

And we did.

Our excitement mounted as the familiar Californian landscape began to flash by. When we dropped off the Pullman on the Yreka platform, just two weeks after we had boarded a similar Pullman, our feet were on our own field. We were at home. At Etna, Henry Shook looked unmoved as we told him about our trunk.

Yep, he would look out for it. Carting it from Yreka to Etna would cost us four bits. Guessed he'd better write out his name for us.

We said we would remember it. We had been at his house the night before to see Mrs. Roberts and had met his wife.

"Oh," said Henry Shook, "that so? Well, your trunk will be all right. Find a place for it in my shed. Won't cost you a cent."

The stage was to leave directly after dinner. Billy, the stage driver with whom we had come down, met us as we came into the dining room.

"Hello, girls," he said. "What you mean not coming back with me? I'm real mad."

He held a ladder so we could climb up onto the front seat. The horses were fresh and we made the twelve miles in an hour and forty minutes. There was a new moon and big stars. The horses scampered over the road without Kruger, our driver, once using his whip.

With every mile the country grew more familiar. Mr. Tyler, whom we had seen at the Forks of Salmon, drove us into Finley's Camp, as usual, very drunk. Mr. Fealy was on the stage. Wherever we went Mr. Fealy was sure to be on the stage.

It had been barely light when we turned out of bed

in the morning, and there was a faint pink glow behind the mountains. Down the hall we could hear the thumps and stirrings that marked the rousing of the other passengers. Mr. Tyler was climbing up onto the driver's seat as we came out. We marked with regret that there was a man standing near the front seat, and that he had put his kodak on it. But here he made a mistake; he went inside for some more luggage.

Mabel put her hand on the coach and then put a tentative foot on the step that leads to the front seat. She threw a glance of inquiry at Mr. Tyler.

"There was a gentleman—" began Mr. Tyler weakly. Then, in a stronger voice, "But I guess it will be all right. You girls climb right up."

The stage was crowded and the horses sweated up Etna Mountain. Then we were swinging along on the downgrade.

"Here you are, girls," shouted Mr. Tyler as we drew up. Tied to the fence were two mules.

"Hand over those saddle bags," said Mr. Tyler to a man inside the coach.

"Good-by, girls."

The stage went on but we did not notice it. We were tightening cinches and fastening saddle bags to our saddles. Ahead lay the trail to Sawyer's Bar. We were home again.

We took the eight miles over Old Man Bennett's road at a gallop. There were smoky mountains all around us. The sky flamed a soft pink and then it was dusk. Mr. Smith came out to take our horses.

"You ladies back?" he said. "Well, we expected you."

Old Lady Bennett had so much to tell us that we hardly got to bed at all. The next day, on the trail to Somes, Mr. Young and the new schoolmaster stopped to gossip. Anderson Grant called out to us as he rode by that he had made it from home in fifty-five minutes. We were certainly back on the Rivers when it counted so much what time you made. The Grants were all waiting for us by the corral as we rode up.

"We have a real good prospect," they told us. "Everyone says it should pan out rich. Just as soon as we get the mules unsaddled, we will show you some pieces of quartz."

And later: "Look at that now. How is that for a rich strike?"

We had stopped at the Grants' on our way out to Yreka. Mr. Grant was a white man. He was tall and lean and old, like many another white man on the Rivers. And like many other white men on the Rivers, Mr. Grant was a squaw man. The Grants lived in a little valley between two high mountains. The mountains were so high that the house and the outbuildings and the corral and the cultivated fields looked like the tiny toys of a child as we saw them from high up on the trail. At supper and all during the evening, it was Mr. Grant who talked to us. The family sat silent. Mr. Grant didn't talk about the people on the Rivers. He talked about the East and the part of the country he had come from. He tilted his chair back and closed his eyes.

"I remember when I was down in Pennsylvany," Mr. Grant would begin.

When we saddled up in the morning, Mr. Grant laid a detaining hand on Mabel's mule. "Wait a minute," he said.

He shouted for his three sons and they came and stood uneasily by the corral.

"These are white women," said old man Grant. "I want you always to remember that you saw them."

We were well up the second mountain from the Grants' house when we saw Rube Morse.

"They are looking for you at Kot-e-meen," he shouted as he rode by. Then, around a bend in the trail, we saw the Klamath and glimpsed the roof of the barn at Somes. We waved our hats and kicked our heels and yelled "ki-yi-yi" and came down the mountain in style. It seemed as if we had never been away. Mama Frame hugged us, and Papa Frame and Sam and Margy stood by looking on. We had chicken for supper. We had watermelon and peaches. And in the evening we had the phonograph.

As we crossed the road from the house to the store, we saw Essie coming across the bridge.

The first night at Kot-e-meen, Essie and Mart came over as soon as they saw the smoke from our chimney.

"Les, he don't live here no more," Essie told us. But even as she spoke there was a step on the porch and Les stood in the doorway. He made the dramatic entrance common with all Indian men, standing a minute, straight and impassive, outlined against the opening, and then he came into the room and sat on the woodpile, just as he had always done. The fire blazed up and everyone talked at once.

Les had been bitten by a rattlesnake just after we had gone. He had been hurt bad. Everybody thought he would die. His mother sent down to us for medicine but we had already left. Les, he was awful sick. He just couldn't do nothing.

We thought of the night before we had left when Les had come over to drum—the bright moonlight and the bark of the fox and the clear, sharp outline of the mountain. And how Les had stopped his drumming and had sat looking out into the night.

"*Apruan,*" Les had said.

And we had asked, "After us, Les?"

And Les had replied, "No, ma'am. After me."

And then he had gotten up and gone away.

And we remembered what Rube Morse had once said: "It's different with white folks, but if you got Indian blood in you and an *apruan* comes after you, you ain't got no chance. You get drownded or some fellow puts a knife into you or you get bit by a rattlesnake. In lessen a month. It's just sure. You watch and see if it doesn't happen every time."

"I go on yother side of river," Les was saying. "I go watch deer lick, but ain't no deer so I come home. I come along trail on yother side of river. Ain't no moon. Pretty soon morning. Trail, he pretty good. Then I 'fraid. I 'fraid. I stop. I look. I listen. I stand still long time. I listen. Everything, he quiet. Nothing there. Nothing there. I go along. Trail, he good. Everything quiet. But I 'fraid. I 'fraid. I take my gun. I shoot. I shoot. I stand still. I listen. Nothing there. I go along. I run. I run. I so 'fraid. I run. I shoot. I run. I stop. I listen. Nothing there."

"The rattlesnake got him in the knee," Mart broke in. "He run a long time, and then he felt something on his leg and he put his hand down and there was a rattlesnake dug in and hanging down his leg. So he pulled him off and sucked out all the poison he could get, and then he got him out a cartridge and ripped it up and spilled out the powder on the bite and touched it off. It blew out a good piece of his leg, but he fixed it up good as he could with a piece of buckskin tied around above the knee and a stick through it to twist it tight. Then he come home."

"I know something git me," said Les. "All time I shoot I know something git me. I don't git home so good. I fall down and I git up and I fall down. I go 'long and I fall down. I think maybe I don't git home. I git to Pich-pichi and Ruther (his brother) come along. He git hold of me so I git home all right."

"Les's mother, she's Indian doctor," said Essie. "She fixed him up good. But all the Indians round here think Les ain't going to get well. They think he's going to die."

"Mabel, he 'fraid laddersnakes," said Les thoughtfully. "I think all white womens, he 'fraid laddersnakes. I ain't 'fraid laddersnakes. Now *tani vee* (I don't like) laddersnakes. Laddersnakes soft. Hang on leg very soft. *Tani vee* laddersnakes. I 'fraid laddersnakes just like white womens."

We have lived on the fat of the land since we returned to the Indian village of Kot-e-meen, in the Coast Range. The salmon run is on. We have salmon for breakfast, salmon for dinner, and salmon for supper. As soon as the smoke rises from our chimney in the morning, some one of our Indian friends catches a salmon in the river and brings it in to be fresh cooked for breakfast. This morning, well fed and replete, we sat outside on the grass with all our bedding spread out on the fence. Lively reds and blues. Very ornamental.

Up on our mountain, Les sang Indian songs at the top of his lungs as he pitched firewood downhill. It was almost eleven, and the entire morning had been devoted to personal cleanliness. We were so very spick-and-span that very few occupations were open to us.

Ever since our return to the Rivers we have been turning over in our minds the possibility of moving to the other side of the Klamath. Only the Kot-e-meen Indians, the Hildings, the Alberses, and the people at T Bar live on this side of the river, and on this side of the river we are hemmed in. Between Kot-e-meen and Somesbar is the Salmon, and horses can only ford the Salmon with safety in low water. Between Kot-e-meen and the main trail from Happy Camp to Orleans rolls the Klamath. As we are well aware, fording the Klamath, even in summer, is not something to be taken lightly. Crossing the Klamath with horses in winter is impossible. When we stopped over in Washington on our way east, the Indian Department promised us horses and supplies and hinted at an allowance for two stations. If we should get enough money for two stations, the first station should be on the other side of the Klamath, and one of the best locations on the Rivers would be at I-ees Bar, in Big Steve's country.

I-ees Bar is on the main trail, twenty-five miles from Orleans and thirty-five miles from Happy Camp. From Orleans, we are only three days from Eureka, on the ocean. From Happy Camp we are only four days from the railroad. Mr. Hunter has promised to survey land for us near I-ees-i-rum, and we are planning a trip up river to see Big Steve.

We have been in low spirits lately and we shall be glad to be on the trail again. Ever since we came back to the Rivers we have had a feeling that all was not well at Kot-e-meen. We know things are not right because there is a shadow between ourselves and Essie. Maybe it is the talk of our going up river and the fact that, if we go to live somewhere else, we can no longer be members of the Essie family. Or maybe it is because of Pic-i-ow-ish, the Indian New Year's. All the Indians in Kot-e-meen ask how can you expect things will be the same when the world has been made wrong, and that everyone is bound to have a trouble with someone, and anyhow we are all in danger of being knifed or drowned or something equally unpleasant.

Just watch out and see whether something does not happen to us.

Of course, on the other hand, there may be nothing really wrong between us and the Essie family. Les *did* get George Leary's mule for us, and Essie *did* say we could have Baby, quite like old times. There are days when every thing seems all right, and that it is the old Essie that we have grown to know so well and to care about. But then, deep down inside us, we know it is not the old Essie, and we are glad we are going away.

The Alberses' place is about six miles beyond the Hildings', on the up-river trail. Their cabin was on a small patch of level ground back from the river and about a hundred feet above it. The dugout was on the Albers' side and Herman said he would put us across. As we scrambled down the trail, a great bend in the Klamath lay below us, and nestled in the bend was the tiny flat, or bar, of I-ees-i-rum. On the little flat were cabins and gardens and wide stretches of sand and bush, and rising sharply above them was the mountain. The sun shone on the river, quiet now in the summer drought, and behind, in shadow, was the great mountain, dominating the tiny flat.

Travel on the Rivers is always a complicated affair. Herman refused to put us back across the river because, in the first place, he didn't want any trouble with the Indians at I-ees and he feared he was likely to have some if he stopped over for a few minutes, and, in the second place, he had to go right down to the Hildings', apparently to avert some trouble that was waiting for him there. However, he was willing to take our two horses back to the Hildings' with him. As there were two horses now at I-ees-i-rum, which the mailrider was planning to take down to Orleans, Herman suggested that we ride them to Hayward's Bar, leave them there for the mailrider, cross the river at Hayward's, spend the night at the Hildings', and pick up our own horses for our return trip down river. All this may seem very involved, but for the Rivers it was really quite simple.

The crossing at I-ees is an easy one, and as the nose of the dugout drove into the sand Herman pointed to a tiny cabin on our right.

"That's where the old woman lives," Herman said. "And that cabin right ahead of us with the garden is Swanny Pete's. But he ain't the one to talk to if there's anything you want here at I-ees-i-rum. Over there, just under the mountain—see the smoke from that chimney? That's Big Steve's house. If you want anything this side of the river, better talk to Big Steve."

Big Steve was standing on the porch of his house as we came up. His cabin was built of rough, unbattened boards. It was very small and the roof was of hand-hewn shakes, or shingles. The door was closed and Big Steve did not ask us to come in. There are tales of Big Steve all up and down the Rivers—the things he has done and the people he has killed. As we looked at Steve, standing there on his porch, we thought it probable that at least some of those tales were true.

Big Steve's face was expressionless as he greeted us. We explained why we had come. Would the up-river Indians like us to come to I-ees-i-rum? Did Steve think that the Indians on this side of the river would like to come to school? If we should decide to come to I-ees-i-rum, did he know of any place where a house could be built?

There was a location, Steve said, not far from the rancheria. It was on the side of the mountain and well back above the river. He thought there would be enough level ground for a house. All the Indians said they liked school. Probably they would come. If we wished, he would look into things for us.

We came away and took the down-river trail for Hayward's Bar. For months now it has been the dry season and the mountains quivered in the warm haze. As we crossed the ridge beyond I-ees-i-rum we could hear the beat of a drum. Some of the excitement following Pic-i-ow-ish must be still in the air. We could hear the tinkle of cattle bells. The cattle must be grazing somewhere up in the hills above us.

Big Steve had said everything would be all right. But would it? Did Big Steve really want us to come to I-ees Bar? Down river at Kot-e-meen things had been different. White influence had been strong at Kot-e-meen and at Pich-pichi, only two miles from the bridge at Somes and eight miles from Orleans. But there was no white influence at I-ees-i-rum. We were in the heart of the Karok country, up-river country, a day's journey from Orleans and a day and a half from Happy Camp. What would happen if we came to I-ees Bar and built a house and spent the Government's money and Big Steve should prove to be no friend of ours?

Would we be members of Steve's family if we went to live at I-ees-i-rum? We hoped very much that we would be members of Steve's family, but as we remembered Steve's expressionless face it did not look like it. As we thought of living at I-ees-i-rum we felt very far from home.

It was after five when we rode into the little clearing at Hayward's Bar. We told Mrs. Johnson we wanted Charlie to put us across. Mrs. Johnson speaks no English, and with difficulty we made out that Charlie was away.

"Then we will put ourselves across," we told Mrs. Johnson. "Where is the boat?"

With difficulty we made out that Charlie had taken the boat with him.

"Will Charlie be back this evening?" we asked.

"*Ha* (yes) ," said Mrs. Johnson.

We pointed at the sun. "Back for supper?" we asked.

"*Ha*," said Mrs. Johnson.

We unsaddled the horses and settled down to wait. Across from us, on the other side of the river, we could just catch a glimpse of some of the Hildings' outbuildings. Someone who must be Mrs. Hilding came down the bank, and we explained the state of affairs in a series of shouts.

We settled down again to wait. Then Lucy came out of the cabin. Lucy speaks English. Yes, said Lucy calmly, Charlie was coming home that evening but he was going to leave the boat up river.

We sat up. We had saddle blankets and we could make a fire, but the Johnsons were no particular friends of ours and supper lay on the other side of the river.

There was another river crossing two miles below Hayward's Bar. We flung on our saddles and dug in our spurs. As we rode we had visions of Jim Covey away from home and night coming on fast. But luck was with us and our shouts brought Jim out of his house. Jim is not a good paddler but the river was low and the current sluggish. In the dusk, we scrambled up the bank on the east side of the Klamath. It was our own legs that took us the two miles of trail back to the Hildings' and it was not quite black dark when we ran up the path to the house.

But only the three children were in the kitchen. Mrs. Hilding had gone down to the river to put us across, they told us.

Our hearts stood still. The Hildings' boat is leaky and Mrs. Hilding is afraid of the crossing, even in daytime. If she tried to make it alone in the dark . . . We cried out to Lewis to show us the way, and ran at top speed for the river. As we stumbled over roots and stones in the dark, we urged the scudding Lewis to run faster. The only result was we lost him in the bush and, coming to a place where the trail branched, we did not know which path to take. Mabel took the most likely one and I took the other. A few minutes later I heard voices calling and made out that one of them was Mrs. Hilding's. She had been trying to launch the boat. We had gotten there just in time.

There was trouble at the Hildings' and it was late when we started for home. The sun had already dropped behind the mountain, and our side of the river was in shadow. In spite of the approach of evening, the air was hot and heavy. Everything was quiet, but I found myself watching the thick bush on the side of the trail. I had an odd sense of something lurking there, waiting for us, something we could not see and that was not friendly. I wished we were nearer home. I wished it was not so late and that the trail was not in shadow.

Maybe there were panthers in the bush. Les said you never saw a panther until he came at you. Every now and then, when we could see nothing, the horses would snuff and shy. Maybe it was just because we were always afraid of night on the trail. Or maybe it was because Essie was no longer a friend of ours. Or it might be only Indian New Year's and that the world was made wrong, but the queer feeling I had had ever since we came back to the Rivers was very strong.

"Darn the Indians, anyway," said Mabel, quite out of a clear sky. She rode in silence for a few minutes but it was evident she was thinking of her wrongs.

"I do wish we ever had good riding animals," she went on. "This mule of George Leary's ought to be called Crawl-i-up-ium. He is the queerest beast and I don't like his peculiarities. And I do wish we had something good to eat. Since the last of the salmon run, I have been hungry all the time. Do dig your spurs into Baby and see whether you can't get something out of her."

I dug in my spurs. There was a faint little breath of

cooler air, and our animals took a better pace. Just ahead of us was a deep gorge spanned by a bridge. When we first came to the Rivers, we used to regard that bridge with considerable misgiving. It was high over a rocky ravine and covered quite a span. It trembled and swayed and creaked, when we crossed it, in a way we did not like. But then all bridges in this country seemed to us rather unsafe and you get used to things. Panthers and rattlesnakes and bridges. Lately, we had hardly noticed it.

Mabel was ahead. I watched her as she crossed, for the bridge did seem rather unusually frail. The ravine below had once been the rocky bed of a stream. The jumble of rocks was still there, with some large boulders and light timber. On the left side of the bridge, toward the mountain, the fall was no more than ten or twelve feet. But the ground fell away rapidly toward the river, and on the river side the drop was nearer thirty feet. Mabel's mule skittered a little as some of the boards creaked under him but nothing happened, and in another minute Mabel and Crawl-i-up-ium were across.

I followed, easing Baby along and thinking of nothing in particular until we reached the center of the span. Then there was a sharp, crashing sound. The next thing I knew, the bridge where I had been was gone and Baby and I were hanging in midair, astride a beam. Baby's middle rested on the beam and her feet dangled down over the bottom of the gorge, far, far below. With extreme speed I got myself off Baby's back and inched a little way up the beam. On the other side of Baby, the beam waved in the air but on my side it was fastened to a crosspiece. It looked likely to give at any minute, and I prayed it would hold until I reached the crosspiece and safety. Then I heard Mabel's sharp voice. She was standing on the bank, shouting to me.

"Pull the cinch strap!" she called. "Pull the cinch strap!"

A trifle unwillingly I inched my way back to Baby and caught the dangling cinch strap. It is from long experience in a dangerous country that cinch straps on the Rivers always dangle to within a foot of the ground and have a slip knot. I held tight to my beam and gave a sharp pull. Instantly the saddle loosened. I made the best speed I could back to the crosspiece. Just as I reached the girder, there was another crash, and Baby went headlong into the gorge below. But the saddle fell clear.

Mabel was already racing down the gorge when I made the bank. By the time I had caught up with her, she had found Baby, not dead as we expected but limping toward us. A fall with that high-pommeled saddle would have broken her back. As it was, under such conditions, it was miraculous that she was alive.

Getting home was not easy. One of us would ride Crawl-i-up-ium and the other would lead Baby, encouraging her along. We were only about eight miles from Kot-e-meen but the trail seemed endless. Poor Baby was so stiff and lame that she could hardly move one leg after the other. Black night was upon us and there were still miles to go. We have never ceased to hate night on the trail. We dipped down into little hollows. We forded creeks in the thick blackness, to the soft gurgling sound of unseen water. The trees almost touched our necks, and the thought that panthers stretched out on limbs could easily drop on us was even less pleasant on foot than on horseback.

It was so dark that we had to feel our way along, stumbling over stones and rough places and trying to make out the trail with our feet. With every mile, poor Baby went more slowly. We began to despair of getting her back at all. When at last we came out on the high ridge above the Offields' and could see far, far below us the dim outline of Ah-o-wich, our own Sugar Loaf Mountain, we nearly wept with relief.

CHAPTER XIV

Moving Day on the Klamath

At long last we are going to have a house at I-ees-i-rum. Dave McLaughlin is going to build it for us. He came in this morning to see us, ate a large breakfast, and said he would start work Monday. He promised that the house would be finished by November thirtieth.

It all started with a letter from Washington. It appears that our official star is in the ascendant. We learn that we are to be allowed the money for two stations, four hundred dollars for each of them. In addition, we are to have two hundred dollars for horses and about forty dollars for equipment.

In the same mail with the Washington letter was one from Mr. Kyselka. He wrote that he had heard from Washington that we were to have all the assistance we needed. But he really doesn't see what he can do. It is impossible for him to leave Hoopa at the present time. He has no secretary and is very much behind in his work. Moreover, he has been informed that he has been promoted to a school in South Carolina. And, oh dear, oh dear (our interpretation of his feelings), it is a dreadful thing to have to leave accounts to be paid by the next superintendent. Of course, we may do anything we think necessary, with his blessing (again our interpretation). Accounts like his really constitute hours of work. He hopes we enjoyed our vacation and he is faithfully ours.

Following hard upon Mr. Kyselka's letter, Mr. Hunter turned up. He sat thankfully on our porch and wiped his forehead with the sleeve of his coat. Yesterday the thermometer had again coasted up to one hundred degrees. Mr. Hunter searched through his pockets and brought out a letter from the Forestry Department. It stated that the ladies therein mentioned were to have the entire forest intact, if they so desired (or words to that effect), and that Mr. Hunter was to see that they were accommodated in every possible way. And please be quick about it. (The language might have been a little different, but certainly that was the impression we received.)

It certainly looked as if our house troubles were over and that there was a clear trail ahead. But here we made a mistake. When you start to build a house on the Klamath, your troubles are only beginning.

In the first place, the house would have to be built by contract, and Indians do not like contracts even under the best conditions. Then, in our innocence, we thought that Mart, who is no longer working at Heinze's mine, would be willing to build the house for us. We talked to Mart about it, and in the very sweetest way he agreed to build the house.

We thought that it was settled. Then Mart disappeared. Day or night, we never caught a glimpse of him. It was true that large cuts of wood would bound past our house from some place up on the mountain, where Mart and Eddy were working, and that some of these cuts would mysteriously find their way to our woodpile. We also would find slices of watermelon on our back doorstep when we opened the door in the morning. From all this we concluded that Mart did not want to build our house and was afraid to come home until we had found someone else to build it.

With Mart out of the running, we tried Sam Stenshaw. Sam is an attractive young half-breed who lives on a flat up above the Hildings'. He is the Indian type of half-breed and has his full share of the charms of the young male Indian. While we talked to him, Sam leaned against a post and looked doubtful. He really didn't see how he could build our house. We did our best, with some of our own charms thrown in. But Sam, with every charm displayed, shook his head, and we came away.

We then went to Dave McLaughlin. Dave is white, and charms of any kind are not on his horizon. Dave was abstracted and not encouraging. He was busy and he didn't think it would pay him. Then this morning he turned up and said he would start right away, and this afternoon we hear that Sam Stenshaw was wounded to the quick when he learned of our negotiations with Dave and is no longer a friend of ours.

Meantime, the rains had begun early and the river was up. Mart said there were still some fine days ahead of us and that the river would fall again, but he strongly advised us to push the move up river before big water began in earnest.

Pete Henry brought us the news that Hilding was back from the trip over Marble Mountain with his pack train. They say he had a tough time of it. He and Goodman were days in the mountain, camping in the open in either rain or snow, and not daring even to stop to eat for fear they might be snowed in. The last day, with the mules in bad shape and the snow getting heavy, Goodman gave up. He wanted to leave the pack train and get out with their horses as best they might, but Hilding stuck it out and brought them through.

"I'll be down for you the end of the week," Hilding had sent word to us.

These are our last days at Kot-e-meen.

We have taken the Indian baskets off the walls in the living room and tied them up neatly in flour sacks. All our personal possessions are in flour sacks, and to get into the kitchen you have to step over endless small boxes, all set out two by two, as though they were going into the ark. For a pack train, you must pack by weight as well as by bulk. The loads for each side of a mule must be as nearly equal as possible in both pounds and size. Unless the two boxes have the same weight and displacement, the load will tend to shift on your mule and make his back sore.

Mabel has spent the morning weighing a pitcher against a teapot or a bunch of pans against three cups and four saucers. Then the pitcher goes into one box and the teapot into another, and Mabel carefully hefts the two to test the result.

Yesterday we saddled for our final trip to Somes for supplies and packing boxes. They did not look like much when Sam got them all assembled, but they cost us eighteen dollars. We had forded our animals as the river was low enough to make fording possible. And Sam helped us load both animals to the ears.

We were just wondering what to do with the stovepipe when Luther Hickox came by and promised to pack both lengths of it on his mule. Then, just as we were ready to start for the trip back, we heard the despairing yelps of Shaw-baby, the puppy that Sam had given us.

Before making the crossing to the store, we had tied George Bernard Shaw to a small tree. He took this in very ill part and his screams rent the air. While we had gone in and out of the store collecting our purchases, we noticed that George Bernard had got loose and was tearing up and down the bank, shrieking his grief. He finally appeared dripping, having swum the Salmon. But nothing would persuade him to swim back again or to cross the bridge. Mabel lured him halfway across, while the animals were being forded, but in the center of it, he grew terrified and scuttled back to the Somesbar side. I coaxed from my side of the bridge and Papa Frame beat him with a stick at his end, but GBS would not budge.

We were at our wits' end. Then Sam appreared and, briskly picking up Shaw-baby in one hand, came over the bridge at a run. Shaw-baby must weigh nearly seventy pounds. He struggled and yelped. The bridge under the best conditions is unchancy enough. Moreover, in crossing the bridge, you try to balance your loads. Being thrown off balance is something no one likes to consider. But with the yelping Shaw-baby dragging him to one side, Sam never wavered. We held our breath while we watched the crossing, but Sam, with an unmoved face, unceremoniously dumped Shaw-baby on the bank and was back across the bridge before we had time to thank him.

Packing over these trails is not a carefree existence. Mabel had two enormous empty boxes on Jane while I had two small loaded boxes on Sally. We had to carefully skirt every tree we came to, lest the boxes become stuck. Sally caught the spirit of what we were trying to do and sort of Virginia Reeled along, bumping into trees she could have quite easily avoided. By the time we got home we were so exhausted that we decided to put off the rest of our packing until the following morning.

Not only all of Kot-e-meen but most of Pich-pichi as well were over to see us off the next morning. In true Indian fashion, they came early, prepared to spend the day. We were just discussing a possible Christmas tree in December, with Frank Offield, and how many bags of candy we ought to have, when we heard the sound of voices and the tramp of mules. We ran to the door, and there was our whole yard filled to overflowing with a pack train.

It was not Hilding the friend but Hilding the packer who strode into the room. He lifted boxes and bundles in his hands to test the weight and found fault with everything. Nothing was right. The boxes were too light and too small. When it came to that, we had been doing our darnedest to keep them light. Hilding checked on everything, then picked up a load and went out muttering something we did not catch. Maybe it was just as well that we didn't. Mr. Hunter came in and helped us take apart benches and shelves. We stuffed the coffee pot and cups we had used for breakfast into a last box that had been left open for them. We rolled up blankets and pillows while the men carried everything into the yard and began placing them in little piles.

Hilding is famed as a packer, but as we looked at the

mules and then at the piles, we did not see how he could possibly handle all that stuff, boxes and bumpy rolls, lumber and our little oil stove. But Hilding stalked about the piles, swiftly making changes, until he had things the way he wanted them. Then he caught one of the mules, led it between two of the little piles, and dropped its head rope on the ground. The mule spread its front legs, laid back its ears, and closed its eyes. The pack saddle on its back looked like a little sawbuck, cinched very tight, with a heavy pad under it that did not reach all the way up the backbone.

Mr. Hilding took his stand on one side of the mule and Mr. Hunter on the other. Mr. Hilding caught up a length of the tangle of ropes on his side of the mule, fastened one end to the front horn of the pack saddle, arranged the rope in an intricate loop, caught up a box, threw the loop around it, and tossed the rope to Mr. Hunter, who fastened it around a similar box on his side. We were watching the throwing of the diamond hitch. The ropes swirled back and forth, over the pack saddle and under the mule's belly, ending in a knot in the middle of the box. Then the men stepped back to let the weight of the box sag into the ropes. The mule groaned and drew its feet under it. The bundles and odds and ends were tucked into the cradle made by the boxes, and something bulky and soft was settled on the top of the load. The whole load was then covered with a square of tarpaulin and securely lashed into place. Then the mule's head rope was tied up and he was turned out to graze.

As each mule was loaded and turned out, we were warned to keep an eye on them to make sure that they didn't try to roll with their loads. The boxes and bundles on the ground disappeared as if by magic. The mule loaded with the oil stove threatened to buck. The mule with the boards lashed to his pack saddle was piled so high with lumber that only his hoofs and his ears were in sight. In less than an hour, Mr. Hunter was leading off up the trail, followed

Top—Mary on Sally. Although "she is a good one to buck you off,"
this shows her in one of her more peaceful moments.
Bottom—On the trail. Mabel on Jane.

Top: left—Carrie; right—Kate.
Bottom: left—Agnes; right—A-su-ná-pee.

Top: left—Steve brought along his drum; right—Steve, at the
Deerskin Dance.
Bottom: left—George McCash as one of the dancers; right—
Dumphrey, with a flint, at the Deerskin Dance.

Top—The Salmon River, where rocks, hidden and in full sight, make
it too dangerous for animals to swim.
Bottom—Cold meant snow in the mountains.

Top—The pack train.
Bottom—Somesbar as seen from the Salmon River.

Top: left—Luther Hickox with
White Puppy; right—Steve and
his nephew, Swanny Pete.
Bottom—Essie.

Top—The Deerskin Dance.
Bottom—Les in Indian dress.

Top — Papa and Mama Frame with Mama's little helper.

Center—Grandma at Kot-e-meen.

Bottom—Our house at Kot-e-meen.

Top—
Molly Bawn. "Lit-
tle cat, he say
hol' on."

Center—
Eddy and Nero.

Bottom—
Our house at
I-ees-i-rum.

Top—the stagecoach.
Bottom—Mabel and Mr. Darcy.

Top—Our skirts were exactly the right length, a little below the ankle.
Bottom—Fort Jones in the early days.

Top—Annie, shown with some of her beautiful baskets.
Bottom: left—Mrs. Mayhew: right—Mart.

Top—Ossi-puk.
Bottom—Cabin of the Essie family.

Top—The dugout.
Bottom—The mountain white men call the Sugar Loaf.

Top—The ranch at Orleans.
Bottom—Orleans Bar.

Top—Packing a live pig across the swing bridge.
Bottom—The swift-flowing Salmon River.

by the pack train, with Mr. Hilding heading in the strays from the rear.

We stood watching them as they bobbed up the trail, turning and twisting up the mountain, until we lost sight of them in the chaparral. The next time we saw those things it would be in our new house, and our new life in I-ees-i-rum would have begun.

The next day, after spending the night at Somesbar, we rode up river. The air was chill with approaching winter after the cold rain of the night before. We hoped the river would not rise. We hoped all had gone well with the pack train. But we found trouble at the Hildings'. They told us Goodman was very bad. Mack Charlie had ridden to Sawyer's Bar for Dr. Kyselka. As Hilding talked to us, his face was covered with sweat. He had come down with rheumatism the night before, he told us, and was just managing to keep on his feet. But he had already been up with the first load and this was the second one. We had better go on and see about getting the stuff across the river. He thought the river was rising.

The trail between the Hildings' and the Albers' has some bad places in it. At one spot we saw a new slide. When we came within sight of the crossing, there was no sign either of Charlie Johnson or the dugout. All our things lay dumped in piles on the bank. We rode back up the mountain to the Albers' cabin. The door was locked and there was no sign of life. We rode back again to the place where our boxes and bundles lay forlornly on a tiny spit of land by the side of the river. We did not know what to do.

As we stood uncertain on the bank, someone came out of one of the cabins on the other side of the river at I-ees-i-rum. It was I-ees Pete. There was no mistaking the thick-set, powerful frame and the sag of the broad shoulders. In response to our signal, Pete launched the dugout and came across. Without a word, he flung our saddle bags over his shoulders and dumped them in the boat. Still without a word, he loaded up the dugout with our stuff until it rode so low in the water we trembled for fear he could never make the other side. Then he got in and paddled across. We waited, sitting on our horses, until he came back for another load. Again he piled the dugout full of our stuff. Then he paused, the paddle in his hand.

"Pretty soon I get mad," said I-ees Pete.

We looked worried.

"Steve, he take my horses," said Pete. "I ain't got no horses. Steve got 'em. I haul rocks two-three days, I don't get nothing. Pretty soon I get mad."

He stepped into the dugout, dug into the water with his paddle, and steadily drove the boat across the river. We breathed more easily. Pete might get mad but he is accounted one of the best paddlers on the Rivers.

It was growing dark by the time the last load made the I-ees shore. We turned our horses and rode up the trail. We were about a mile on our way back when we met a worried Hilding. There had been a fresh slide on one of the bad bits of trail and the mule with the oil stove on its back had slipped and gone over the embankment. It had been a fall of more than two hundred feet, Hilding said, and he didn't know how bad the mule was hurt. It had taken him pretty nearly an hour to get him back on the trail. We did not dare to inquire about the condition of the little oil stove. In the dark, Hilding unloaded our things and piled them on the bank. We left them there and rode slowly back to Hildings' house.

As we sat in the kitchen and the Hilding children dragged the wretched Shaw-baby around by the tail, Mrs. Hilding told us that Dr. Kyselka had said Goodman had cancer of the stomach and would die in six months. Poor Goodman. He only said when they told him: "I wouldn't have minded paying him the hundred if he'd told me I would get well, but it's pretty hard to pay a hundred just to be told you're going to die."

When Hilding came into the kitchen for supper, his rheumatism was so bad he could hardly stand, and he had to help himself with a cane to get to the table. They had almost no money, Mrs. Hilding told us, and did not know what they were going to do.

At best, supper at the Hildings' is a depressing affair. Mrs. Hilding is not a good cook and on this night the grease on the potatoes seemed more than usually uneatable and the bacon more rancid. For the most part, we ate in silence. Mr. Hilding moved uneasily when he felt a twinge of rheumatism. There was a smart shower pattering on the roof. We thought of all our possessions, lying unprotected on a spit of sand by the river, and moved uneasily in our turn. The children fidgeted and snatched at the food. In the next room we could hear poor Goodman groan as he turned in his bed.

We were helping Mrs. Hilding with the dishes when Dave McLaughlin came in. He wanted to speak to us, he said. There is little or no privacy in the Hilding household, but Dave and I huddled over the sink in the kitchen, and when Mrs. Hilding took possession of the sink we squeezed ourselves behind the dining-room table.

In a low tone, Dave told us that he was desperate for money. He had to have it. He just had to have it, he said. He owed money for the stuff for his mine. He owed Steve for the work on our house. He owed a man who had helped Steve. He couldn't pay for anything until we paid him. This was the beginning of the mining season and he couldn't get anything without money. He'd got to have money in order to pack in his winter supplies. The rains were starting early. Didn't we see? He'd just got to have the money we owed him.

He was worried and insistent, and more than a little threatening and ugly.

We told him that fifty dollars was all we had to spare, and that we needed money for our own winter supplies.

It wouldn't do, said Dave. He'd got to have the entire three hundred dollars. We'd got to get that money somehow. He must have it.

"The Government does not pay that way," we said. "You know that, Dave."

"Well, you've got to pay me," said Dave. "I gotta have that money."

We thought hard. "We promise you nothing," we told him. "But we'll ride to Hoopa tomorrow and see what we can do."

"All right," said Dave. "Ride to Hoopa and get the money and I'll be satisfied."

We went to bed that night with troubled minds.

The sun was shining as we swam the horses across the river and landed on the broad flat that was I-ees Bar. Piled high on the sand lay our things. Steve came down to meet us. Some Indian women and two children stood a little back from the sand spit, watching what was going on.

"Steve," we said desperately, "we must ride to Hoopa. Will you put those things in our house? Will you see that nothing happens to them?"

"Ain't nothing going to happen to them," said Steve noncommittally.

We turned up the mountain and made our way to the down-river trail. It was a beautiful morning. We were on a good, well-traveled trail. The horses were in fair shape and we made good time. But behind us, on a sandbar, lay everything we owned and everything we needed for a winter in I-ees-i-rum. The Indians who had watched us cross the river had looked at us with expressionless faces. There were no white men at I-ees Bar. This was Indian country. We had come to make our home with up-river Indians. They were standing now, looking down at our stuff, scattered over the sandbar. We did not know these Indians and they did not know us. We did not know how friendly they might be or what they might do.

Ahead of us lay Hoopa. Was there any chance at all

that Mr. Kyselka would pay us the money for the house? We had given Dave fifty dollars. That left us with just twenty in our little buckskin bag. We had not been paid our traveling expenses for the last quarter. The check for Mabel's salary had been lost in the mail. Unless we could get money in Hoopa, we ourselves would not have enough to live on. We must pay the I-ees Indians for what they did for us. Dave had been ugly. It would not be pleasant if we did not pay him what we owed him. We rode with our heads down. Though the moving was behind us and we were across the river and on the trail, the prospect ahead was a bleak one.

The hotel at Orleans was full of men. Mrs. Devon, the schoolteacher, and the cook and ourselves ate at the second table.

"Mrs. Richards isn't back yet," they told us. "She is waiting until Mr. Richards can bring her up here."

Well, our things were scattered on a sandbar behind us and there was a strong possibility that there would be no money for us at Hoopa. But, at least, we were not sitting waiting for a husband to bring us up onto the Rivers.

"If I lived the life of some married women," said Mabel, "I'd commit hara-kiri on our nice new hatchet. Do you remember that Essie told us that when one of the Bennetts at the Forks wanted to marry her cousin, the cousin refused him. Yet young Bennett was one of the wealthiest men on the Rivers and her cousin was an Indian."

"Woman marry white man," Essie's cousin had said, "stay home all day and cook. Woman marry Indian, take her baby on her back when she want to, and go along trail."

Certainly Mrs. Hilding doesn't leave home from year's end to year's end. Women who marry Indians pack their babies on their backs, take the other children, and go to all the dances while the men stay home and tend house.

Early the next morning, we struck out for Witchpec. The night before, Shaw-baby had never moved from an exhausted little heap on the foot of our bed. When he saw the horses saddled, he lay down on the trail and wailed. There was a heavy mist when we set out, but as the sun started to come through it, the mist took on wonderful, opalescent colors and the mountain peaks loomed out in beautiful greens and purples. Then the sun burst through and everything was shining, with a clear, blue sky overhead.

But by this time Shaw-baby was lying down in the trail and wailing whenever we stopped for a minute. We tried carrying him on our saddles, but we lost so much time that we finally left him at the Moonharts' and made the best speed we could for Hoopa, across the Klamath and still twelve miles away, with night close upon us.

All Sunday we struggled with an embattled Mr. Kyselka. He said he couldn't tell when the house money would come through. It might be one month and it might be three months. As for Mabel's salary, its loss in the mail would complicate things. It might take six months to get it straightened out. He couldn't pay our traveling expenses because he had paid Mrs. Mayhew out of the wrong fund and he was afraid he would be held personally responsible for the money.

With our backs against the wall, we took Dave McLaughlin's position. Every thing he said might be true but we must have the money, and what was more we must have it now. Somehow Mr. Kyselka would have to get it for us, and what was he going to do about it? The day wore on. It was not a restful Sunday for Mr. Kyselka. For that matter, it was not a particularly restful Sunday for us. By two o'clock in the afternoon we had resigned, written an impassioned letter to Commissioner Leupp, in Washington, and were composing a telegram to our respective families, begging them to send us three hundred dollars immediately.

At five o'clock, with no Sunday dinner for anybody and night closing down upon us, a kind but completely exhausted Mr. Kyselka, who had kept his temper and been kind and considerate through all the long hours of that trying day, gave us our traveling expenses, all his own personal money, and promised to hold up his plan to send some Indian children to Riverside the following day. Taken together, it totaled three hundred dollars. It was half-past seven when everything was finally arranged.

Mrs. McKimmon had warmed-over food waiting for us, a very special kindness here on the Rivers where all women expect you to come to the table when the food is served or go hungry. We gulped it down and ran over to beg Mr. Mills to have horses ready for us in the morning. Back in the office again we signed checks and vouchers. And thanked Mr. Kyselka. It was difficult to put into words the extent of our gratitude to Mr. Kyselka. Then with three-hundred dollars in gold safely stowed in my little buckskin bag, we took the trail home the following morning. Three hundred dollars in gold can lie heavy on one's stomach. What is more, it leaves a black-and-blue place there after even a mild burst of speed. But I did not care. The clink of that gold as we trotted over the soft grassy hills of Hoopa was the pleasantest sound we had ever heard.

Fifteen miles from home, our new home at I-ees-i-rum, while Mabel was nursing along a whimpering Shaw-baby, we passed the Hickoxes'. Mrs. Hickox ran out to speak to us with something cuddled in her hand. It was an adorable yellow kitten with a stumpy tail. I put it carefully inside my sweater and it bore up pretty well until I had to dismount to look for a stone in the Trinket's shoe. When I tried to remount, I faced a difficult problem. The kitten was ensconced on my stomach, under my sweater, riding unhappily on the little buckskin bag, with its three hundred dollars in gold. The Trinket always starts off at a lively trot as soon as I put my foot in the stirrup. If I tried to mount with the kitten pressed between the gold and the saddle, there was a good chance of its getting squashed. Mabel had unfeelingly gone on ahead. The kitten and I were alone. I finally eased it gently around to the back of my sweater, where it dug its claws into my backbone.

Praying it would not escape in the excitement, I climbed back gingerly into the saddle. It did not escape, and when we rode into I-ees-i-rum it was sound asleep, with its claws still embedded in my person.

We saw the last little fleck of sunshine as we scrambled down the trail to our own house, with our saddle bags flung over our shoulders. The brush was so thick along the little path that leads from the main trail to our back door that we had to force our way through it. Coming down from the main trail, you enter directly into our kitchen. It is a small, square room and was very dark when we came in because of the thick bush that crowded so close around the windows. From the kitchen a door opens into a large living room, all across the front of the house. On one side of the room is the fireplace, and on the other, three windows set close together. We are going to have a breath-taking view of the river and the mountains from those three windows as soon as the brush is cleared away. In the center of the front wall of the living room, a door leads out onto a porch.

Except for the noise of the river and the jingle of our spurs as we stepped into the living room, everything was very still. The spruce and pines pressed up close around the house. As we opened the door onto the porch, we saw a faintly trodden trail leading into the bush from our front steps. We followed it with our eyes until it lost itself in the dim light. Then we came back into the house. Neatly piled on the floor of our living room lay our things. Not a box or a bundle had been disturbed. The bundles had been roughly tied with bits of rope. Not a string had been untied. Shavings lay scattered over our floors. The shavings lay untouched. Our door was unfastened but none but the carpenters had ever entered that house.

We were daunted a bit by the stillness. We caught up some shavings and made a fire.

I-ees-i-rum was Karok country. Up-river country. That is what they said at Somes. "That's Karok country you're going into. There ain't nothing but Indians up there."

Across the river from us lived Herman Albers and his family. Herman was a half-breed. But Herman was the Indian kind of half-breed. Twelve miles up river was Siwillup, where the Elliotts lived. But after our last experience with Old Bob, we didn't expect much comfort from the Elliotts. And between the Elliotts' and the Hickoxes' were Indians, Karok Indians. Now we were going to see what living in Indian country was really like. As the fire of shavings blazed up, faint but distinct at a bend in the river we could see the outline of a mountain. We stood for a long time looking at that faint, beautiful outline. We felt very far from home.

We heard a step on the porch and turned to find Steve standing in the doorway. After all these years, we never think of I-ees-i-rum without thinking of Steve as he stood in the doorway. Steve, very Indian in his presence and dignity. No white man standing there could have looked like Steve. Steve always made the same dramatic entrance. He would fling open the door and stand with his head thrown back and more than a hint of arrogance in his manner as he took stock of the people in the room. Then, with complete assurance, he would cross the floor and seat himself. We never saw Steve lack assurance. He took in his stride, quite literally, whatever he might find.

That first day at I-ees-i-rum, as Steve stood arrogantly in the doorway, he looked at us and we looked at him. We were quite uncertain how things would turn out. Steve made us feel we belonged to a different race. We hoped very much that the white race, as represented by ourselves, would conduct itself with credit. We hoped it would not be found wanting.

We had hardly time to say hello to Steve when Pete came in. The two men are much alike in build. They both have the same dark, clean-cut features. But no one, even at a distance, could mistake Pete for Steve. Pete is a burden-bearer. He is a kindly burden bearer. It is hard to imagine anyone who would be afraid of Pete. Without a word the two men set to work. They put up the stove and finished nailing up some boards on the wall near the fireplace. They unroped the lumber and helped us knock together tables and benches. When black dark fell, things were to rights, and we were at home in our new house. As the two Indians stood on the porch, ready to go, rain began to patter on the roof. All evening it rained steadily. But the fire burned bright. Molly Bawn, the new kitten, and Shaw-baby curled themselves up on the hearth, and wrapped in blankets we slept soundly on the floor until morning.

All the following day, Indians drifted in and out of the house. According to Indian etiquette, you may neither enter, nor even glance in through a window of a vacant house. There is no need to lock your door against your Indian neighbors when you leave home. If you are absent, you may rest assured that they will not come in. But on the other hand, if you are at home there is no place in your house where it is not proper for your guests to go. As the months went on, we regretfully became accustomed to our Indian friends coming in without knocking and hunting us down, no matter what our occupation. But we never became resigned.

In the morning, Steve's woman came in, looked at us impassively, stood around for a while, and then went out again. Herman Albers arrived a little later. After he left, some women from the rancheria came over, followed by several children. Jim Covey, a tall, dignified Indian with a limp, came in, sat impassively for a time, and then went out again. But it was not until evening that Dave McLaughlin came for his money. We borrowed a leaf from Steve's book and showed a bit of arrogance on our own part as we spread the gold pieces out on the table.

"Here are two hundred dollars," we told Dave. "We have already paid you fifty."

"But there is still fifty coming to me," said Dave. "How about that?"

"Not until you finish the battens on the outside of the

house, Dave," we said. "You remember that was the agreement,"

We looked at Dave and Dave looked at us. His eyes did not waver and neither did ours. There was a movement behind us, and Steve stood at my side. There was no question now as to the arrogance in Steve's bearing or the look in his eyes. If there was going to be a fight, we could count Steve in on it.

"I think maybe he better go away," said Steve, and his eyes were hard and malevolent. "I think maybe he better go way."

Slowly Dave got up and put the money in his pocket. He turned toward the door. We watched him in silence but he did not turn back. He closed the door behind him and went down the steps.

Indians at Home in Up-river Country

From what the Indians say, it is not possible to belong to more than one family when you live on the Rivers. In Kot-e-meen, we belonged to the Essie family. Here at I-ees-i-rum we are part of Steve's family. It made a difference to Essie and Mart and Les when we told them we were going to live up river. Things were never quite the same again. We should have liked very much to have continued to be members of the Essie family, even after we had come to live in I-ees-i-rum, but now Kot-e-meen seems very far away. As far away as Somes did after we had gone live in Kot-e-meen, or as the Sacramento Valley did after we had come up into the Indian country, or as Somerville, New Jersey, does now, and all the things they do back east.

Every day we grow to feel more a part of the life at I-ees-i-rum. We like belonging to Steve and being a part of his family. What white people thought and did impinged a good deal on our life at Kot-e-meen. It even brought a faint restraint into our life with Essie and Mart and Les. But when you live at I-ees-i-rum, there may be white people at Orleans, twenty-five miles down river, or at Happy Camp, thirty-five miles in the other direction, but what they think or what they may do does not concern you at all.

Steve can remember when the first white men came to the Rivers. He can remember the time when the Indians had no weapons but bows and arrows and flints. Especially he can remember what it was like to have no tools. When Steve handles a pick or an ax or a knife or a saw, you can tell by the way he looks at the tool in his hands what a magic thing steel is, and how much easier it makes life for everybody. It is hard for us to imagine a world without steel. But Steve remembers well a world without steel, and what a very different world it was from the one we live in today.

Steve has a quick intelligence. It equals that of anyone we have ever known. He takes agriculture and carpentering and engineering in his stride. He is interested in the food we eat and the books we read, though he takes them with a certain reserve. But it is different when he speaks of iron or steel. All the tremendous, latent power that is in Steve comes into his voice when he speaks of iron or steel. One night when we sat talking late over the fire, Steve spoke of himself and of his only son, who is now dead.

"My boy, he die," said Steve. "Every day I think of my boy. All time I think of my boy. But if my boy he don't die, I think," and Steve's eyes flashed and there was a passionate emotion in his voice, "I think maybe he get to be a blacksmith."

Our first days in I-ees-i-rum now seem very far away, but sometimes during those first days we were not sure how things were going to turn out. At Kot-e-meen, we had grown to feel very much at home and not at all like white people. But as strange Indians stalked in and out of our living room with expressionless faces, we felt very white indeed and very far from home. If we had been four-footed, our tails would have drooped. But when on the third day we awoke in our own bedstead, which we much feared Steve had made for us out of some of the flume from the Russell mine, our spirits bounced up. We were at home in our own house, and if we were going to live up river in Karok country it was time we went about it.

When Steve and Jim Covey came over, we picked up an Indian basket.

"*Yuc-ca* (see)," we said. "This basket has a pattern. It goes so. We are going to make a pattern on the walls of this room just like the pattern on a basket. We will put *muroks* like these on the walls. We will put *sip-i-noks* like these on the shelves."

I held a *murok* against the wall by the windows. "Does this look well?" I asked.

There was a long silence and then Steve nodded gravely. "You put the murok there," he said. "I will put this one here."

Jim Covey limped around the room with a basket in his hand, trying it out in different places. Mack Charlie came in and was given a basket. A new young Indian named George McCash came in and was set to work. We tried different baskets over the fireplace. We took them down and tried others. The Indians had a sense of form and color. The room took shape. It was charming.

But only men worked on the decoration. The business of life in an Indian rancheria is in the competent hands of the women. They have no time for the lighter things of life, like decoration. Steve's woman came in, looked at what was going on, and went away. Pete's wife came in. She was a slightly built Indian woman and moved quickly and competently.

"Pete, you come," she said. "I got dinner ready."

The men turned to her and pointed to the baskets on the wall. There was a burst of Indian language while they explained what was being done.

Pete's wife looked contemptuous.

"Money makes *yarmuch* (pretty)," she said. Then she went out. If you have enough money, she had said succinctly, it will make anything look pretty. We had heard the same sentiment expressed by some white men in our own country.

At Kot-e-meen, it was the women who sang. But at I-ees-i-rum, it is the men. All week, we practice for Sunday school. We may have trembled a bit the first Sunday-school day in Kot-e-meen. But we are no tremblers these days when faced with a Sunday school. We carry on with a masterly hand.

All day long we sing carols. We write the first verse of a hymn on a piece of blackboard cloth. Then with a stick I point to each one of the words and say them over slowly, many times. No one can read and only a few Indians understand English, but everyone watches the pointer and speaks the words after me. When nearly everyone can say the words quite quickly, we repeat them without the pointer.

While I use the pointer, Steve stands by arrogantly, looking out the door and apparently paying no attention. But if anyone makes a mistake he swings around. "You say it so," he orders haughtily.

At this point, Mabel is usually called in. She not only guides the tottering voices of the Indians, she guides my tottering voice as well. But at I-ees, the Indians have little need for guidance. In short order, Steve's voice and the voice of Jim Covey ring out clear and true. We sing the same verse over eight or ten times, the sound rising in volume and intensity. Then we stop, draw a long breath, and get ready for the next carol.

"Peautiful song," Jim remarks gravely.

The singing is a far greater success here than it ever was at Kot-e-meen. But the Lord have mercy on the people who wrote the words in our Episcopal hymnbook. They will not do. They simply will not do.

"Veiled in time the Godhead see, Hail the incarnate Deity."

When the Indians are completely stampeded, we hold up everything and compose entirely new words.

The Lord Bishop better not try visiting this parish. He will think something is the matter with his hearing.

Everyone on both sides of the river turned out for the first Sunday school. The room was full to overflowing with Indians. Suddenly we did not feel white at all. We felt Indian, just as we had felt at Kot-e-meen. The singing had beauty and volume. We sang until it grew dark, and then Steve built up the fire. Pete went out and came back with a great load of logs in his arms. Steve brought out his drum.

"This is my song," said Steve. "Nobody else he sing my song."

All Steve's power and intensity was in his singing.

"Ai-yah. Ai-yah. Ai-yah," sang Steve. The fire blazed up. Every Indian face was intent.

"Now I sing," said Jim Covey. Jim's singing was softer and lacked the passion that was in Steve's song.

Together the two men sang a hunting song. It is a medicine song and is about the two little pine trees up on the mountain.

"When you go hunting at night," they told us, "everybody he sing and pretty soon deer he come right off."

They sang for a long time and then everybody began to drift away.

"Now what I make tomorrow?" said Steve as he went out.

With an allowance of four hundred dollars for a station at I-ees-i-rum, we are planning not only for a house, but also for a barn and a picket fence. Steve is going to build the barn for us with poles for studding and rafters, and shakes for the sides and roof.

And George McCash has already started work on the picket fence. The fence is of prime importance because of the depredations of Black Dog. Black Dog belongs to old I-ees woman who is too poor to feed him. Black Dog therefore lives on us. No matter how carefully we close our doors, somehow Black Dog manages to get in and eat everything in sight. As our own supplies are scanty enough, the situation is serious.

We tried arguing with old woman. But old woman only said humbly, "I like dog." And there things stood.

There was nothing for it but a picket fence.

George agreed to build the fence for us on contract. But George is an Indian. When George had finished the fence, he felt that something was lacking. The fence was fashioned the way fences are built on the rivers, with the pickets cut straight across the top. But as he looked at it, George remembered a fence he had once seen in the valley. So he took down all the pickets, sharpened the tops to a point, with his ax, and then put them up again. Both George and ourselves agreed that the effect was very beautiful. But when George was paid he only took the money we had agreed on, and threw in the extra time for sharpening the pickets. When it comes to the finer things of life, like putting pointed tops on your pickets, we like very much living with Indians.

But a barn and a picket fence are not the only blessings we enjoy in our new life at I-ees-i-rum. We have often read of people who had retainers. Now we know what it is like to have one. It appears that Pete is going to be our retainer. He used to be Steve's and now he is ours. Before Pete makes a move of any kind, he now puts his head in the door and announces it.

This morning, he came all the way in and sat down. He ate all seven of the corn pones we were saving for tomorrow's breakfast, without the butter Mabel had given him, and then he ate the piece of butter all by itself.

Then he got up. "A man, he want two dollars. I got to have two dollars," said Pete firmly. We gave it to him.

He then opened the door. "I cut wood this morning," said Pete.

"No, you don't, Pete," we said. "You go up river and pack down hay for us."

"All right," said Pete placidly. "I go up river."

All the rancheria tell us joyfully that Pete is *une-une* (crazy), and everyone in the rancheria makes fun of him. But then, Indians make fun of everybody. Kate, who is Pete's wife, is devoted to him. She came over this afternoon to see the picture we had taken of Pete. Pete was very much set up because we had taken his picture, and he leaned over Kate's shoulder to look at it.

"Who is that old man in the picture?" asked Kate gravely. "I ain't never see that old man before."

Pete looked completely taken aback, and all the other Indians laughed until they wept.

Later in the afternoon, Kate became completely absorbed in the fascinations of a primer.

"I don't like that old man," said Kate, looking coquettishly at Pete. "I cook, cook, all time cook. I don't like that old man no more. I like book. I think maybe I don't cook no more. I read."

Observe the effect of higher education on the Rivers.

For the past two weeks now, Pete and Jeff have been packing hay for us from T Bar. We had taken this trail on our way back from T Bar, and, though we are accustomed to bad trails in this country, it was only trusting in the Lord that brought us back with no serious damage to life or limb. We had just got through a quarter of a mile of one big boulder after another when we met poor old Pete looking like an animated hayload. All three of us gladly stopped to rest. Pete pointed serenely back over the trail.

"Only that one," he said mildly. "I don't like it."

From what we hear, it looks as if the hay were going to involve us in a minor growl at I-ees-i-rum. It was the day after we had come back from T Bar, and the bread was sitting sullenly before the fire. Mabel is worried about it because it has been that way now for two days, and she is afraid it may have decided not to come up at all. It was just then that Jeff put his head in the door, followed a little later by the rest of his person. Then Herman came in and we learned that they were both waiting for Pete. Mabel went over to the Pete household to see what was the matter and learned that there was a Jeff-Pete growl, and that Kate was openly unsympathetic and had sent Pete across the river to Sam Stenshaw's.

When they learned of this, both Jeff and Herman went off looking stormy.

The following morning the door opened and Annie came in, followed by Steve, followed by Pete, followed by Jeff. The growl was on. For the most part, it was in Indian. First,

Pete and Jeff exchanged what appeared to be fitful recriminations. Jeff plainly had the most potent tongue, so Steve, who has a very poor opinion of Pete as a brother and is not on speaking terms with him, hurried to his aid.

At first, Steve's manner was judicial, with a becoming mixture of sarcasm and contempt. Then suddenly things took a personal turn. Jeff became wildly excited and Steve's voice trembled with anger. Finally Jeff's voice broke with emotion. It was plain that Steve was driving his point home. At length, Jeff got up and, with a tragic gesture, plunged his hand into his pocket. He drew forth a coin, and, with an air of surrendering his all, crossed the room and laid the coin on Steve's knee. It was two bits.

"Yes,," said Steve bitterly, "he owe it to me for one year."

After that, things quieted down and Pete's affairs came again to the front. It appeared that when Pete had contracted to pack down hay for our animals he had asked Jeff to help him. Pete's claim was that "Jeff, he pack half the hay, he get half the money," while Jeff argued doggedly, "Pete, he say he pay me one dollar a hundred."

Things were at a deadlock. Steve argued. Pete argued. Jeff argued.

"But what did Pete say?" we asked when everyone stopped for breath.

Jeff looked blank. Pete looked blank. Steve remained noncommittal.

Finally we lost patience. "Well," we said, "what did Pete say? Did he say *I-o-qui* (hello) ?"

Everyone went off into fits of laughter.

"No," said Jeff, still grinning. "He ain't say nothing. Only say, "You want to pack hay?""

We looked at Pete and Pete nodded. "What then?" we asked.

"Pete, he say I get thirty dollars," said Jeff, warming to his subject. "And I say, all right, you pay me a dollar a hundred. And Pete say all right."

"Did you say that?" we asked Pete.

"Yes," said Pete.

"Ask him in Indian," we told Steve. Steve made the inquiry in a subdued tone. Pete nodded his head.

There was a step on the porch and Kate came in. Kate was in a lively temper. She is not Steve's equal but she would like to be. Everyone was silent while Kate had it all her own way. The trouble seemed to be that poor old Pete had thought that a thousand pounds made a ton and that Jeff had taken advantage of him. Kate was not resigned.

"But Pete he *une-une* (crazy)," said Kate.

"Pete he *une-une*," said Annie, who up to this time had kept out of the conversation.

"Pete he's *une-une*," said Steve.

"*Tani une-une (I'm crazy),*" said Pete modestly.

"Well, if Pete is *une-une*," we said grimly to Kate, "you better not let him make the bargains for the family. As it is, he will have to stand by what he said."

We looked at Steve.

"All right," said Steve, just as grimly. He nodded at Jeff. "Pay him."

We looked at Pete.

"All right," said Pete sweetly.

"He say all right to everything," said Kate bitterly.

"Well, is there anything more you want to say?" we asked Kate.

There was and Kate said it.

We told Kate firmly that the law was on Jeff's side. But Pete had made a mistake and Jeff knew it. If Jeff wanted to do right, he would help Pete pack the rest of the hay. But if he wanted his money, he should have it.

"Is that right?" we asked Kate.

"Yes," said Kate sourly.

"I take my money," said Jeff.

We gave it to him and Jeff went out the door.

"Herman, he's gone across river," said Steve, and his face relaxed a little. "I think old woman now she make Jeff pay two bits to get across river."

Pete started to go.

"You know," said Mabel, "I think that, as it was our hay, we ought to pay Pete the four dollars, so he will get his money just the same."

"All right," said Pete serenely.

But Steve drew a long breath and sat back in his chair. Steve is a lover of poetic justice.

For several days, Steve and Pete have been cutting away the trees and brush from below our house. We had found a beautiful little spring back up the mountain, and when we came back after cleaning it out we could see the whole stretch of the Klamath and the great mountain at the bend of the river. Steve tells us that the name of the mountain is O-we. Yesterday, breakfast was delayed. We can see O-we from our south window as we lie in bed. When we waked yesterday morning, behind O-we was a broad band of white light and above it clouds tipped with pink. We could only see the two peaks of O-we, because below, at the base, everything swam in mist. It really was a day that called for the efforts of three able-bodied field matrons, but instead we propped ourselves on pillows and watched the sunrise while the clock ticked from seven to seven-thirty and then to eight. At quarter-past eight, I hopped wildly out of bed, but already the door was opening and we heard Steve's voice commenting on the fact that the fire was not lit. We told Steve reprovingly that we had been watching the sunrise, so, of course, we couldn't get up. And Steve replied reprovingly that he had been up at six and had also been watching the sunrise. When it comes to sunrises, Indians are very sympathetic.

Steve stayed to breakfast on the strength of his sympathies, and we had hot cakes.

"I catch six that time," said Steve with considerable satisfaction.

For days, Steve has been prophesying storm. After the bright pink sunrise, when we went out to gather wood there were heavy clouds over O-we. By suppertime we could hear the rain pattering on the roof and beating against the windows. With the mountains towering above us and the river roaring below, we feel very sheltered and safe in our kind little house, sitting so warm and comfortable before the fire. Moreover, Steve says the storm will not last long, and that he is going to sing the Grasshopper Song.

"I go make medicine," Steve said. "Maybe you don't think I make medicine. Pretty soon you find out. I go sing Grasshopper Song.

"Long time ago it rain and rain. You can't see no river, just mist. By and by Grasshopper, he come out. He walk down to river. But ain't no river. Just mist. It rain and rain. Grasshopper, he sit by river and sing his song. He say, 'Ai-ai. Ai-ai. Ai-ai.' Then he say, 'Puff.'

"And he blow like this. Mist, he break and go down river. Rain, he go away. Sun, he shine. Grasshopper, he go back and he say, 'When mist, he come on river; and ain't no sun; and rain, he rain and rain; everybody sing my song, and say, "Puff."'

"Then mist, he go down river; and sun, he shine; and rain, he don't rain no more."

Whether or not because of the Grasshopper Song, the day after Steve made medicine turned out to be so pleasant that we decided to paint all our furniture. We had found a can of green paint, the last time we were in the store at Orleans, and we couldn't help feeling that painted furniture would make a profound impression all up and down river. It did. But not quite in the way we had expected. First, we painted all our straight chairs, one after another. Then I fell to on what serves us for a dining table and painted it. Meantime, Mabel painted the phonograph table and the box we keep the records in. Then we both painted the bench. While we were working, Steve was nailing battens on the outside of the house. As a result, everything started to fall off the walls, so we took down all the Indian baskets and put them on the floor. After that we put the legs of all the chairs and tables on little islands of newspaper to protect the floor from green paint.

When we were completely exhausted and it had grown too dark to see, Annie and Steve came over, and we sat on little kerosene oil boxes and sang songs in the twilight. After a long time our supply of wood gave out. The fire was so low that Mabel went out onto the porch for more wood. I heard her emit a little, feeble, inarticulate sound from her throat, so I went to the door to see what was the matter. There on the porch stood Mr. Hunter and Mr. Wilder, the two foresters. They had come to make a formal call on us in our new house in I-ees-i-rum, and, of course, expected to stay to supper.

Now Mr. Hunter and Mr. Wilder are white men. They take us very seriously, and coming to call on us was an occasion. The Indians do not take us at all seriously. We are just friends of theirs. But to Mr. Hunter and Mr. Wilder we are not only *white women,* we are *ladies*—the kind who have Sunday schools, and never say a bad word, and rustle around in a lot of silk petticoats.

It is true that we wear divided skirts and Stetson hats, and never rustle, but the foresters make nothing of that and cling to what we ought to be as womenkind. We do the best we can and listen to what they say and try to act as though we never, never did such unladylike things as ride trails and cross rivers, but it isn't always easy for the foresters. And here they were on a dark and possibly stormy night, come for a quiet evening with two perfect ladies, and not a chair or a table or a box that didn't have green paint on it.

Mabel, with no thought of anyone but herself, hurried out into the kitchen to get supper out of her imagination. I sat Mr. Hunter and Mr. Wilder on the two kerosene-oil boxes, which Steve and Annie had vacated (both had vanished by way of the kitchen), and talked brightly about the sort of things that interest white people. I still talked

brightly while I took the freshly painted chairs and tables
off their little islands of newspaper. After that, I sacrificed
our only centerpiece by putting it on a painty table. (It has
since been soaking for three days and is still a bright green.)

Then I faced the choice. Painty chairs and tables or
sit on the floor? I was sure, quite sure, that ladies, real
ladies, back where Mr. Hunter and Mr. Wilder came from,
never ate their dinners off the floor. So I chose the paint.
We all drew the painty chairs up to the painty table and
delicately sat down. We could not give the foresters unblemished suits to take back with them, but we could give
them style, and we did our best. I think it was more than
even they had anticipated. As course followed course and
clean plates followed dirty ones, both foresters were so
agitated that they only occasionally cast nervous glances at
the stripes of green paint that were rapidly appearing on
their coat sleeves. Meantime, to keep things going, we guyed
Mr. Hunter in our best manner, and, in every way we could
think of, tried to persuade both of them to eat. But they
had manners and one thing they had learned: never do more
than pick at your food in the presence of a lady. With plenty
of ragging, we managed to get Mr. Hunter through a serving and a half. But it was evident that Mr. Wilder was
carefully counting the number of his mouthfuls.

They were plainly only too much aware of all the dangers that beset them (of which painty clothes were evidently
the least), but in spite of all their efforts a frightful thing
happened. Mrs. Richards told us about it the next time
we saw her in Orleans.

It seems that Mr. Hunter had come to her in great
agitation of spirit.

"You know the ladies at I-ees Bar?" he said.

Mrs. Richards said she did.

"You must know," said Mr. Hunter, "how much I respect them. We all respect them. Every man in the forestry
service respects them. But a terrible thing has happened."

Mrs. Richards looked grave. "What was it?" she asked.

"I wouldn't have had it happen for worlds," said Mr. Hunter. "I don't know what they will think of me."

"Do go on," said Mrs. Richards.

"Well," said Mr. Hunter, "you know the nice way they talk to each other. One of them said, 'Pass the butter, dear.' And—and—I passed it."

It is not white men but Indians who are at home with ceremony on the Rivers. Steve is the man for functions. He could ride out a ten-course dinner, no matter what the array of knives and forks and strange dishes, and come through with glory. When we have guests in to dinner, it is Steve who keeps the conversation going. When the room is full of strange Indians, it is Steve who knows when the time has come to stop drumming and start the phonograph. It is Steve who senses every light change in the atmosphere of our guests and knows what is going on beneath the surface, and what we should do about it.

So far, the only person who has defied Steve to his face and gotten away with it is Emmott. We were just finishing a leisurely breakfast when all the Indians from the rancheria came over with the air of something in the wind. It appeared that Kate, who is Pete's woman, had been fixing dried beans. Kate's two children, Maud and Emmott, were playing quietly in a corner.

"Maud, he cry out," said Kate. "Maud, he say that Emmott got a bean in his ear." When she investigated, Kate found that Emmott had put a bean in his ear and, what was more, pushed it in as far as it would go. The rancheria had forthwith come over to see what we would do about it. We hunted up an orange stick and a fountain syringe and did our best, but nothing came out but screams from Emmott. While I poked around as gently as I could, Mabel sought counsel of the little first-aid book. It was its usual unhelpful self.

"The ear is a delicate organ," said the little first-aid book. "In case of any emergency, send at once for a surgeon."

With Dr. Kyselka two days away across two mountains,

we did not feel that the advice entirely met the situation.

Meantime, Emmott, with nothing happening to him, screamed himself hysterical, and Kate egged him on. All Steve did was to sit by with a reserved expression. He obviously does not approve of Kate's method of bringing up children.

After some attempts, it became evident that the syringe was worse than useless, and that nothing could be done with the orange stick unless Emmott would keep still. While this was going on, Pete, who is the father of Emmott, seemed to feel his presence was not needed, and went on placidly piling wood behind the house.

After a half hour of Emmott's screams, Kate became completely unnerved and left. We placed a row of presents before Emmott, and then Steve held his head and Mabel held his hands. But Emmott only yelled and twitched the harder, and after every trial failing we gave up in despair. What we needed was a small pair of tweezers, and it was probable none could be found short of Witchpec or Hoopa.

We finally decided to send Emmott down to Mrs. Mayhew, the field matron at Witchpec. If she could do nothing for him, Pete would then take him down to the doctor in Hoopa. We wrote letters to Mrs. Mayhew and to Dr. Anderson at Hoopa, begging them to help the child if they could. Pete waited for the letters, and after he had gone we settled down to draw our breath. Steve lingered a minute to make it quite clear what he thought of Emmott's behavior.

A little later, Steve dropped in on his way to cut some poles for us and told us that Pete had got off. We groomed Shasta and Siskiyou until we saw the entire rancheria coming along the trail. First came Annie, and then Maud. Then Grandma and then Kate. Last of all came Emmott. We thought we were seeing a ghost.

"Kate," we gasped, "didn't Pete take Emmott?"

"No, he don't take him," said Kate placidly. "Pete, he say you give him letters. Down river they fix him."

Without a word, Mabel caught up the saddle bags and ran to the mules. Pete had four hours' start. I caught Kate by the arm.

"Take Emmott and start down the trail," I ordered. "Go fast and get as far as you can. Pete will come back for him."

We thanked the Lord for the mules. You think in terms of your animals here on the Rivers. You breathe them going uphill and ease them going down. But we dug in our spurs and rode. We made Ross's in two hours. At Ronell's Creek was an Indian cabin. An old woman came to the door as we clattered up.

"Seen I-ees Pete?" we cried.

"Pura fata (no more)," said the old woman, giving the equivalent phrase of "he is gone." We rode on. Ed Mann stood outside the shaft of his mine,

"How long ago did I-ees Pete go by?" we shouted.

"Hour and a half," said Ed Mann. Our chances were poor. If Pete got as far as Pich-pichi, we might lose him in the multiplicity of trails. By this time both mules were breathing hard. A mile farther on we met Ross.

"Seen I-ees Pete?" we called.

"At the Hickoxes'," said Ross.

"Ride," said Mabel. We did. It was a fairly level bit and we took it at a gallop. Luther himself came to the door.

"Pete here?" we asked.

"Just gone," said Luther. "You can take your time," he shouted after us. "He should be going through the mine now."

Mabel was the first to top the rise that leads down into the deserted placer mine. I was just behind her. Climbing out of the mine on the other side, we could just make out a squat figure on horseback. It was Pete.

"Pete!" we yelled. "Pete, come back!" Pete drew up and waited.

"You will have to go back for Emmott," we gasped as we caught up with him.

"All right," said Pete serenely. "Maybe better."

We had made fifteen miles in three hours. Record time on the trail. We should not like to do it again. Even Luther, the horse-killer, nodded respectfully.

But Luther is not only a horse-killer. He is a tooth-puller. His eye brightened when he heard of the bean. He brought out his forceps and looked at them doubtfully. Then he went off and came back with two tiny pieces of metal, which he fashioned into a little pair of tweezers. While we held beans as tightly as we could in our fingers, Luther picked them out with force and precision.

"Get Emmott and come back to Luther," we told Pete. "Luther will fix him."

We thought of the menace in Luther's eye. It had cowed many a man on the Rivers. We thought it equal even to Emmott.

But what a neighbor Luther was going to be if we should decide on another station at Ossi-puk, only three miles away. Tooth pulling and bean extracting! If necessary, it was worth marrying such a man. But as a neighbor he would have all the assets and none of the liabilities.

We rode back slowly, letting the mules take their own pace. Near Flower's Flat we met Pete, with Emmott safely up behind him. We were home a little after six.

"What time you get down?" said Steve.

"Three hours," we said.

"Well," said Steve, "you ride pretty good."

The next day, Pete came back with Emmott, minus the bean. You can safely bet your money on Luther.

CHAPTER XVI

The Baby Growl

There is trouble in the rancheria over Agnes' baby. Agnes' baby has a bad name, they tell us. And it is not a white man who is the father of Agnes' baby.

"White man, he don't care," Steve had once told us sadly. "White man, he just get kids anywhere."

Nor is it a question of rape. Rape is unknown among the Indians and is regarded with horror. No, the father of Agnes' baby is an Indian.

Last winter while Kate was away, Clint Albers, from across the river, used to come over and see Agnes. When the baby came, everyone thought Clint would marry Agnes, Indian way. But instead, Clint went off to work in the valley, and now the baby has a bad name.

For the past few days Rube Morse has been staying with the Pete family, in the rancheria. There is talk that Rube would be willing to marry Agnes. There is also talk that Clint may be coming back from the valley. In every cabin there is a sense of impending trouble in the rancheria. Yesterday, Steve came over to ask us about white law. Steve was grave and plainly concerned. He was withdrawn and very Indian in his attitude. And there was the faint, intangible sense of menace in his manner that one always feels when in the presence of Luther Hickox.

"Clint, he don't come back," Steve began. "Agnes' baby, he got bad name. Indians don't like it when baby got bad name. I think maybe there is a trouble. Agnes say maybe she marry Rube Morse."

We were standing on the porch, and Steve was looking across the river.

"What you call trouble about baby?" Steve asked.

I shook my head. "What do you call it, Steve?" I said.

"Indians call it baby growl," said Steve, and he went back up the trail to his house.

A little later the door opened and Agnes came in. She is a pretty girl. She had a white father. That happened when Kate was only a little girl herself, long before she married Pete. Agnes sat on our settle and had a cup of coffee. She kept twisting her fingers and looked very unhappy. Presently she began to talk.

"Rube likes baby. Rube says he will marry me if I go along with him. Maybe it would be good for me to get married. I don't know, but maybe it would be good. Rube wants someone who can cook. I guess Clint ain't coming back. All this summer I thought maybe Clint would come back and we would get married."

"Maybe Clint will come back this Christmas," we suggested.

"No," said Agnes. "No, he won't come back. I wrote him twice and he won't answer." She cried a little, and then got up and went away.

The next day was the day for school at Kot-e-meen. After school, we went over to Somesbar. At the store, everyone was talking about the baby growl. Sam Frame said Rube Morse was marrying Agnes Indian way and was paying seventy dollars for her. Of course, that is very handsome of him and shows his appreciation of Agnes as the regular price is sixty dollars. But both the Frames were loud in their indignation.

"If they get the benefits of the law, make 'em follow the law," said Papa Frame. "That's what I say."

It is not quite clear in our minds just what the benefits of the law are here on the Rivers, but as white women and field matrons and representatives of the Government, we tried to look sympathetic.

All the Indians down river tell us there will be a trouble, and that someone will get shot. We can't make out whether it will be on our side of the river or at the Albers'.

On our way up river we felt the cloud of impending trouble. Mack Charlie, our Indian friend from T Bar, stopped us to discuss the possibilities.

He didn't know nothing about Clint, he said. "But Herman now (Herman Albers is Clint's father), he ain't much good with a gun except at close range, but the Albers boys, they can shoot pretty good."

"Pretty soon big row," said Pete gloomily, as he put us back across the river.

At the rancheria there was bad news. We found everyone waiting for us, when Pete drove the dugout into the spit of sand.

The Alberses had stolen Agnes' baby. It had happened when Rube and Agnes had crossed the river that morning. Rube had got the horses from Herman and they were all ready to go down river. They sat on the horses and Herman came out of the house and talked. Then all the rest of the Alberses came out. The old woman come over to where Agnes sat on her horse and talked nice and friendly to her. Then she leaned over and quickly snatched the baby out of Agnes's arms and ran with it into the house. Then all the Alberses went back into the house and locked the door. Rube beat on the door and told them to come out and give Agnes back her baby, but they wouldn't come. Then he went and got his gun.

Later, Kate came over in tears.

"Agnes, he get married to Rube Morse," said Kate, weeping. "I think maybe Rube, he don't want baby. Agnes and Rube, they go away. And I think," said Kate in a burst of grief, "I think that maybe I keep baby."

There may be babies who have a bad name on the Rivers but there are no unwanted babies in the Indian country.

Kate was no sooner gone than Rube came over to air his point of view.

"Herman, he's just down on me, anyhow," said Rube. "It was when we were over there playing smit. Maybe-Joe had a card and Clint had a card. 'If I let you out,' says I to Clint, 'will you go on playing?'

"Clint, he says he wouldn't.

" 'Well, will you?,' I says to Maybe-Joe.

"So I played a diamond and Joe, he went out. And Herman, he was back over by the counter, and he come across the room and hit me in the face.

" 'Let 'em fight it out,' said Maybe-Joe. But Clint, he jumped in, and Joe, he jumped in, and I took Herman and rubbed his head in the dirt.

" 'You can't fight,' I said, so I sat on him. So I got my sleeve tore and the old man, he give me another shirt. And Herman said it was all right, but I guess he's had it in for me ever since."

In the evening, we discussed white law and Indian law with Steve. We told him of the status of a white, unmarried mother, and asked him what was the Indian way.

"Well," said Steve, "when Agnes, he don't get married, baby, he got bad name. If Clint, he don't pay no money for Agnes, baby, he don't belong to Clint, he belong to Agnes."

We said it was the same, white way. The baby belonged to Agnes. That was white law. It was bad for Rube to go and get his gun. Frank Offield was sheriff and Hilding was deputy sheriff; we would go down river and see what could be done.

Hilding is the only white man in the twenty-five miles between the Alberses' and the Salmon River. He said he didn't hold with mixing in Indian matters, but he told Rube he had better be careful. Rube said he didn't care, he was going for his gun. He said he had bought the woman and he'd bought the baby and he was going to have the whole damn outfit.

We tried to find Frank Offield, but it looked as if he might be keeping out of our way. We left a message for him, asking him to come up to the Alberses, and straighten things out. At Somesbar, they were not encouraging. We wrote a letter to the district attorney in Yreka, but we were not banking much on it. White law in Yreka, four days away over trails and wagon roads, doesn't mean much to the Indians on the Rivers, or to the white men either, for that matter.

Everything conspired to delay us on our return, and it was several days before we again crossed the river at I-ees-i-rum. There was no one at Steve's house, so we went over to Pete's. As we came up the steps of the porch, we heard talking. Then the door opened and all the rancheria Indians came out—Steve and Pete and Rube and Jim Covey, and Kate and Annie and Agnes and the two children. There was excitement in the air and every face was tense.

They had been waiting for us, they said. There had been a call from across the river. Clint was back. All the Alberses were waiting for us. Maybe we better go.

Down on the strip of sand, Pete was already in the dugout. As we walked past Steve's house, along the trail and through the low bushes to the little beach, we tried to give an impression of confidence we were far from feeling. Everyone was watching us. This was white law we were carrying across the river, and everyone wanted to see how it would work.

"Do not shoot," we repeated over and over again. "The baby belongs to Agnes. Herman will have to give it back. Everything will be all right. It is Indian law and it is white law that the baby belongs to Agnes. Do not shoot. Everything will be all right."

We hoped, most earnestly, that it would.

Rube and Agnes were getting into the dugout when Steve went back up the trail to his house. We were fairly certain he had gone for his gun, and our hearts sank. As he came out of his cabin, his woman followed him. We have never felt that we knew Annie very well. She speaks very little English, and when she comes over to see us her face is expressionless. But Annie's face was not expressionless now. She caught up with Steve and clung to his arm. Steve tried to shake her off but she only clung the harder. Then with a swift, impatient movement Steve pulled himself away, and striding down the strip of sand stepped into the dugout.

No one said anything as Steve and Pete paddled us across. We were silent as we climbed the mountain to the Alberses' house and remained silent until we stood before the Alberses' door.

"Speak English," we then urged our crowd. "Be sure to speak English."

By the time the door was opened, Steve had disappeared. Herman stood in the doorway. We asked him if we might come in.

"Yes," said Herman. "Come in if you are not afraid."

We entered a large room. It was relatively narrow and long and extended the full length of the house. We entered at one end. To our right, as we came in, was a stove. It stood well out from the wall, halfway into the middle of the room. Behind the stove sat all the Albers women, on a long row of chairs. In the very center of the row, directly behind the stove and protected on either side by the sitting women, sat Herman's wife. In her lap she held a baby. We had no need to ask what baby it was. This baby was the cause of the baby growl. Across from the stove and near the doorway through which we had entered sat all the Albers men and the male friends of the Albers family. In the center of the group sat Mack Charlie. He gave us a feeble, propitiating smile as we came in.

To find seats for ourselves in the room, we had to pass through this narrow passage: all the women on one side, protected by the stove; all the men on the other side. We did not see any six-shooters but we had a notion that every hand was ready. All the men sat with their chairs tilted back, looking at us.

Herman had taken a seat near the center of the room. Like the other men, he had tilted his chair back against the wall, and his right hand was in his pocket. Directly across from him was a high bench. On this bench sat a young Indian. As he stared at us, his face was mean and not pleasant. He did not look at Agnes, but there could be no doubt from his expression that he was Clint, the father of the baby. Like Herman, Clint also had his right hand in his pocket. A few more Alberses were ranged at intervals about the room. At the end of the room, farthest from the door, two or three children were playing quietly together.

Kate, Rube Morse, and Agnes found seats as near the door as they could get. They crowded into some chairs near the row of men. Mack Charlie made a place for them. Pete stood still, looked around for a minute, and then crowded in beside them. I picked up a chair, put it at Herman's right, and sat down as close to him as I could get. I was pretty close, because I could feel the full length of Herman's right arm at my side. If there was going to be any movement of that right arm I wanted to know about it. Mabel swiftly crossed the room toward the rather startled Clint. She hitched herself up onto the bench and pushed close against Clint's right arm. Both men were at a disadvantage. If a lady sits beside you and squeezes herself close against you while everyone looks on, you rather hesitate to do anything about it.

The conference began. We were just warming up with a few opening remarks when there was a sound at the door. Everyone looked up. Steve was standing in the doorway. He stood silent and impassive, with every eye on him. There was a studied insolence in his look as his eyes slowly surveyed the room. There was a faint smile on his face, but the room might as well have been empty, for in his glance there was no recognition of anyone in that silent, watching crowd. The seconds ticked by as he stood there with that faint, half smile on his lips. Then, with an insolent and contemptuous swagger, he slowly walked down the full length of the room, past the women behind the stove and the men across from them, past the cross fire of Herman and Clint, directly opposite each other, to the other end, where the children sat playing. He seated himself negligently on a table while we all sat watching him. One of the Albers children came up to him. His face broke into a smile and he leaned over and spoke to the child.

The room relaxed and we went back to the talk that had been broken off. But we thought, as we sat close to Herman and Clint and their guns, that if it should come to shooting, Steve would never leave that room alive.

It might be white law that we represented but we approached it with Indian tactics. I joked with Herman about his Happy Camp trip, and Herman smiled unwillingly while the rest of the room giggled at his expense. Mabel joined in and we both kept it up until Herman outmaneuvered us and said something to Agnes in Indian. Agnes began to cry. I broke in and said white people always wanted to find out what the facts were, and what the law was, before they did anytling. We had written to the district attorney in Yreka. He was the representative of the white law for all this district. He had written us. I asked Rube to give Herman the letter.

Herman took the letter and turned it over in his hands. Our party said nothing, and the Alberses ate apples belligerently. After a long while, I asked if they would like me to read the letter aloud, as sometimes it was hard to understand just what lawyers meant by what they said. Herman rather thankfully agreed to this. After the letter had been read, Herman said he guessed it didn't make no difference what they said in Yreka. Did we know that Clint had come home? Well, Clint had come home. He guessed the baby belonged to Clint. There wasn't many people who didn't know that. The baby was here and he guessed that was all there was to it.

While Herman talked, Clint leaned forward a little, his eyes hard and mean. He drummed with his feet against the bench on which he sat.

We explained the question very slowly: first, from the standpoint of Indian law; then, from the standpoint of white law.

"Now," we said, "you all understand just what the white law is in this case. It is not good to go against the white law. Will you give back the baby? That is what we have come to find out."

Peaceable relations came abruptly to an end. They would not give back the baby. There would be no compromise. Herman had been drinking and his breath came a little hard.

I leaned forward a little. "We need this as evidence before witnesses," I said pleasantly. I looked at Clint. "You will not give back the baby?"

"No," said Clint angrily. "I won't."

"All right," I said. "That is what we came to find out."

Mabel and I got up. We smiled pleasantly at Herman. We smiled pleasantly at Clint.

"That was what you wanted, was it not?" we asked Rube and Agnes.

Rube and Agnes agreed rather doubtfully that it was.

"Very well," we said, "then we can go."

We nodded at Rube and Agnes. They looked at us dubiously and then got up. Slowly they went out of the room. Kate followed them, and then Pete.

We looked at Steve. "That is all, Steve," we said. Then we waited.

Steve looked at us. His face was expressionless but we suspected that a good deal was going on in his mind. Slowly Steve got off his table. He waited an instant and then, still slowly, walked the length of the room to the door. He hesitated a minute at the door. Then he went out.

"That is everything we wanted, Mr. Albers," we said formally to Herman. "Thank you all for being here."

We followed Steve out of the room.

It was bluff. It could be nothing else but bluff. But at least we were all out of that room in one piece. What would come of it, we did not know. Our only comfort was that the Alberses were in even greater doubt about what would come of it than we were.

We were very aloof as we came down the mountain to the dugout.

"Very satisfactory, wasn't it?" we said to Rube and Agnes, who were already in the dugout. They nodded doubtfully.

We left the others on the spit of sand and headed toward our own house. But before we turned to go, we looked grimly at Rube.

"It would be just as well," we said, "if you and Agnes got married white way just as soon as you can. We want no trouble about that with the white law."

"Yes," assented Rube eagerly. "Just as soon as we knew there would be a trouble, Agnes and me were going to get married white way the very first thing."

As we took the trail to our house we had the mild comfort of knowing that no one knew how things stood or what would happen, and that they would probably wait to find out. We were staking our bottom dollar on that fact. And we were staking our reputation on the Rivers. All evening we sat reading magazines we had read before. But we had no notion of what we read. Our thoughts were on what might be going on at the Alberses'.

Steve came over just before luncheon, the following morning. He was in good spirits. We talked about the flume he was going to make for us and where we wanted the water brought down into our kitchen. In the course of the talk he said he had been across the river.

We asked casually whether he had seen anyone, but our hearts beat fast.

Yes, said Steve, just as casually, he had seen Herman. Frank Offield had been up before breakfast and had taken the baby. He had taken it down to Somes. It was all right, just as we said it would be. Rube and Agnes had gone right off down river. They were going to be married white way

Then they were coming back to Sunday school. Everyone was coming to Sunday school.

Everyone *did* come to Sunday school. We were in full volume of "Hark, the Herald Angels Sing" when the door opened and Herman and Clint came in. They found themselves seats and promptly joined in the singing. Not a six-shooter was in evidence. No one at Sunday school kept his right hand in his pocket. Both Clint and Herman were extremely pleasant when they took their leave. Everyone was pleasant.

The baby growl was over.

Several weeks before, when there was no sign that a baby growl was imminent, we had discussed the advantages of white marriage with Rube Morse. Rube had not been impressed. He had settled back in his chair and stretched his long legs out in front of him.

What he wanted, he said, was a good, hard-working woman, and from all he could hear there wasn't no kick from anyone about Agnes. If they should get married, he'd go back to the Forks. He'd been thinking about marrying white way but he wasn't sure about it. When you came right down to it, Indian way was pretty good.

We made as good a case as we could for what was considered on the Rivers our rather inferior white method, but Rube shook his head.

"You see," he pointed out, "you must have a good deal of regard for a woman if you are willing to pay money for her. Now there are some men who pay thirty dollars and then have to support all the family. Of course, if you haven't much money, that is the best you can do. But if you are pretty well fixed and have done all right, you pay down your sixty dollars and let your wife's family look out for themselves.

"Now white way you only pay two dollars for a woman, and you pay it to the Government instead of to her family. You can't have much respect for a woman that you can get for two dollars. You hold her pretty cheap, and that isn't a good thing, no matter what white people say about it."

It was plain we were making heavy sledding of it. We shifted our ground and began to describe the glories of a white wedding party. Here we struck pay dirt. Rube listened with close attention and it was plain that he was impresseed. By the time we had described the wedding cake in full detail, there was no doubt that white marriage was forging ahead. Rube said that up to then he hadn't really understood about it but evidently it had its points.

We redoubled our efforts, and in our excitement went so far as to say that if Rube and Agnes should get married white way, we would produce the cake and the festivities.

With Rube and Agnes actually getting married this very day at Somesbar, it was certainly up to us to make good.

It was a time for rejoicing. We set the wedding party for the day of Rube's return. All day I cleaned while Mabel cooked feverishly in the kitchen. We were just hoping for a sorely needed rest when Hilding arrived for his first call on us at I-ees-i-rum. It was plain that he felt that the happy termination of the baby growl had been entirely his affair.

But this wedding party was to be entirely an Indian affair, so Hilding shortly slipped away to carry the news all up and down river, just as the first guests began to arrive. Of course, as a wedding reception it was not quite conventional from the standpoint of Somerville, New Jersey, but we were omitting no bets that might add to its popularity.

We opened with a donkey party. I cut out a donkey of sorts, very large and impressive, to pin on the wall. Everyone, in turn, was blindfolded and given a tail to pin on its rear end. It was the first donkey party on the Rivers and it was an unqualified success. While everyone was concerned in finding the proper place to pin his tail, I-ees Old Woman and Mrs. Pepper came in. Mrs. Pepper was slight and serene-looking. No one would guess from looking at her how many of the other side she had wiped out in the Schenck-Pepper feud. She accepted her tail with poise and dignity and pinned it about four feet away from the donkey. Jim Covey and six-year-old Maud tied for first prize.

We then threw cards into a hat. Steve won and received as a prize two little beans that jumped when you put them on the table. They had just come from New York, and we were saving them for a very special occasion. Steve was a trifle apprenhensive at first. We told him they were *apruan,* and they certainly jumped convincingly. But later he became vastly taken with them, and Rube Morse openly mourned because he had not won the prize.

The final event was a mold of flour. Each Indian, in turn, was given a knife and told to slice off a piece of the mold. A dime had been stuck in the top of the mold. The purpose was to cut off a slice and leave the mold still standing and the dime undisturbed. When the flour mold finally collapsed, dime and all, it was the unfortunate Rube who had to pick the dime out of the flour with his teeth.

Of course, the really high light of the whole affair was the cake. I am not sure, but I think it was the first wedding cake ever introduced into our whole two hundred miles of territory. Mabel had done her darnedest, and the icing was beautiful to behold. I unwisely ate all of my very large slice, to my regret later in the day. After all, a baby growl was something to live through. Everyone else had two rounds of cake, Pete and Steve hungrily dividing the last slice between them.

The afternoon ended with drumming, Indian way. But long before this it was plain that the whole affair had gone over big, and I think it has put white marriage on the map.

As usual, after the others had gone, Steve and Annie stayed and sang sweat-house songs. We sat in the firelight, listening.

"There is a big wind," sang Steve in Indian. We could just make out the words. "A big wind comes in the brush, and all the brush, he move in the big wind."

We slumped down in our chairs and listened. The fire burned bright, and outside there was the steady beat of rain on the roof.

We were glad to have been in on a baby growl, but of all the people concerned I think we were the most thankful to have it over.

CHAPTER XVII

We Introduce White Customs in the Form of Two Christmas Trees, and, for a Moment, Fear We May Regret It

Christmas is now appallingly close. We spend every minute feverishly adding to our store of gifts. In spite of all we can do, the men are only scantily provided for. Every minute she can spare, Mabel is knitting mufflers or making tobacco pouches out of bits of cotton or silk.

All the presents that people from all over California have sent us, as well as those that have come from home, are in a long-shaped, boxlike pile, under the eaves in our sleeping room. We call this pile "McKinley lying in state." It is covered by a piece of old rotten canvas that we found in a deserted mine. The displacement under the canvas is about six by two and one half feet. Its resemblance to a concealed corpse is impressive.

The number of presents stands at forty fancy bags, thirty plain bags, twenty dress pieces, fourteen shirtwaist lengths, and a large number of toys. But we have only twenty-six articles that, in a pinch, can be given to the men, and we have reckoned about fifty Indian men among our rather close personal friends, not to mention about fifty more whom we know slightly but on a less intimate basis.

I wish there were some way we could make our Indian male friends believe that white men in the East relished little dolls. We have those and to spare.

Mabel says all she does, day after day, is to sing the song of the shirt—stitch, stitch, stitch. The shirt she is mak-

ing now is for Tintin. She regards with bitterness the fact
that I am no seamstress, and says she had all she could do
knitting mufflers. Then someone sent us a huge roll of
red flannel from Lord and Taylor's and there was Tintin
and four other shivering old men, and it did seem as if making shirts for them was the least she could do. The most
troublesome part of it was that she had no shirt pattern.
She thought she knew something about the way her brother's
shirts were put together, but she found she had forgotten
some important details. Yesterday, when Jim Tom came
over, she eyed his shirt so piercingly that he got very nervous and kept looking down at it to see what was the matter,
so she had to stop before she was quite certain about the
piece down the front that carried the buttons and the but-
tonholes.

Friday was the last mail day before Christmas. We are
on the main trail from Happy Camp to Orleans Bar, and
mail is delivered once a week on our side of the river. The
main trail is about two hundred feet up the mountain from
our kitchen door, and Mr. Wright, the mailrider, is due
about ten o'clock in the morning. From breakfast until ten
o'clock, when we hear the clump of the horses' hoofs on
the trail, we are good for nothing. If by ten o'clock we
do not hear the clump of hoofs and the creak of the packs
on the saddles, we know something is wrong. When you ride
trail on the Rivers, you plan to come in on time.

It was nearly twelve noon, after we had vainly raced
up to the main trail a dozen times, when we finally heard
Mr. Wright call. He already had loosened the pack and
taken our bags off one of the mules, when we scrambled
into sight.

"Well, girls," said Mr. Wright, "you came near not getting your Christmas candy. One of my mules rolled down
the mountain where the trail was kinda washed out, but
I guess your things ain't mussed up too bad."

We persuaded him to stop just long enough to drink
two cups of coffee, and then we dragged the two mailbags

down the mountain to our house. The Lord was good to us. In spite of their misadventure, everything was unhurt.

But a week later, on the twenty-third of December, it looked as though the auspices were not favorable for Christmas trees. It was beginning to rain when Steve came over and tied up the two boxes of Christmas things we were planning to take with us to Somes. They weighed about fifty pounds each. Steve shouldered both boxes and prepared to carry them to the dugout.

"Steve," we said, "too heavy. It's a quarter of a mile to the dugout. You take one at a time."

In response, Steve gave a delighted war whoop, and with the two boxes on his back tripped down our flight of steps as lightly as though he were seventeen instead of seventy.

A friend of Sam Frame's is supposed to have stopped at Herman's and loaded up the rest of our stuff on his pack mule, but by the following morning the rain was coming down in a deluge, and there was no sign of the man from Somes.

All during breakfast, we listened to the pounding of rain on our roof. It seemed to be raining inches at a time when we went upstairs to put on our boots. It was a deluge when we went down to the corral to get the mules.

Meantime, Steve stood on the porch and took no part in what we were doing. He made it clear that he washed his hands both of our going and our coming back.

Yes, he thought the river would rise. . . .

If it did, he did not know how we could get back. Maybe at Sandy Bar. . . . (Sandy Bar is at Orleans and would be twelve miles out of our way.)

No, he did not know anyone at Sandy Bar who would put us across. . . . (This was simply not true. The Sandy Bar Indians are Steve's cousins.)

Maybe big water when we come back. Bad to swim mules in big water. . . .

Trail pretty bad in big water. Maybe we don't come back at all. . . .

Did we want him to put mules across river? (A long silence. Steve stood with his back to us, looking out on the raging Klamath.) Very well, he would take them.

Steve's irrigation ditch had swollen to a torrent. We waded it, and in one place it was over our high boots. Then we found we had forgotten our quirts and had to wade back again. The rain poured down. Nothing we had on was going to resist that amount of water. When we got down to the dugout, Steve was already on the opposite bank with the mules. It was Pete who put us across.

"We are coming back two days from now, Pete," we said.

"All right," said Pete, "I put you across."

"Maybe big water," we ventured doubtfully.

"I put you across," said Pete firmly.

Our spirits rose. Pete may be crazy, but not even Steve is better on a river crossing.

But it was not only big water and the chance of not getting back to I-ees that lay heavy on our spirits; there was the Christmas tree at Somes.

While we were still at Kot-e-meen we had talked over the question of a Christmas tree at Somes, with Frank Offield. Frank appeared to be in favor of it. He said probably he and Luther Hickox could arrange for a tree, and he guessed all Orleans would come and maybe some from the Forks of Salmon.

But the last time we were down river the climate had changed. Frank was obscure and withdrawn when we mentioned the tree, and Luther was not only obscure but a trifle menacing. Now when you live with Indians and you find the atmosphere has become clouded, it is because they mean it to be clouded. When they are obscure, it is because they mean to be obscure. When they look at you with expressionless faces, it is because they are holding out on you.

We were not sure what it was that was wrong with the Christmas tree at Somes, but deep down inside us we had a faint, clear sense of danger. Something intangible was not right, and we felt that we were strangers in a strange land.

In the store at Somes, we had found Sam Frame. Sam was not obscure. White men are not obscure. But Sam was offish. He indicated that he was not interested in Christmas trees, and he was not friendly. The thing we had sensed with Frank Offield and Luther Hickox was here at Somes, too.

Should we go ahead with the tree at Somes? we asked ourselves. For that matter, what excuse was there for not going ahead with it? It didn't do to stumble on a bad bit of trail, or when you were fording a river. It didn't do to stumble in these queer physchological currents in the Indian country. And it wasn't so good for a man who hesitated and turned back.

Before we had returned to I-ees-i-rum, we had grimly made arrangements for a Christmas tree at Somes.

It was still raining heavily when we reached the Hildings', and they urged us to come in. But there was fifty pounds of candy fastened to our saddle bags, and fifty pounds of presents. We resisted the urge to get warm and dry, and pushed on. The rain drove in our faces. It trickled, cold and uncomfortable, down our breastbones. The mules bunched themselves and no amount of spurring would get them off a walk. It had been warm when we started, but as we climbed Sisson Mountain my fingers began to tingle, and the cold began to strike in. But for all that we lifted up our voices and rejoiced. Cold meant snow in the mountains. Snow in the mountains meant a fall in the river. Maybe we could make it back, after all.

At Kot-e-meen we stopped to get Eddy. Even with a fall in temperature, we did not dare to ford the river at Somes. The Salmon can rise in a couple of hours, and the hidden rocks make it too dangerous for animals to swim. Once on the Somes side with our mules, if there should come a rise in the river, we were caught indeed. Eddy trotted along behind us. He would take the mules back to Mart for the night. We crossed the river over the swing bridge, thankful to get over safely on that wet and slippery single plank. Sam promised to send over for the hundred pounds of presents and candy, and Eddy assured us he would have the mules on the other side of the bridge early Christmas morning. Maybe our luck had turned.

But at Somes there was bad news. Frank Offield had gone away. He had said he would come back but he had not come. Sam was grim and silent. There was to be a dance at Carrie's. A white, not an Indian, dance. That meant plenty of drinking. The lid would be off. Plenty of whiskey, and men and women lying together. Probably it meant trouble. The menace we had felt was out in the open.

As we crouched upstairs in our bed, in the cold, we talked it over. If there was trouble in our own district, and under our very nose, the responsibility would be ours. Ought we to go to the Carrie dance and see what we could do?

But in other parts of the Indian country, wherever this had been tried, it had failed to work. No man or woman had ever succeeded in putting a brake on a white dance, once the dance was under way. Any attempt to stop it only added to the fun and raised the excitement to a higher pitch.

On the other hand, our methods had been different and seemed to work. When our half-breed friends asked us to go to white dances, we always smiled and said, "Oh, do you go to white dances? We thought nobody much went to them any more."

Then we backed the Indian dances to the limit, with all we had. Month by month, the Indian singing and drumming became more popular. Month by month, the popularity of the white dances had waned. They said not enough Indians came to white dances to make them pay.

But the Carrie dance at Somes was a Christmas dance.

All the Indians from up and down river who were coming to the Christmas tree would find it convenient to drift over to the Carrie dance. It would be a good joke on us—people coming to the Christmas tree and then getting drunk and having a trouble at a white dance. It was the kind of joke that would go all up and down river. So far, we had ridden on the crest of things, but the Carrie dance might pull us under.

Did we dare stake everything on the Christmas tree drawing the crowd away from the Carrie dance? Suppose the crowd would not even come to the Christmas tree? That was evidently why Frank Offield and Luther Hickox were refusing to back it. Suppose there was talk that we were afraid to go to the Carrie dance? We could not stay on the Rivers if a question like that was ever raised.

We pulled the covers closer around us and felt very cold. We were staking everything on one throw. Suppose we lost? It was not easy to go to sleep. The rain still beat down on the roof. We lay listening for sounds from Carrie's that would tell us the drinking had begun. The night seemed very long.

A little after midnight we heard the clatter of hoofs. Someone was riding fast. We got up and ran to the window. The door below us opened and the light within streamed out and lit up a horse and rider. The man was Frank Offield. We could have wept with relief. We crawled back into bed and went to sleep.

All the following day we decorated the tree. Sam's friend picked up the rest of the presents at the Alberses' and arrived in time. The celebration was set for Christmas eve. Melissa and Maggie Grant arrived. Essie and Ida came. Mama Frame was in and out. There was no sign of Frank Offield, but it seemed better not to ask what had happened at the Carrie dance. If there had been a trouble, we would have heard of it.

By the middle of the afternoon the tree was finished, and we went upstairs and grimly went to sleep. No one could tell what the night might bring forth. Just before supper we sorted the presents into little piles. One for men. One for women. One for children. We tried to fasten in our minds where special gifts were to go. Every few minutes someone would run upstairs and poke a head in the door.

"Say, you ought to see the crowd over to the store."

Five minutes later. "Why, they can't get in the door."

Still later. "Just look at them coming over the bridge."

Meantime, below in the dining room, the mailriders, very drunk, ate and ate. Mama Frame and Ida waited on them with very red cheeks. Finally, when it was nearly eight, Mama Frame pushed her way into the dining room.

"I'm going to take these things off now," she said. "I guess maybe you don't think there's anything else going on here tonight."

I was up on a very topply chair, lighting the Chinese lanterns, when the people began to come in. At first, they came in twos and threes, and then in a great, pushing throng. Sam and Mabel and I worked at top speed to light the candles on the tree. While we worked we could hear the steady tramp of feet coming up the stairs.

"They're all pretty sober," Sam whispered to us.

If they were sober, we had won out in our competition with the Carrie dance. The steady pound of feet went on. It sounded as though a hundred people were coming up those stairs, and when we turned around, crowded into the room on every side, we saw a sea of dark, upturned faces.

While the candles burned we sang the carols. At Kot-e-meen, Essie had gathered together all the women we knew, and we had practiced carols until we thought they knew every one by heart. They did. But we had reckoned without the Grant girls, who had white blood, clear, high voices, and had never heard of a carol or of carrying a tune. Essie and Kot-e-meen stood no chance. We averted our minds from the singing, and, with the lighted tree before them, we hoped that everyone else was doing the same.

Delivering the presents was breathless work. Everyone had waited silently to hear the Christmas story, and then the excitement blazed. You would snatch something for a squaw, leap over Carrie's baby, who sat in the center of the floor, and deliver your gift. At the same time, Sam Frame would fly by, murmuring anxiously, "Haven't we any more of those handkerchiefs? The men are crazy about them."

The giving went on and on. Most of the crowd eagerly put anything given them behind their backs and looked hopefully around for more.

But we saved the nicest thing we had for Essie. And we heard Ida cry out over something that had been saved for her, "Oh, isn't that the very best of all!"

A strange old women from Pich-pichi looked up at me with a radiant smile when I gave her a piece of gingham. Two more babies added themselves to Carrie's baby in the middle of the floor and beat the floor boards with their toys. Small boys appeared blowing horns. I think everyone got something. It was a success. The candles burned down. The Indians began to drift away. The first Christmas tree that was ever seen on the Rivers was over. As I pulled the last doll off the tree for Melissa Grant, an old white man named Anderson, who had come with Luther Hickox, came shyly up to me.

"I just wanted to thank you, ma'am," he said. "You see, my getting something was so kind of unexpected."

All night we pulled the tree apart and packed the decorations. It was after eleven when we heard Frank Offield's voice from somewhere outside on the trail.

"Sam, Sam," he called. "I say, Frame, where are you?"

Thank the Lord, his voice was perfectly sober, which must mean that he meant to keep order at Carrie's. We heard later that nothing happened and nobody got hurt but "tam little Chim," who got into a drunken row, and Frank wanted Sam to help put handcuffs on him. The next morning Essie told us that the Carrie dance had been a very mild affair. Most of the Indians had gone home early.

But there had been a big fight at the Forks of Salmon, and Mart had got badly cut up. As we crossed the bridge and mounted the mules, we met Essie's special enemy, Johnny Pepper. He was evidently in a pleasant humor, and waved to us. The Christmas tree at Somes was over, and it looked as though everything was all right.

It was not Pete who answered our call as we stood on the banks of the Klamath, at I-ees-i-rum. It was Steve who stood there waiting for us and it was Steve who put us across.

He followed us into our house and said noncommittally, "You going to have Christmas tree?"

We most certainly were, we replied.

"All right," said Steve briskly, "I got him."

He was back in a few minutes, not only with the tree but with all the rancheria as well. They brought with them great armfuls of cedar, covered with yellow berries. Everyone took a hand in the decorations. The room was beautiful when they had finished, and we all sat around making garlands until it was too dark to see. Then we gathered around the fire and sang Christmas carols in the twilight.

It was white blood that had taken the Grant girls off the trail when we sang as Somes. But there was no white blood to lead us astray at I-ees-i-rum. The roaring fire of logs that Steve had built for us lit up only dark faces, and it was only soft Indian voices that sang the familiar words. Steve and Jim Covey led the singing but everyone joined in, their voices sweet and true. And everyone knew the words. We sang Indian way. Only one verse for each carol. But we sang that verse over and over, with mounting intensity, until "Hark, the Herald Angels Sing" had a passionate force.

The Indians are a musical people. Their intervals are different from ours and it is as hard for them to understand our music as it is for us to understand theirs. But once our music becomes familiar to them, all the passion and emotion of the Indian people goes into their singing.

Jim Covey sat with his dark face rapt and absorbed, giving full value to every note. Steve leaned forward a little, his broad shoulders and clean-cut Indian features very clear in the firelight. His voice had depth and power, and rang out clear and strong. His silent drum was in his lap. His eyes were fixed on the blazing fire.

"Hark, the herald angels sing."

The room rang with the clear, beautiful sound. Annie, Kate, and Pictoria carried the high notes. Their eyes were also fixed on the fire. The music rang out very clear and sweet.

"Glory to the new-born King."

Jim leaned back and drew a long breath.

"Peautiful song," he said gravely.

We knew six carols and sang them again and again, until the emotion was almost too intense. Six-year-old Maud and eighty-year-old Grandma joined in, both voices clear and sweet. Then Kate took the children home for supper, but Steve and Jim sang on.

"Silent night, holy night, Christ the Saviour is born."

It was after everyone had gone away that we had our Christmas dinner of corn-meal mush and real, honest-to-goodness cream, which kind Mrs. Hilding had sent us as a Christmas present.

Steve was over at daylight in the morning to get things under way early. Gorham Owl and Emmott, two twelve-year-olds, went out for mistletoe and came back with a bunch as big as a washtub, which was hung from a rafter in the center of the room. While George McCash was finishing putting up the garlands, a strange old Indian man came in, followed by all the rancheria, and we began the decorating of the Christmas tree. By twelve o'clock the room was filling up, and Steve began to play Christmas carols on the phonograph.

When everything was ready, we lighted the candles on

the tree and sang the carols while they burned. The room was packed with people, and every face was dark, with clean-cut features and high cheek bones, for only Indians came to the Christmas tree at I-ees-i-rum. There was not a rustle, and not a person moved, while the candles burned. Steve and Jim led the singing, and clear and true Indian voices joined in, but when the singing at last came to an end and the candles had burned down, everyone drew a long breath, and relaxed. For a moment there was quiet, when the first candy and presents were given out. Then the roomful of people broke into unrestrained enthusiasm. These were not people from Kot-e-meen and Pich-pichi and Somesbar and Orleans and the Forks of Salmon, many of whom we hardly knew at all. These were our own people. They were our friends and it was their Christmas tree. They could be as gay and as Indian as they chose, without any loss of dignity, because we had been adopted by I-ees and were not white any longer but Indians like themselves.

George Pepper, a pale-blue muffler with a ravishing border around his neck, ecstatically waved a fan, out of which popped a cigar. Jim Tom had an expression of idiotic joy on his face as he clutched a large green handkerchief and tried to get two dolls for his little girls into a quite inadequate pocket. Herman shot an insect on a ladder at Steve, and Steve responded by blowing a puffy thing with a long curling tongue at Herman, who showed all the proper alarm when it just touched his nose. It would have been poor taste to remember that less than a month ago they had looked at each other in quite a different way, with six-shooters in their pockets. All the while the little girls clasped dolls and the little boys blew horns and everyone ate candy. We had California candy and New York candy and everyone dutifully sampled both varities.

"New York candy, he prette-e-e-e good" was the verdict.

All the Indians sat watching us while we opened our own presents. A beautiful basket from Annie and Steve, the wonderful, fine basketwork that you find nowhere short of

Alaska except among our own Karok Indians. And no Indian on the Rivers can make baskets finer than Annie's. A
basket from Kate with a straggling M E A woven across
it. Hair ornaments from Pictoria. A very old little hollowed
stone to hold the paint for coloring arrows was the present
from Jim. And two little baskets from Essie, one with a
black bear woven into it, and the other with a brown bear.
Of course, the brown bear was A-chay-wish and the black
bear was My-er-is. As it grew dark, we sat down and finished
the candy, and soon the Indians began to drift away. Christmas was over.

Only Steve stayed on. He began carefully to take the
tinsel off the tree and put the shiny balls back in the box
from which they had come.

"You put him away," said Steve sternly. "Next year, we
get very big Christmas tree."

Crouched on the steep stairs to our upstairs room, the
only place where we might be concealed from our friends,
by the light of a candle we opened the things from home,
and I think we wept a little. There was package after package, so like the family and so like other Christmases. We
did not talk much; we just sat fingering what had been
sent.

Then, to our surprise, there was package after package
from California. And such very sweet messages. We wept
a little more. There was a rag rug and a Navajo blanket
and a shawl and pillows and home-made candy, and a message from Mrs. Kelsey saying not to tell anyone but it was
the "packages for the girls" that she really cared about
getting ready.

The family had better stop worrying about us off here in
the wilds of the Coast Range. When we do come home, we
plan to greet Somerville and Plainfield, New Jersey, with
a war whoop, and it may be that our skin will have become
a trifle dark, that we will have high cheek bones, and will
have turned into real live Indians.

CHAPTER XVIII

Ti Postheree

We were saddling Shasta and Siskiyou for a trip to Hoopa when Steve come over. Yesterday, when Mr. Wright, on his way from Happy Camp to Orleans, dropped off a mailbag with our weekly mail, we found a letter from the new superintendent. It informed us that he wanted to get acquainted with all the workers in his field.

Steve stood watching us as we came out with the saddle bags, and then observed noncommittally, "You lock door."

We shook our heads, got the saddle bags tied on, and prepared to mount.

"I think better you lock door," said Steve more persuasively.

We grinned at him. "Not in Indian country, Steve," we said. "You don't lock doors in Indian country."

Steve looked unconvinced. "I think better you lock door," he said firmly. "Maybe white man, he come along the trail."

It seemed that although Steve recognizes honesty as an Indian characteristic he did not feel that it applied to white men.

We had looked forward with some eagerness to meeting the new superintendent, for we doubted whether he would take all the things we wanted for a winter in I-ees-i-rum in the proper spirit. But after some discussion of the suitation in up-river country, he proved genuinely friendly and gave us three hours of his time. Not only are we to have mules but oats. Think of it! And horseshoeing.

Toward noon of the following day we had progressed so far that Mr. Mills was sent for in order to discuss the kind of animals we ought to have. Mr. Mills was quite the same Mr. Mills, and not at all averse to our open admiration. As for us, did we ever give the impression that we were indifferent to flattery? You should have seen our faces when Mr. Mills, who has ridden everything on legs from Texas to Alaska, turned to Mr. Mortsoff and said, "And you bet those girls can ride."

That moment remains with me yet.

Mr. Mills thinks he can get mules for us—good ones. Mr. Mortsoff thinks he can do something about the unsafe bridges in the up-river country. It certainly was a red-letter day.

Twenty-four hours later, as we ate dinner at the Moonharts', two miles out of Witchpec, with ourselves on one side of the river, our mules on the other, and the raging Klamath between, we were not so sure about the red-letter part.

But that was later.

It had begun to rain as we sat talking with Mr. Mortsoff. By afternoon, the campus at Hoopa was two inches deep in water. It rained steadily all night, and in the morning, when we went out to take a look at the weather, even the mild Trinity was leaping and tumbling between its banks.

At the breakfast table three men from down below caught our attention. In the first place, it is not often that we see anyone from down below. These men wore black clothes that looked strange even in civilized Hoopa. They wore high collars and cravats, they had on new riding boots, and their hands were white. We thought they must be prospectors. Not the kind of prospector that goes out with a pick and a pan to look for gold, but the kind of prospector who sells the prospect.

We caught snatches of their talk at breakfast: "quartz . . . will pan out so much to the ton . . . placer mining . . ." The younger member of the party nodded while the two older men talked. We became a bit sorry for the younger man. Poor lamb, if they were trying to sell him a prospect, he didn't know what he was in for.

We thought of Elder's mine on Prospect Hill, where Mart had worked a year and a half without pay—the investment of ten thousand dollars in machinery; all of it collected from Elder's family, mostly from his mother and two aunts; the tragic failure of the whole venture; the two-dollars-to-the-ton yield instead of sixteen dollars to the ton as they had expected. The Klamath was no place for innocent-looking young men, with black suits and high, white collars, who didn't know what they were getting into.

Meantime, the steady, persistent downpour went on while we ate breakfast.

"Gist will never run the ferry to Witchpec today," said Mr. McKimmon. "River's too high." Then, as he saw our faces, "What you girls worrying for? You're lucky to be here instead of one of those god-forsaken places up river. You just sit quiet and draw your salaries and nobody'll be the wiser."

The prospectors were in their saddles as soon as we were. They had good animals and we gave them the lead. When we caught up with them, they were sitting on their horses, the picture of dismay, looking down at the raging Klamath tearing at its banks. The river was high above its customary level and seemed to whirl along in one great solid sheet of furiously moving water. Whole trees would suddenly appear, up-ended in the flood, and then fall back and disappear beneath the surface. As we stood looking down at the water, we saw two men descend the bank on the other side and ease a dugout into the river. The prospectors looked at it with white faces.

"They can't expect us to cross in that," they said. "Where is the ferry? They told us there was a ferry."

As the boat grounded on the sandspit beneath us, we saw that the two men in the dugout were Witchpec devils.

They looked inquiringly at our party. Without a word the two older men climbed into the boat.

"Better wait for the next trip," they told their companion. "Four is enough for this load." The younger member of the party gave us a frightened look. That would leave five and a dog for the second crossing.

The Witchpec devils grinned and raised their paddles as we clambered in.

"*Ti postheree,*" they said gaily. "Maybe drown."

"*Ti postheree,*" we laughed back at them. "Maybe drown."

It is good form to jest on bad river crossings, but we had forgotten our young man. He gave a gasp.

"I think I'll take off my coat," he said. "It's better to be ready if you have to swim."

But after all, the crossing was not nearly as bad as we had expected, and Mr. Gist promised to get hay across to our animals and to have horses waiting for us in the morning.

We made Orleans Bar with very little difficulty, but the following day the Sandy Bars washed their hands of our getting up river.

"*Ti postheree,*" they said. "*Ti postheree.* Mailrider, he don't make it so good when he come down Tuesday."

For all that, the sun was struggling through the clouds, and when we stopped at the foresters they received us in excellent spirits.

"Leave the Indian Service and join the foresters," they urged us. "Then you won't have to ride in the rain. We haven't been able to do any work for the last four days."

But at Ten Eyck, where we stopped for the night, Luther Hickox shook his head.

"Better stay over," he said. "There's a bed and food here and I've got twenty new phonograph records. Big water like this won't last. Better stay a week."

He went on to say he was going to fix up the house at

Ossi-puk for us. (We have had it in mind as a second station.) Wasn't no need to hurry back up river. Just settle down and stay as long as we liked.

As we sat in the parlor after supper, and he played us the "Holy City" on the phonograph, it was hard to imagine Luther shooting holes through anyone's hat. The Hickoxes may be desperate characters, but we thought, as we rode up river, there were no people we would rather have as neighbors.

It was after we had crossed the mountain that the low place on the trail lay before us, with the Klamath already swirling over it in spots. But after all, the water was not as deep as we had feared, and in short order we were over it, with only five miles of good, high trail between us and home. The fire was lighted when we came in and all the rancheria were waiting for us. Molly Bawn, fat as butter, was coming down the mountain as we turned into our own trail. Kate told us that after we had gone the children disappeared and did not come back for several hours.

"Why don't you come home?" Kate had asked, and Maud replied, "I stay over there with little cat, and every time I come away little cat, he say hol' on."

We found our mail waiting for us and a box of new records. We longed for supper and bed. Then we saw that Steve was standing quietly by the phonograph.

"Some new records have come," said Mabel. "I suppose we could open them."

Yes, said Steve with dignity, he had known there were new records. They had come with the mailrider, two days ago.

All the rancheria gathered around. We played all the records through once, and then the Indians went away. As Steve went out on the porch we followed him to the door. There below us lay the Klamath, one straight expanse of water from bank to bank. Not a familiar rock in sight. The river had reached its high-water mark just three hours after we had come through.

"You come now, you don't make it," Steve said as he went down the trail.

We are getting up in the morning now, turn and turn about. First, I stay in bed while Mabel crawls out, pours ice water over her shivering person, and then goes downstairs and gets breakfast. The following morning, I slink out of my nice, warm blankets, cover my person with ice water as fast as my frozen fingers will permit, and then scurry downstairs to get our two fires lit. Then if Steve comes to breakfast, as he very often does, we exchange confidences about the advantages of cold water. Breaking the ice in our pitcher each morning and dousing ourselves with ice water seems to result in our thriving in a climate where everyone else suffers from colds or pneumonia. That is, most white people.

Steve is very approving. In the old days, it was obligatory for every male Indian to jump into the Klamath, morning and evening, during the entire rainy season as well as during the more attractive parts of the year. When Steve feels out of sorts and we offer him medicine, he shakes his head and says, "I think maybe I catch cold. I go jump in river."

We are very much annoyed by an article we have just read that refers to what it calls an "Indian odor." Indians on the Klamath have no distinctive odor any more than we do. Of course, to some perceptions, both Steve and ourselves may have an odor, but it is pleasanter to avert our minds from such a possibility. There is an "Indian smell," as we call it, in most Indian cabins, but it is the smell of dried fish and eels. It may be these Klamath Indians are unusually cleanly in their habits. The Indians certainly keep themselves much cleaner than do the white men in the country. You can't jump in the Klamath twice a day and not get rid of some surplus dirt. When to this you add the custom of the sweat house, it is hard to see how Indians could be cleaner.

Day after day, the rain continues. When we come downstairs in the morning we go out on the porch to look at the weather. The skies seem to rest on our roof, and on the trees around it. Above us everything is gray. The mist lies so low we can only see halfway up Herman's mountain, on the other side of the river. The entire top is cut off by low-hanging clouds. Day after day, we listen to the pounding of the rain on the roof. Day after day, we listen to the roar of the Klamath as it races in one smooth torrent of water from bank to bank. We have forgotten we ever did such a thing as ride the trail. We have given up all hope of ever seeing our mules from Hoopa. Inside the house it is so dark the Indians have to strain their eyes to read their primers, and their voices are drowned in the roar of the Klamath.

But in times like this, of big water, we have our fill both of white and Indian music. Steve adores the phonograph and plays it continually. Yesterday, when two new Indians were down from Siwillup, we came into the room to hear Steve say haughtily, "Now I play just one more song and then I do my work."

For the most part, Steve's work consists in carpenter jobs for us, and he is making our house beautiful to behold. But it is also causing a rift in the Steve-Pete relations. Now that the trees are cleared out, and our wood cut for the winter, and an interruption in packing down hay from T Bar, there is little left for Pete to do.

Yesterday, when the phonograph had been turned off and all the rancheria sang sweat-house songs, Pete sat grimly silent, staring at the fire.

"Pete, he don't sing," said Annie.

"Too poor to sing," said Pete ominously. "Rich man, he sing all time. "Too poor to sing," said Pete, glowering at Steve.

All the rancheria, even Old Woman, laughed until they wept.

After the Pete family had gone home to get dinner, Steve told us about the money he had found at Happy

Camp. He was going along the trail with another man when he saw something in the bush, by the side of the trail. It was a small tobacco pouch. When he opened it, he found in it four twenty-dollar gold pieces.

"The other man, he say, ain't that nice, let's divide," said Steve.

"But I say, ain't no hurry, maybe we hol' on."

Steve's idea was that some inquiries would certainly be made by the owner of the money but the next day went by, and then the next, and no one mentioned the loss.

"I think anybody he lose money he say so," said Steve. "That night I go home. I think and think. I guess I ain't sleep that night at all."

The next day he went back to the saloon in Happy Camp and asked Mr. Monaghan, the saloon keeper, if anyone had lost any money.

"How much?" said Mr. Monaghan.

"Well," said Steve, "maybe I tell him when I know he los' it."

Mr. Monaghan went into the saloon and asked the men there if they had lost anything. One of the men at the bar said, "Wednesday night, I did have eighty dollars, but I was so drunk I thought I had blown it all in."

Steve handed the money over to him without a word.

Of course, we then went on to discuss devils. No conversation is complete in Indian country that does not end in a discussion of devils.

We said we thought that an *apruan* came under our porch each night and bumped against the flooring. We thought it must be an *apruan* because of Shaw-baby. Ordinarily he greets all enemies with a series of barks, but when the *apruan* bumps against the floor he only says, "Weh-weh-weh," in a trembling voice.

When Annie heard there was an *apruan* right under the place where she was sitting, she hastily put her feet up onto the settle. And Steve got up with great dignity and went to the front door and flung it open. Outside, it was very dark. Steve peered out as if he was frightened. He stepped back into the room and feigned the wildest alarm.

"Maybe *apruan*," he said, and made his voice tremble very realistically.

Then he grinned and again became a very dignified Indian, gathered up a rather reluctant Annie, and went placidly out onto the porch. After that he cheerfully said, "*Jimmy-co-yap* (good-by)," and went off into the darkness, humming to himself.

We stood on the porch with a candle until we heard his gay "all right" as he and Annie disappeared in the bush.

It is weeks now since the beginning of *ti postheree*. Our barn is no longer a few poles sticking up into the air. It is a genuine barn with sides and a roof. The picket fence is completed and encloses us on all four sides, and Black Dog beats himself against it in vain. The water from Steve's irrigation ditch, diverted from the creek about a half mile up the main trail, comes down through a flume to our back door. We have planted sweet peas on the inside of the entire perimeter of the fence, and they are to have their own tiny irrigation ditch from the surplus water from the flume. But all these riches profit us little, for there is trouble between ourselves and Steve.

It is not a little ordinary trouble such as we might have with Kate or Pete or Jim, or one of our not-so-very-intimate friends. Many times we feel quite cross with something someone has done, and then forget it entirely before they come over the next day. We do not feel cross with Steve about little ordinary things, but when there is trouble between us, as there is now, the sky is very black and all the pleasure is gone out of our life on the Rivers, and we want to go home and never come back and never see Steve any more.

It is always the same trouble between Steve and ourselves. Steve is our friend. The friendship between us is very close. Sometimes we think it is the closest friendship we have ever had. We forget that Steve is Indian and we are white. And then something like this happens. We look at Steve and Steve looks at us and all we see before us is an Indian, and we feel that we have never really known him at all. We feel that Steve is not our friend, that Steve could not be our friend, for a second and a third time he has overcharged us and cheated us and taken advantage of us because we do not know the prices of things on the Rivers, so without any question we have paid him what he asked.

This time, it was the poles Steve used in building our barn. We had agreed with him on the price, and then George McCash offered to do the work and told us what the current price of poles was all up and down river. It was a lower price, a much lower price, than the one Steve had given us.

With the lowering sky above and the roar of the Klamath in our ears, Steve and I went out onto the porch. But neither Steve nor I saw the heavy mists across the river or heard the pound of rain on the roof or listened to the roar of the Klamath. We walked up and down the length of the porch, not looking at each other.

He could charge us anything he liked, I told Steve, but he was no friend of ours. We would pay him anything he asked, but we were no longer friends. Friends were not like that. You could trust a friend in anything he asked you or anything he did. It was not the first time he had overcharged us. Before Christmas, he had overcharged us for horses, and now it was the poles for the barn. Of course, we would pay him anything he asked. But he was no longer a friend.

While I was speaking, Steve stood looking out across the river. His face was not impassive. He kept it turned away from me. Then he turned around. He talked in Indian as well as in English, so it was hard to make out what he was saying. But it was something like this:

Whenever we wanted anything, he would do it. Always, whatever we wanted, he would do it. No matter what it was we wanted. If it was a trouble, it would be the same. He would do it, no matter what happened to him. Even if he got hurt bad, he would do it.

If he built a barn for us and we did not pay him, it would be all right. He would build the barn for us just the same. He would do what we wanted. Any time. Any place.

If we did not pay him, it would be all right. And if we paid him too much, it was all right. If we did not pay him, it was bad for him, but he would do it just the same. But if we paid him too much, it was good for him. The horses had been good for him and the poles were good for him. But if we did not want to pay him, it would be all right.

He moved quickly so we could not see his face.

We both stood silent. It was a deadlock. We belonged to different races and we did not think the same. Without looking at me, Steve went down the steps and along the trail to the rancheria. He walked heavily, and he did not once look back.

The next day, he came over with the rest of the Indians. On the surface everything was pleasant, just as it had been before. But when it comes to a trouble or a quarrel, Mabel and I are not white. We are Indian. Things were not right and they were not as they had been before. Not by any means.

In the afternoon, Steve started to make us a wire closet over the sink. We had already talked it over. It was to be made of rough boards and was not to cost too much because our money was getting very low. While he was working, we learned Hilding was across the river at Flower's Flat, and we walked down to see him. When we came back, the closet had one door on. It was not a rough closet. It was carefully planed and fitted. I stomped down the steps and went under the porch.

"You are making that closet too expensive," I told Steve. "That is not what we agreed on. The way you are making it, that closet will cost four or five dollars. You told us you would make a rough closet that would not cost much."

Steve said nothing. His face was impassive. I climbed back up the steps and went into the house. After a long time, we heard him gather up his tools, and then the click of the gate as he went away.

We spent the rest of the day on a detailed report to the Indian Department. But it was no use. We could not keep our minds on the report. After all, what was the use of white people and Indians trying to be friends and live together? People like ourselves had much better go home where they belonged. The day seemed very long. None of the Indians came over. We went to bed.

As we washed the dishes the following morning, there was a familiar sound under the porch. It was the plane going hard. In the evening, Steve came in and said the closet was finished. It was a lovely closet, beautifully planed and finished. We asked Steve how much we owed him.

"Nothing," said Steve with dignity.

He owed us one dollar for horseshoe nails and we owed him one dollar for the closet. We could call it square.

We thanked him but the Indian Steve and the Indian Mabel and the Indian Mary knew that things were still far from right between us. The rancheria came over and everyone struggled with their primers. But Steve did not look at us nor we at Steve. Two days passed. It was mail day, and we came down the trail with our mail. The door opened and Steve came in. It was the old Steve, and he came in with the old swagger. Everything was as it had been before. There was no trouble between us. It felt as though there never had been any trouble between us. It was peace.

Steve stayed to luncheon and we had Maryland beaten biscuit, which Mabel made. It was a huge success. Philip Donohue came over and brought his drum. Steve had brought his drum, too, and we listened as we had always listened to Steve's singing.

"Ai-yah. Ai-yah. Han-o-way."

As it grew dark, the men brought in more wood for the fire, and we practiced "Scotland's Burning." "Scotland's

Burning" has suddenly leaped into popularity on the Rivers as the Indians have learned the excitement of attempting to sing a round. At first, when we started in to practice with Steve and Annie, they went into such fits of laughter that everything was held up. But now Steve is a master hand. His face was a bit strained as Mabel's voice rang out very loud and clear on "Look out, look out," when it was his turn to come in with "Scotland's burning, Scotland's burning." But after he had weathered the difficulty of the start, he swept down on "Fire, fire, fire, fire" with so much force and volume that Mabel was completely drowned out. Philip Donohue, who was making hard going of it, was deeply impressed. Then he and Steve sang sweat-house songs till all hours, and after Philip had left and Steve got up to go I saw Mabel secretly feeding him our very last piece of preserved ginger.

It is very, very pleasant to be friends again.

With nothing but continued rain outside, the rancheria has developed, one and all, a love of learning. When Sandy Bar Tom was here last week, Steve told him haughtily, "I go to school now." Steve listened with discreet gratification when Mabel explained to Tom that Steve learned *jam-i-ach* (very quick). Sandy Bar Tom was very much impressed and said, very well, he was coming to school, too. "Big water now. *Ti postheree.* Stay here all time and go to school." He put a magazine in front of his face and grinned at Steve. "Come to school tomorrow," he said. "This school for old men."

When we pass Steve's cabin now, we can hear him saying gravely, "I see the cat. Do you see the cat?"

Last week, Jim Covey made a spurt and read fourteen pages in his primer while Steve watched darkly. Then the magnifying glass arrived. It was in a small package with the rest of our mail. At first, the Indians could make nothing of it, but one day Steve must have gotten it focused properly. We heard him draw in his breath sharply and cry "*Yuc-ca* (look) ." All the other Indians crowded around him. At first, they thought Steve was making medicine and then they became as excited as he was. Annie sat crying "E-e-e-e-eyah," when she found she could see the words in the primer. Later, they sent us from home a pair of glasses from the five-and-ten, and Annie carried them home in triumph.

The next day, with the glasses on, Steve opened his book. "What's that?" he asked.

"I see," I replied.

"I see," repeated Steve. "And what's that?"

It was long after supper when Steve finally went home, but in one afternoon he had read fourteen pages and written his name on the first page to boot. Meantime, Kate is nearly through the primer and Jim Covey is pressing her hard. Yet Jim must be over sixty and Steve at least seventy. Talk about the difficulty of acquiring a new language after twenty-five! All you need is to be an Indian.

But though school is all serene in the Indian village of I-ees-i-rum, at Sunday school there are indications of trouble. It is between Steve and Mack Charlie. We knew something was wrong because all the Indians were so obscure, but we thought it was because Mack Charlie had sided with Herman in the baby growl. After Sunday school, Mack Charlie took our new drum off the wall and touched it with his fingers.

"Damn good drum," he said, and settled down with it before the fire. Then Kate and Annie came in and looked genuinely startled when they saw Mack Charlie, and we began to think doubtfully of the undercurrent of talk we had heard.

After the others had gone, we asked Kate about it.

"Well," said Kate, "Mack Charlie, he awful good man. But Dan Charlie, he awful mean. Dan and Steve, he have a trouble. Dan, he look at Annie. All time he look at Annie. Maybe Steve, he shoot Dan. Maybe Dan, he shoot

Steve. I don't know. Mack Charlie, he think Dan pretty good brother. Maybe he shoot Steve. I don't know. But maybe big trouble sometime."

But Dan is not the only trouble at I-ees-i-rum. We said nothing to Kate but we had already spent a sleepless night. It was several days ago when it happened. The steady pound of rain on the roof had gone on and on, and late in the afternoon Annie came over for a knitting lesson. A little later, George McCash came in. Mabel was showing Annie how to take off, and I was sitting by the fire, trying to make out a report for the Indian Department. Then I noticed George. He was looking at Annie. I tried to think it didn't mean anything, but a little later I saw George again look at Annie. This time there was no mistake. It did mean something. From Mabel's face, I saw she, too, had seen it. Annie sat looking at the fire. Then, very slowly, she put her hand on her breast. Her shirtwaist opened a little and we could see her warm, dark flesh.

Steve is up on the mountain, I thought, after they had gone away. Steve is up on the mountain.

We were very Indian after that. We did not say anything or do anything, but when George came over to school, the next day we did not see him. When Annie came into the room, we did not see her. We talked and laughed with everyone in the rancheria, just as we had always done, and no one but George and Annie knew that we did not look at them or speak to them.

Meantime, the steady pound of rain on the roof and on the porch went on and on. The room was always dark, and by two o'clock, even when you sat by the window, it was too dark to read. Drops of rain came down the chimney and hissed on the hot logs. A wall of rain pressed against the windows. When we looked outside, the low ceiling of clouds lay close above our heads. We felt as though we were living in a well with a top over it.

The light was always dim, both inside and out. There was no color anywhere. Below, the dark, rain-soaked ground sloped down to the muddy, mist-covered Klamath. Above us were leaden-gray clouds. It seemed as if the rain would never stop. It seemed as if the mules would never come. If we could only get away from I-ees-i-rum! No wonder, George and Annie! The steady beat of rain. The steady roar of the Klamath.

But Steve! No, we couldn't forgive George and Annie. We could never forgive George and Annie.

The rancheria had been over all morning but they had left early. We sat over the fire, straining our eyes to finish the report to the Indian Department.

"Darn the rain," said Mabel suddenly. "Is it never going to stop?"

The room was very, very dark. I stopped working to rest my eyes. There was a little sound at the back door. Then there was a step, and George McCash stood in the doorway. In his arms, and so many he could hardly hold them, and so bright they were like a flash of sunlight in the room, was an enormous bunch of daffodils. They were a wonderful golden yellow. They were the loveliest things we had seen in all those long, dark, dreary weeks. After days of mist and dark and rain, the beautiful golden yellow transfigured the room and made it come alive.

"George!" we cried. "George!" and we ran across the room and took the daffodils in our arms.

And then we paused. But it was too late.

When you shoot at a man, you pay him twenty-five dollars. When you kill a man, you pay a hundred. But when you pay the money to the family, and they take it, the shooting is forgotten and you are friends, just as you were before.

And when you look at Annie and bring an armful of gorgeous, yellow daffodils, and they are accepted, no more can be said.

George and Annie and Mabel and I were friends again.

CHAPTER XIX

The Open Trail

After six long, weary weeks of rain, last night the clouds broke away and today the sun shines from a clear blue sky. It was a sparkling outdoors that smiled back at us as we opened our front door. O-we, our own mountain, stood out in all its glory, clear to its very peak, with all the mists rolled away, so that we could even see the top of the mountain on the Alberses' side of the river.

As though the shining morning itself was not enough to raise our spirits, we heard the sound of horses' hoofs and someone shouting to us from the main trail. This was later in the morning, when we were deeply engaged in sawing wood for our fireplace and had gone up our own little trail to pack some of it in. We had a glimpse of loaded animals through the trees and Mabel said, "Who do you suppose is going up to Happy Camp?" And then we saw that the little pack train had come to a stop, and heard someone shouting at us.

They were our own mules. After all these weeks of waiting, they were our own mules, safely across the Klamath and in our own back yard.

There were seven animals in all. Besides our own two mules, there were three animals that belonged to Witchpec George, and Shasta and Siskiyou. They were on their way back to Happy Camp, all loaded down with oats. We tried to preserve what dignity we could until the men had finished unloading the oats, and then we gave vent to our feelings and behaved in a way quite unbecoming field matrons and representatives of the Government.

The brown mule—Maria—is to be mine. I have named her after a very popular phonograph record. "Maria, Maria, you set my heart on fire. It's you I most desire of all the girls in town."

Oh, Maria-riar-riar, when I think you are actually safe in our own corral, it is impossible to express my feelings.

Mabel's mule is white and somewhat larger than Maria. He is to be called Mr. Darcy. This is because a copy of Jane Austen's *Pride and Prejudice* had turned up in the crate with our little music box. Mabel says she is calling her mule Mr. Darcy because he has a proud and reserved disposition and does not make friends easily. But she thinks he is melting under her attentions. We are planning to be on the down-river trail tomorrow morning. We wish it could be this afternoon, but it seems proper to wait until Witchpec George and the other Witchpec Indians have come back from a call on Steve, and are off on their way back to Hoopa.

It is wonderful to have young animals after all the old scarecrows we have had to ride. Mr. Hilding gives Maria only six years. Both mules have been badly handled and are very nervous. Maria is spoiled about the head. You cannot touch her head without a very lively set-to. She wears a halter into which you must snap the bit. But in spite of the past, today she ate oats out of my hand. It is true, she took one small nip at me, but it was done without any particularly evil intent.

Meantime, Mr. Darcy stood by blowing hard through his nose. He very much wanted the oats but was not sure he liked the way he must get them.

We rode up to the Johnsons' in the early morning and then crossed over to the Hildings'. Instead of an hour and a half on the trail, which is our regular time, we made it in fifty minutes. The Johnsons have been making a clean-up in their mine, and they have high hopes of getting as much as a hundred dollars. But while we were there Fred came in looking very sad. He spoke in Indian so we could not make out all that he said, but plainly they had made very little and it was a bitter business.

We have not seen the Hildings since big water. It had been a hard winter, they told us. One horse was dead as well as three of their steers. Hilding said the winter had been hard on all the Indians on their side of the river. Charlie Hickox had made no money from his mine.

"They say," said Mr. Hilding, "he's getting kinda crazy over it. You know as well as I do," he went on, "there's plenty people around here who have to go to bed hungry."

As we rode back, little storm gusts blew down from the tops of the high mountains, where the rain of the past week had fallen as snow. They ended in a smart shower just as we reached the rancheria, with two rainbows, both extraordinarily vivid. The end of one of them, it seemed, was only a few feet from our corral. It is wonderful to live in the track of rainbows. We must dig for the pot of gold. We shall never have a better chance than right here in the gold country.

While we ate supper, Mr. Darcy showed his masculine prerogative by chasing Maria around the corral and nipping her shrewdly. So when we went to bed we tied Mr. Darcy and left Maria loose. In the middle of the night, we were awakened by a terrible rumpus, and leaped out of bed and into our boots. Outside, in the corral, we found that Maria, imbued with the spirit of the times, had taken advantage of the situation and was kicking Mr. Darcy viciously. Mr. Darcy was extremely glad to see Mabel and myself. We promptly tied Maria to a post. But today, Mr. Darcy's spirit is broken, and Maria chases him around the corral.

The sun was rising clear over the mountain as we scrambled out of bed and into our riding skirts. Little soft white mists curled up off the river and disappeared in the sunlight. As we flung things into our saddle bags, all the rancheria came over to see us off. During these long, long weeks of rain, with the swollen, dun-colored Klamath and the clouds pressing down on our heads, our tempers have grown worse and worse. We scowled at Jim and Pictoria. We scowled at the rancheria. And when the Alberses and the Charlies came over, we cast an occasional scowl at them. But with the clear air and the sunlight our tempers vanished with the mists from the river. It is wonderful to live with Indians. They were as gay as we.

"*I-to poo-a-rum*," said everyone. "*If caro yar-much.*" That is one of Steve's songs. It is Indian for "I'm going away. Oh, ain't that nice."

We waved. Everyone waved and smiled at us. We were off, and on the trail.

The mules scrambled up the mountain. Steve waved us a last good-by. Ahead was the main trail for Orleans. Flowers were on every side—snowdrops, fawn lilies, bluebells. They were thick along the trail, like a continuous carpet. Whenever we passed a cabin, near it were peach trees in bloom. They made the little clearings look like bouquets. On the top of Sisson Mountain, we jumped off the mules and lay on a rock in the bright sunlight and watched the Klamath sparkle far below us.

All the Hickoxes came out as we rode by. The house at Ossi-puk that Luther promised to fix up for us is just as we left it, it is true, but Luther promises to get right to work on the repairs. And the next day, with an equally glorious sun and blue sky, we rode into Orleans.

"*I-o-qui*," shouted the Sandy Bars as we rode by their flat.

"*I-o-qui*," we shouted in return as we waved to them and rode by.

In the store at Orleans, we found Mr. Gent friendly and glad to see us. Everyone in the store wanted to tell us the news. In the gorge below Witchpec, the Klamath had been eighty feet above the summer level. Big water, everyone said. This winter, big water.

On the wide, level expanse that is Orleans Bar, we spurred the mules to a lope and, in a clatter of small stones, came upon the Richardses in grand style, swinging our quirts. The effect was somewhat spoiled by the fact that there was no one to see us, and we had to pound on the front door until Mrs. Richards heard us.

As we went into the still, close atmosphere of the house, after the bright sunshine of the out-of-doors, the Rivers and the trail and the Indians were shut out behind us. It was a different world, and could just as well have been Morristown, New Jersey, instead of Siskiyou County, California.

The winter and the long, rainy season had told on the ranch as well as on the rancheria at I-ees-i-rum. Mr. Hale, the superintendent of the mine, was a walking skeleton. The eleven weeks of downpour had meant one break after another in his flume, and two weeks before they had been afraid the whole mountain was going.

Tempers were short at the ranch as well as up river, but like us they rejoiced in the blessed sunshine. And then there were the picture puzzles. All evening, Mrs. Richards sat with a medley of little pieces before her.

"Perfect nonsense," said Mr. Hale, as he gummed himself to the cutting table where the half-done picture was in progress.

"They're not all there. Can't you see? They're not all there. What's the use of trying when you haven't got all the pieces? There, just let me try that one, Mrs. R. Now just look at that. Jiminy crickets! Didn't that go in well? Now, I'm the boy for this. Just look at this, Mrs. R. Isn't that one a daisy?"

"You seem to forget," said Mrs. Richards coldly, "that I was the one who put the hands around the snowball. You only fitted in one of the coatsleeves."

In the intervals between the picture puzzles, Mrs. Richards drew us aside and told us all that had happened to her and to every member of her family in the long and seemingly unending rainy season. We did our best with our own past histories, but Mr. Hale outdistanced us both.

He had no chance that evening, as Mrs. Richards had the floor, but as we saddled the mules in the beautiful early morning, with the soft green of the grass and the budding fruit trees all around us, Mr. Hale made the best use of the time that remained to him. In the two hours after breakfast, he told us the history of his grandfather, a partial history of his father and his two brothers, a detailed account of Fayettesville, North Carolina, from its founding to the present day, a history of engineering, Mr. Hale's own personal relation to engineering and all his other past occupations, how he came to California, his history since he came to California, the present condition of the store at Orleans, his attitude toward the whites and the Indians in Orleans, and the entire history of his adventures in the Spanish-American War.

Now what do you suppose that leaves him to talk about next time? We can do pretty well ourselves when we get started, but we lack Mr. Hale's advantage of a long and varied career.

As we rode away, the glories of the Orleans Bar Gold Mining Company shut behind us with the pasture gate, and we were again in Indian country. Johnny Spinks, the Indian who works for the company, gave us an Indian greeting and waved to us as we rode by. Jim Rutner, the gardener, waved his arm at us and shouted. At Sandy Bar, Jim's squaw Mamie ran out and hailed us.

"Old woman, he sick," said Mamie, "Maybe you stop and see old woman."

All along the trail we met Indians. Solinda was on her way up river. Penny Tom and his woman passed us, followed at a little distance by their dog, which was followed at a little distance by their cat. It was a heavenly day, and when we stopped at Ossi-puk we found that Luther had been as good as his word. The fireplace was finished.

Fireplaces in this country are made of mud and stones. You trust to the fire to bake your mud into brick. On the outside of your house, you stick one of the large pipes from a deserted mine into your mud-and-stone construction, wire the pipe to the outside of your house, and there is your chimney. Very simple, and it stands up remarkably well. As we were admiring the fireplace, Luther came in looking as though he had never committed a crime in the world and with only the faintest hint of menace in his eye. But we thought, a bit doubtfully, of the story we had just heard in Orleans, when we stopped in at the store to see Mr. Gent. Instead of Mr. Gent, we had found Mr. Hale, who was sorting mail and arranging to bury a man. Praise be, it was not Luther this time who had been too quick on the trigger. But for all that, there was ugly talk about Luther in Orleans. The body of poor old Anderson has never been found in the mountains. A force of twenty-five men from all up and down river have been out looking for it without finding a trace. Anderson was the white man who came to the Christmas tree at Somesbar, and we remembered he had once said to us: "Hereabouts is the selfishest place I've ever lived in."

But now the talk runs in Orleans that Anderson was last seen at Luther's house, and that maybe Luther knows more about what happened to him than he is telling anyone.

The next day we were up at daybreak. With really young riding animals, we are making good time these days, due to an invention of Mabel's. Maria and I take the lead. Mabel follows on Mr. Darcy with a long switch in her hand. With the long switch, she is able to beat Maria, who promptly bounds ahead. Of course, when Maria bounds ahead, Mr. Darcy bounds after her, trying to keep up. It seems to work very well. That is, on ordinary occasions.

But this particular trip down river was not an ordinary occasion. We had stowed in my saddle bag some medicine for the old woman at Sandy Bar who is badly crippled with rheumatism. We have an honest-to-goodness medicine closet these days, and before we left I-ees-i-rum we went through it and picked out a beautiful gallon bottle of oil of organum with which to start a medicine closet at Ossi-puk. We then put some turpentine in a large empty vanilla bottle and took with us an assortment of "bills." (We spell the word as it is pronounced on the Rivers.) We packed the bottles and the pills on one side of my saddle bag and added a nice, woolly shawl as a precautionary measure. Then we set off down river.

When we came to Sisson Mountain, the day was so beautiful that we got off the mules and, whooping and hollering, chased them down the mountain, making even better time than we had expected. Halfway down, as I raced along, Mabel caught up with me.

"You know," she said, "there seems to be an awfully queer smell along this part of the trail."

I thought so too, and the nearer we got to the mules, the worse it got. It came over me that there was something very familiar about that smell. I put on a sprint and caught up with Maria. There was no longer any doubt. The fumes of oil of organum and turpentine struck one like a blow. Maria's back was stained a dark color. So was a place on the trail. The organum bottle was neatly broken in two and the cork was out of the turpentine. The shawl and the pills floated in a nice mixed liniment. All the rest of the way to Ossi-puk, Mabel kept as far behind me as possible. She said I was as good as an aniseed bag and she could have trailed me in the dark.

All day, at Ossi-puk, while we scraped evil-looking paper off the walls with a broken knife and our fingernails, we received a round of calls. First, the two Joe girls and Hackett, and later Mac-i-a-rum Joe and Eddy Owl. We served tea with crackers and sardines. Late in the afternoon, Luther and Mr. Hunter came over. As he came into the room, there was no mistaking the look in Luther's eye. It was plain he was out for blood. Mr. Hunter hastily kept out of the way when Luther pointed out that he had no time to put in the four panes of glass, or fix the porch, or make a gate. He threw in a few extra wrongs by way of good measure.

It seemed best to take the offensive.

So far as we were concerned, we said politely, it really did not make any difference what he did. It was a pity he had to bother himself about the house at all. We were leaving early for up river. There were a great many things at I-ees-i-rum we had to attend to. Perhaps he had better let things slide.

We were a little doubtful about the result of our attitude, as this was the first time we had seen Luther with the gloves off. But early the next morning he was back, extremely friendly and sunny. We were saddling the mules, and Luther watched us with a courtly air.

Of course, we knew, Luther began, that it was going to be a pleasure for him to finish the house. Why, he was going right down to Orleans now, that very minute, to get hinges, and by tomorrow he would have the whole thing done. As for the mules, he'd buy some tools when he was down river and shoe them for us himself. If we should want any lumber, he'd take four animals down to Orleans and pack it up. As to the bill, we need not bother about it. We could pay him anytime.

We took this last statement with a reasonable degree of doubt. But the next time we saw Luther was two weeks later, when we were coming back from Orleans. We got his signature on the house vouchers for the Indian Department, and, to our amazement, Luther charged us just what he said he would and was as friendly as possible.

Yet Orleans was ringing with the last affray in which Luther had been involved. It seems that Mr. Sims, the Brizzard store manager, had given Luther a statement of his store account, and in response Luther had told Mr. Sims just what he thought of him in particular and of the Brizzards in general. Then he left to get his revolver. Mr. Sims wasn't surprised because it is common talk that Luther disputes every bill on principle. Of course, when Mr. Sims saw the door open a minute later, he shot on sight, and got a peaceful citizen who was coming in for a bag of flour. It was a clean shot, and the citizen dropped dead. But after all, as they said in Orleans, it wasn't Mr. Sims's fault, and you could hardly blame the peaceful citizen. So the judge sent word to Luther that this was the second death that had come about through something he had done, and the next time anyone got killed Luther had better look out.

The only thing that bothered us as we finally rode back up river was that Luther muttered something under his breath about Tintin, and how he was going to get him. But we hope that affair has blown over.

Yesterday, we rode down river, our saddlebags filled to bursting with supplies, ready to move in. The decorations at Ossi-puk are to be very classy. We have tacked building paper over the remaining bits of scrofulous newspaper on the walls. The building paper is gray with a blue border. When you add to this the turkey-red curtains we have put up, the effect is very dashing. In the evening, Luther came in to get paid. A check for two hundred and seventy-five dollars in one lump sum, the total amount of our indebtedness, was plainly too much for his proud spirit. He was completely subdued and never offered to pop a single shot at us.

A little later, he brisked up enough to say, "What's that gold crucible for?"

"Why, Mr. Hickox," we said, "that's a flower vase. Mr. Gent at the Orleans store gave it to us. Don't you think it's charming?"

"Yes," said Luther dubiously, and looked more subdued than ever.

Thick pepper bushes grow all around Ossi-puk, and underneath our house live all the little wild hogs in the neighborhood. We do not object to the little wild hogs, that is, we do not object to them very much. But we do object, more than we can put into words, to the fleas that they leave behind them. Maybe you think you know fleas. Wait until you have spent two days at Ossi-puk! Seven fleas on one of my legs and nine on the other, a few minutes after I came into the house, is the record so far.

To date, our only method of meeting the problem is with water. Before we open the front door, we arm ourselves with a pail and go up to the spring. At the spring, we find all the little wild hogs who are not living under our house. We chase them away from the spring by brandishing our arms and beating on the pail. Then we fish a lot of pepper leaves out of the water and wait for the spring to clear. By the time we have managed to get a full pail, we return down a sharp decline to the house. Mabel throws open the front door and I cast the full pail of water over the threshold onto the floor. We return to the spring, chase out more hogs, and get another pail of water. When the floor is about two inches under water, we gingerly step inside. Not a flea. At least, not a flea until we forget and let a spot on the floor dry out. Then one or two brave spirits come to life.

We were sweeping the living room in preparation for our first Sunday school at Ossi-puk when Louis McClellan rode up. Louis is the mailrider with whom we started for Somes, our first day across the Klamath, from Orleans. But times have changed. We no longer run out and catch at Louis' bridle and murmur sweet nothings in his ear. Louis leaned eagerly over the fence to talk to us. He said maybe we remembered him. He said that once he had been at our house, and then he settled himself in his saddle and told us about all his private affairs, to which we listened noncommittally. As we stood looking out at the thick pepper bushes, the Sandy Bar white mule appeared, followed by the brown mule, followed by Sandy Bar Jim himself, with all our goods from Orleans to set up housekeeping in Ossi-puk. Jim put up the little stove, and after he left we made two closets for our cups and saucers and groceries. Now we are ready for anything.

There was still one bit of unfinished business about which we were a little doubtful. When we paid Luther the two hundred and seventy-five dollars for the house, he owed us thirty dollars that we had advanced him for some lumber. We owed him eight dollars for some small jobs he had done for us, so that left twenty-two dollars still coming to us. We told him he could leave it at the company store in Orleans when he went to get his check cashed, but when we asked Mr. Gent if Luther had left any money for us, Mr. Gent said no. We were not entirely surprised. We thought our chances of getting the twenty-two dollars were probably slim. Still, it was government money, and we ought to get it if we could, so before we took the up-river trail we rode up to the Hickoxes.

Mrs. Hickox ran out to speak to us, as friendly as usual, and I said inquiringly, "Of course, I don't suppose Mr. Hickox is here now?"

Mrs. Hickox hesitated. There was a queer look on her face.

"Yes, he's home," she said, "but I guess you couldn't see him this afternoon."

The words were hardly out of her mouth when the door opened and out sprang Luther. He looked rather black but he was quite sober, and he gave us the twenty-two dollars without a word.

Now what do you know about that? Luther, who is supposed to receive unpaid bills at the point of a gun. But as we rode back along the trail, Mabel murmured to me that she would like to know what had been going on in the Hickox household before Luther bounced out of the door.

We did not expect many people at the first Sunday school at Ossi-puk, because there is such a wilderness of pepper bushes around the house that almost no one could see us

ride in. But we were hardly unsaddled when there was a
step on the porch, and George McCash came in. Of course,
it was a special compliment for George to walk all the way
from I-ees-i-rum for Sunday school, so we welcomed him
warmly. We were still finding a place for George to sit when
in came Dora and Ida and their two babies from Kot-e-meen,
followed by Kot-e-meen Pete. Then Mrs. Offield panted in,
dragging a small boy after her, followed by Willy Jones.
Sunday school at Ossi-puk was evidently going to be more
popular than we had anticipated.

Mabel had just started "Joy to the World" when the
bushes outside the fence became alive with people, and
in came Jessie Hickox with Mr. and Mrs. Chester, from
Orleans, and a strange white man. There was so much excitement that we hardly noticed Gorham Owl and Albert
Joe, who, with accustomed modesty, found seats on the
woodpile.

With our room fairly bristling with a congregation, we
came to order with great formality, and had prayers and
the Bible before we went back to the singing. But it was
not I-ees-i-rum. There was marked restraint from everybody but good old George McCash. We hastily abandoned
"Joy to the World" and struck into "Nearer, My God, to
Thee." Instantly a voice like a brass file filled the room. It
was the strange white man. The volume increased. Mr.
Chester, who had just said he couldn't sing, had thrown
back his head and was doing his best. Willy Jones seized a
hymnbook and bellowed forth. Then the door opened and
in stalked Luther, with Louisa at his heels.

We chose safe and assured ground and sang "Rock of
Ages" and "Jesus, Lover of My Soul" twice and "Nearer,
My God, to Thee" indefinitely. Luther cast restraint to the
winds and roared forth, while Mr. Chester and the strange
white man sang until the rafters rang. The white man explained that he had sung tenor in the choir back home,
and bitterly lamented his ignorance of our "new tunes."
Luther went home with an Episcopal hymnbook clasped in

his hand. As the white man prepared to leave, he stopped in the doorway.

"Now if we could only get a guitar," he said. "We certainly could make a go of this."

We drew a long breath as the last of the congregation disappeared behind the pepper bushes. Then we looked up as we saw a shadow in the doorway. It was a little, slight, old Indian woman, with an Indian cap on her head and a long shawl that fell straight to her knees.

"*I-o-qui*," said Á-su-ná-pee.

She crossed the room slowly and seated herself on a little stool by the fireplace.

It was at Kot-e-meen that we had first seen Á-su-ná-pee. She was the mother of Swanny Tomer, who had fallen off the bridge at Somes, a year ago last December, and had been drowned.

Later, Mrs. Hilding had told us about Á-su-ná-pee. She belonged to one of the oldest professions. The Greeks had a name for it. It was said that any man in Orleans, or in Happy Camp, would gladly pay four bits for a smile from Á-su-ná-pee. As she sat on the little stool by our fireplace, we did not wonder that any man would pay four bits for a smile from Á-su-ná-pee. She was not beautiful. She was a little old woman with an *aphon* on her head. But as A-su-ná-pee sat quietly in our room, not looking at us, we kept hoping she would move or speak. She was not beautiful and yet she had a quality of beauty that made us breathe more quickly, and her slightest movement was the nearest thing to beauty we had ever seen.

As we saw more of Á-su-ná-pee, and she became a friend of ours, we learned that her voice is very soft, and she always speaks in Indian. We began to speak Indian ourselves. We had to. Á-su-ná-pee completely lost patience with us if we did not understand at once what she was saying.

At Kot-e-meen and at the Hildings' and at I-ees-i-rum, the Indians are very humble when we are teaching them English. But we are very humble when Á-su-ná-pee is teaching us Indian. And we are very much alarmed when we make a mistake and Á-su-ná-pee loses patience with us.

All the Indians on the Rivers are very pleased when we ask them to eat with us. But we are very pleased when Á-su-ná-pee is willing to eat with us, or when she accepts anything we offer her.

Á-su-ná-pee never comes to see us when there is anyone else at Ossi-puk. It is only after everyone has gone away that we look up and see her shadow on the doorway. But after forty years, something that stays with us, and something we can never forget, is the shadow of Á-su-ná-pee in our doorway.

It was the day after the first Sunday school at Ossi-puk. We had settled down for a quiet evening with Á-su-ná-pee. Then we saw agitation in the pepper bushes outside the gate, and Luther and Louisa came into view. Á-su-ná-pee gave us one look and left by way of the kitchen door. We built a small fire, as it was growing a little chill, and after Luther and Louisa had settled themselves we admired for the seventh time the fireplace Luther had built us, and Luther was very civil about the decorations.

Luther was in excellent form. He told us about having pulled out eighteen teeth and about the time he licked the Chinaman. But the high light of his stories was the time he had gone down below, to San Francisco. He said it was a very dangerous affair.

"I was taking a thousand in dust down below with me," said Luther. "Everything went pretty good until I come to get off the train. Then they were waiting for me. There was a lot of them and they all had little red caps on. The minute they saw me they made a rush at me. I had the dust in my valise and I saw right off I was in for trouble. One of the fellows grabbed my valise and the others closed in on me. I stood there and I looked 'em in the eye.

" 'You git' I said, and I showed 'em my automatic. They saw I meant business and they kind of drew back and I got through. I'd of nailed 'em all right but I won't pretend I wasn't scared.

"I had to see a feller and he kept talking and talking until it was pretty late. I didn't like it getting dark like that so I said, 'Say, walk home a ways with me, will you?' But he wouldn't come. Scared, I guess. He just said. 'Why, you'll get along all right.'

"So there I was. And worst of all, like a fool, I'd left my gun at home. Yep, I was there with one thousand in dust and no gun. It was pretty dark. I walked as quick as I could but pretty soon I heard steps following me. I guessed maybe I was done. But just then I passed a house that was being built. I jumped in and got a brick and put it in my pocket. As I came out I grabbed it hard in my hand.

"Now, says I to myself, you come along and I'll fix you.

"But I guess the feller must have seen what I done because he shied right off and I could hear his footsteps going the other way. So I got home all right."

Louisa moved a little impatiently and Luther got up to go.

"Yep," he said, "I've been in some pretty tight corners." (From what we had heard we thought it was probably true.) "But, do you know, I've always thought that was the closest call I ever had."

CHAPTER XX

The Schoolmarms Come Down Like Wolves on Yreka, and Then Celebrate the Fourth in Indian Country

We have just learned that one of our neighbors near Ossi-puk is in trouble. He is an Indian called Mark-faced Steve. Last winter, he built a bridge for the county. Now the county refuses to pay him for the bridge and we cannot make out what is the reason or what went wrong. Steve owes money to Luther Hickox, and Luther says he wants his money and that Steve has got to pay it. Mark-faced Steve rightly feels that it is not wise to be on bad terms with Luther and has come to us about it. Several weeks ago, we wrote the county but have had no reply.

"You fellows better go to Yreka," Luther called out to us as we rode by. Luther was in high spirits. He had been mining all day, he said, and he expected to strike a core of metal any moment.

"I wouldn't take twenty thousand dollars for that mine " he called after us.

"We could go to Yreka," said Mabel later, as we sat on the porch at I-ees-i-rum. "If we went by way of Happy Camp and Hamburg, we wouldn't have to ford the Klamath with the mules."

Our Karok country extends from Happy Camp to Witch-pec. Steve says that when the Great Spirit came down the Klamath, wherever he camped for the night he changed the language. The Great Spirit certainly made better going of it than we do, for after he had changed the language at Happy Camp he made over a hundred miles in the next lap, and did not change the language until he drew in to Witchpec.

It was late in the afternoon of our second day on the trail when the mountains opened out and we could see the Klamath and the great gashes of red that mark the deserted mines of Happy Camp. This was one of the great mining districts of 1852. The country swarmed with white men. There were placer mines on the river and quartz mines in the mountains. Everywhere, men searched for gold.

When the white men came into the country they found the Indians living on little flats along the river. Now the white men have gone and the Indians have gone and only the abandoned mines mark the trail.

About a couple of miles back, before we hit Happy Camp, we were riding through thick woods when we struck a hard road. A few hundred yards farther on, the road led into a large clearing and what looked like a little village. It was very still and nothing moved. The houses stood rotting in the bright sunlight. Roofs had fallen in. Porches sagged. There were poles along the little street for electric lights, and the houses were wired, but the wires lay trailing on the ground. There were fences around what must have been gardens, but behind the fences the weeds stood waist high. A little distance from the houses were the tailings of a mine. Machinery stood rotting, almost rusted away, in a tangled litter of tumbled rock and stone.

It was very, very still. The sound of the mules' feet on the hard ground was unpleasantly loud. We felt uncomfortable and a little afraid. We had spurred the mules and were thankful when the trees closed around us again and we were back in the friendly solitude of the woods.

Just short of the town, at a very bad brook with caving sides, where the ground shelved away, Mr. Darcy did not like the look of things at all. He was just beginning to indicate how much he distrusted that particular brook when we came upon an Englishman, with dozens of little neat canvas bundles spread out over the ground in every direction. This was naturally the last straw for Mr. Darcy's already shattered nerves, and he did not attempt to conceal his agitation. At this, the Englishman became quite as agitated as Mr. Darcy. He gathered up his impedimenta, hurried behind a tree, and called out to ask whether we were mailriders.

But installed in the bedroom of our hotel, we found a basin and pitcher. Believe it or not, there they were. True, there was no water in the pitcher, but that was only a minor item. At the Hildings' you bathe on the back porch from a water trough. There is a communal towel handy, and an inconspicuous piece of pink soap. At the Elliotts', there is a tree stump in the back yard on which are two grimy tin basins. You dip water out of a greasy pool under some bushes, where the females of the family wash their pots and pans. After you have washed your hands, you wipe them on your pants unless, like us, you are wise and travel with a towel up your sleeve. But at Happy Camp you draw up before a real hotel, which is called the American House, and find your way upstairs to a bedroom with a door. And behind the house is a privy.

We are in a very civilized community.

In the dining room, someone who seems to be a friend of ours lent us a Yreka paper and gave us the latest up-river gossip. John Reese, who sometimes gets Mabel's mail and on the strength of it once wrote her a long personal letter, has shot old Bob Shasta, and Siskiyou, the little mule that Mabel rode and who was always very polite to us, spilled Mrs. Bickel's grandson and kicked him in the back. Happy Camp appears to be quite a town.

After supper, we sat talking to Mrs. Bickel, who runs the hotel. Two Indian women came in. Their faces were impassive and they sat down without a word.

"Did you want to see Mrs. Jenkins?" asked Mrs. Bickel.

One of the Indian women shook her head. They sat silently for over an hour, while we went on talking, and then Mrs. Bickel went out. There was a slight movement from one of the Indian women. We looked at them and found they were no longer impassive. The atmosphere had changed. They were smiling. They were friends.

"You know my sister down river?" asked one of the women. "She live at I-ees-i-rum." The woman was Annie's aunt. All of us relaxed and began to talk and laugh. We had a good time. We told them all the gossip from down river. Dumphrey Pepper's woman was sick bad. There had been a big run of eels at Kot-e-meen. They responded with the news from Happy Camp, which we were expected to carry down river with us. We felt at home in Happy Camp. It was nice to be there.

At Hamburg, we were clean out of our field and in new country. Hamburg was not inspiring. We had left the mules in Happy Camp, as the sight of a wagon road seemed to affect them most unpleasantly, and took the stage, which as usual turned out to be a spring wagon. A sharp rainstorm came up in the afternoon, but in spite of it our driver suddenly drew up and got off his seat.

"Got to get him," said the driver.

"Get what?" we asked. There had been no sound but the sharp, staccato buzz of the locusts.

"Young rattler," said the stage driver. "Can't you hear them? All along this road down there in the bushes. There goes one now."

We thought about the trail between Somesbar and Kot-e-meen. Apparently those sounds we had heard so many times on that trail had not come from locusts. They had come from young rattlers. From the continuous buzz, when we had passed along that trail on foot, they must have been so thick that they practically lay head to tail. We had traveled that trail many times, at all hours, both afoot and on horseback. But, after all, what you don't know doesn't hurt you.

It was still raining when we drew up at a handful of dismal houses, early in the afternoon.

"Where is the hotel?" we asked meekly. Our proud

spirits were quite broken, now that we were out of our own field.

"Down there," said the stage driver, pointing to a house with a row of doors. We tried two of the doors and found them locked. The third door admitted us to a dining room, with a table swathed to keep off flies. At our call, a woman came in and gave us a hard look. She put us in a dank, dirty bedroom and left us.

We were in a man's world at Hamburg. Snatches of song and laughter came from the saloon. Any man who travels in this country can be sure of warmth and comfort and companionship, although maybe a little unsavory. But women have not much chance in this white man's country. Well, well. When you come to think of it, strangers are none too welcome on the Rivers.

Supper was very bad. We are pretty well conditioned to bad food, but this was even worse than the Forks of Salmon, and that is speaking very strongly. We left the food uneaten and went out on to the road, in the dark. The lights were on in the saloon. A strong smell of whiskey permeated the air. A man began to sing what sounded like a pretty dubious song. We looked longingly at the saloon, smells, song, and all. Then we turned and walked up the road in the rain and the dark.

After an hour, we came back and snuggled down under the dirty covers of our bed. We thought of all the little brothers who were undoubtedly sharing that bed with us. But, after all, in this country a bed is a bed. We went to sleep and slept soundly until morning.

The next day, all along the road to Scott's Bar, we saw white people. There were no longer any dark faces. The people in all the cabins we passed were white. They spoke English as if they were quite accustomed to it. When we changed horses at Scott's Bar, there, standing waiting for us, was a real stage. The kind you see in pictures of the West. The kind that Deadwood Dick would undoubtedly hold up at the proper moment. We were coming nearer and nearer to civilization. Tomorrow, the driver told us, we might even ride in an automobile.

But the cabins and houses that we passed were more shiftless and dirty than they had been in the Indian country. We were in the land of the saloon. This was gold country, and what was the use of mending a fence or making a garden when tomorrow, or next year, you might strike it rich and never do a stroke of work the rest of your life?

When we finally drew up to the hotel in Yreka and were installed in the ladies' parlor, we tried to live up to its reputation. We tried to look the way that ladies ought to look in this country. We have hats and veils, and, from what they tell us, we shall need every advantage that a dressy appearance can give us, for it seems that our case is considered hopeless. The appropriations have been made without any allowance for Mark-faced Steve and the bridge he built for the county. It is the opinion of everyone that the best thing we can do is to return to the Rivers. We have seen Mr. Glendenning, who is the representative from our district. He was friendly and discouraging. He could do nothing for us. It was a pity we had taken such a long trip for nothing. Then he left us.

From Mr. Glendenning we had learned that there was to be a meeting at the courthouse at ten the following morning. We went to the courthouse at ten and could find no trace of Mr. Glendenning. But we succeeded in making a friend of the man who was sweeping down the steps, and he pointed out the door that opened into the room where the session would be held. We stood outside the door and waited. No Mr. Glendenning. Finally a man with a very red nose came by. He was a stout man and looked approachable.

"Could you tell us where we could find Mr. Glendenning?" we asked meekly. The stout man looked benign.

"I'll get him for you," he said. He did get him for us. Mr. Glendenning seemed to be much cast down by our appearance.

"I really can't do anything for you," he said.

We stood there.

"Oh, well," said Mr. Glendenning, "come back at one-thirty. But I don't think you will gain anything by it."

We ate as much as we could of a very bad dinner and came back at one-thirty.

We opened the door into the room where the session was held and went in. The room was full of flies, and five men were seated around a table. Mr. Glendenning got up and introduced us to the other four. Then he sat down. We learned that George (Mr. Helmouth) was not there and that nothing would happen until George got there. We looked as pleasant as we could, and a half hour went by. Then a very stout gentlemen who sat across from us at the table said, in a voice that would have downed a lion in a zoo, that he thought Indians ought to be paid. We said we thought so, too, and gave him the best smile of which we were capable. There was another long wait in which all five men at the table consulted books and wrote diligently. Then the door opened and George came in. We were introduced to George, who did not seem pleased to see us. There was another pause, and then one of the men got up, went out, and came back with Mark-faced Steve's bill.

Everyone at the table agreed that it should be paid. Everyone also agreed that it had not been paid. But no one saw how it could be paid now.

Mr. Glendenning said he wanted to be on the right side of the law. The stout man gave an inarticulate roar and said something we didn't catch. Mr. Helmouth appeared to be down on paying anything as a general principle. Mr. Luxell, the district attorney, was called in. Mr. Luxell looked very legal, made some doubtful remarks, and went off with the bill.

There was a long silence, and then we presented our side of the case, bringing in all the local color we could. Mr. Helmouth looked unconvinced.

"Of course, that bill should have been paid," he said. "But I can't see how we can possibly pay it now."

There appeared to be a general agreement to this. Then suddenly the stout man got to his feet.

"And I say pay 'em the money," he roared. "Pay 'em all that's coming to 'em. Pay 'em now. And send 'em home happy."

Mr. Luxell came back while the roar of the stout man still rang in the room.

"There really is no legal reason why the money should not be paid," he said.

The dam broke. Mr. Glendenning and Mr. Helmouth and the stout man with the roar all talked at once. Before we had quite taken in what was happening, a small, elderly man came in and took us into another room. He opened a safe and laid out on the table before us four twenty-dollar gold pieces.

A young lady beside us was saying, "I represent the Yreka *News*. If you will just give me your names——"

After the eighty dollars in gold was safely disposed on our persons, we went back to the session room and told everyone how grateful we were, and everyone leaned back in his chair and looked very pleased with himself.

"Now what you want to tell those Indians down there," said Mr. Glendenning, and Mr. Helmouth in chorus, "is not to do any work without a legal authorization from me."

Then the entire group asked questions about conditions on the Rivers, and we told Mr. Glendenning what fine, well-kept trails he had in our district. We paused. "Now, if Mr. Helmouth would only fix up his trails, so all the trails were in good condition——" we murmured.

"Well, why don't you do it, George?" asked the stout man. George looked mutinous.

"Some day, Mr. Helmouth, when you are walking on a nice dry pavement," we said very gently, "just think of us trying to push our way through the heavy, wet brush on the trail."

"Oh, well," said Mr. Helmouth, "all right. Tell 'em I said to go ahead."

We thanked everyone individually all over again. They said good-by. We said good-by. Then we waited.

"Was there anything else?" asked Mr. Glendenning.

"We were just waiting for Mr. Helmouth's written authorization," we said meekly. There was a shout of laughter. Mr. Glendenning slapped Mr. Helmouth on the back. Mr. Helmouth sheepishly wrote out an authorization, and we came away.

The next day, we left Yreka as marked celebrities. The chauffeur of the auto stage put someone out so that we could get in. Mr. Morrison flew out of the hotel to say good-by. Mr. Glendenning hurried across the street to give us a final handshake. Eugene, who had actually handed us the eighty dollars, took three side steps and almost ran down an old lady, trying to bow to us.

We sat back in the stage, taking our ease. Before us, like a misty wraith in the sky, was the beautiful white cone of Shasta. Fort Jones greeted us with a good supper, and life had no more to offer us.

Back in Happy Camp, our foot was on our native heath. As we drew in, one of our companions on the stage spoke to us.

"They say you live way down on the Klamath in an Indian ranch."

We said we did. He leaned forward eagerly.

"Be you married or single?" he asked.

"Single," we said modestly.

"Well," he said, drawing a long breath, "such is life."

We were not quite sure how to interpret this, but it seemed to be well meant.

As we rode down river, everywhere we stopped there was news from Somesbar. The old man was sick bad and Mama Frame wanted to see us. We only stopped long enough at Ossi-puk to give Mark-faced Steve his money, which he received with truly Christian resignation. Evidently it was

no more than he had expected. Then we went on to Sandy
Bar, where they swam the mules for us, and we reached
Somesbar just as the light faded.

The old man had been sick for almost two weeks, they
told us. They thought now that maybe he was dying. All
evening, we sat and talked in a low voice with Mama Frame
while the old man dozed, and Sam and Margy and a daughter from down below came in and went out of the room.

The next day, we took the familiar trail from Somes
to Kot-e-meen on our way back up river.

Just where the little trail leads off to A-o-wich, the sugar-
loaf mountain, we found Essie on the trail, waiting for us.
As we stopped and talked, the queer shadow that had
been between us was gone. It was the old Essie. We felt
as though we were still a part of the Essie family and still
lived in our house at Kot-e-meen. Les didn't live there no
more, she said. Mart was down to the Forks, working in
the mine. She had been sick bad. An hour went by as
we stood talking. Essie stood leaning against Mr. Darcy with
her fingers wound in his mane as though she could not
let us go.

We begged her to come to school at Ossi-puk. We begged
her to come to I-ees-i-rum. But she only shook her head,
then turned and went slowly up the trail.

We came away sick at heart to be leaving her.

Getting the mules back across the Klamath proved more
of a job than getting them over. Instead of crossing at
Sandy Bar, we had decided to swim them at Ten Eyck, across
from Luther Hickox's house and only a few miles from
Ossi-puk. At this time of year, the water is low at the Ten
Eyck crossing and there is a long, low bar on the east side
of the river. At one end of this bar there is quicksand. We
had heard that Luther would be on the east side of the
river, and we thought Luther's help would be worth something. But we reckoned without the mules.

The mules had been peaceful and well behaved at the
Sandy Bar crossing. But at Ten Eyck, they were not peace-

ful and they were not well behaved. We had Luther and Mark-faced Steve and Hackett and Eddy Conrad and Mr. Hunter and Willy Jones to help us. But we were all as nothing when it came to handling the mules. They reared and plunged. They used their heels on whoever came near them. They leaped in the air and shied on the very edge of the dangerous quicksand, with all of us trying to ward them off. When we attempted to make the crossing in the dugout, Maria pulled Luther out of the dugout, across a stretch of water, and up the bank. The boat leaked and we nearly upset. The mules plunged and snorted down upon Eddy Conrad, who hastily retreated to a safe position far up the bank. We tried everything we could think of. It was no use.

At last, when we were all completely done in, Mr. Darcy put one foot in the water. I held Maria off a little distance away, behind a bush. All the men got behind Mr. Darcy and clubbed him. Our mules swim like ducks. Mr. Darcy took the water and was across the Klamath in no time. We then centered on Maria. We clubbed her until we were all black in the face. Maria would not budge. We sat down on the sand to catch our collective breath while Maria stood quietly by. Then she caught sight of Mr. Darcy on the other side of the river. She walked down to the water. She stepped in and swam across.

We invited the perspiring Luther and Mr. Hunter to come to dinner with us at Ossi-puk. We thought they deserved it.

It is now very close to the Fourth of July. It seems to us proper that the Fourth of July should make a pleasant impression on the Rivers, as up to this time, apparently, none of the Indians have heard of it. We are therefore planning a celebration of the Fourth at I-ees-i-rum. Mr. Gent has been down below, and we asked him to bring some fireworks back with him. We stayed overnight at the Richards' and were waiting in the store when Mr. Gent rode up. He not only had fireworks in his pack saddle, he had something more for us. He had two bananas, one in each pocket, which he had packed all the way from San Francisco. Real bananas. Think of it. We ate them later as we rode up the trail.

But to come back to the fireworks. Mr. Gent had brought some firecrackers and some Roman candles. Then, in a rash moment, we also yielded to the lure of some rockets. We rode back up river with our prizes packed carefully in our saddle bags.

For a week we spent our time telling everyone up and down river that a Fourth of July celebration did not begin until after dark. This was a terrible blow. Indians expect any festivity to begin early and last all day and far into the night, with meals at frequent intervals.

"Don't come until nine o'clock in the evening," we told everyone.

Pictoria and Sophia arrived at eleven in the morning. They hung around hopefully for about three hours and then went away. By seven in the evening, the porch was crowded with Indians, and we set Mack Charlie to playing the phonograph while Pete acted as ferryman and paddled dugouts full of passengers, crowded to the point of foundering, from the other side of the river. It was still too light for fireworks, so we desperately passed refreshments—cakes, raisins and nuts, and some candy left over from Christmas. We gave the refreshments to the rancheria to pass around, so we wouldn't know how soon the meager supply was exhausted.

At length, it was really dark, and surrounded by eagerly helpful young Indians we began on the firecrackers. They went well enough, but it was a breathless assembly of Indians that watched the Roman candles.

Steve and George McCash and Mack Charlie and Herman were in charge. The Indians crowded on the porch, which is high above the river, on the steps, and on the high ground, from all of which they had a clear view of what was going on in the little flat below them. Between the high ground and the river stood four dark figures, silhouetted sharply against the sky, each holding a Roman candle in his hand.

There was a long wait. Nothing happened. What could be the matter with Steve? What did they think they were doing? Then a brilliant shower of sparks lit up the sky. A Roman candle had begun to whirl. Then there was another and another.

"*Ya-a-a-rmuch* (beautiful)," breathed the watching Indians. "*Y-a-a-rmuch.*"

But the great event of the evening was the rockets. They were to be the crown of the entertainment. Steve had them in charge, and we stood anxiously by. There was a long wait, and the crowd sat tense. Steve tried desperately to brace the supports of the first rocket in the hard, stony, shelving ground. Suddenly there was a hiss and a splutter. The crowd leaned forward.

Siss-boom-ah went the rocket, and, without warning, it crossed directly over the heads of the crowd of Indians and entered the corral, where the mules had been drowsing, missing Mr. Darcy by a hair. The mules left the corral without more ado, taking most of the fence with them.

It was an even better show than the Indians had anticipated.

The next rocket nearly got Mabel, while Steve and I watched it with horrified eyes. It bounced past her, taking a low course along the ground, and fizzled out at the very feet of the Indians crowding the porch. The crowd drew back their feet and watched it in awe-struck silence.

We managed to extinguish the third rocket before it set the roof on fire. But the three remaining rockets rose with gorgeous trains of fiery sparks, lighting up the river and the mountains until they broke in scintillating showers over our heads.

Singing and drumming was rather an anticlimax after the fireworks, but it was late before we could shoo our reluctant guests away, and crawl into bed.

CHAPTER XXI

We Cross Marble Mountain and Find the Indian Ain't Got No Chance in White Men's Country

At long last we are to see Marble Mountain. Ever since we came to the Rivers, they have told us of Marble Mountain. It lies in a jumble of mountains somewhere between the Klamath and Scott's Valley, and famous packers like Mr. Hilding pass over it as they cross the mountains with supplies, instead of taking the long way around, by the Forks of Salmon and Sawyer's Bar. Now Mr. Mortsoff has written us from Hoopa that an Indian in Scott's Valley is in some trouble with the whites. He thinks it is in regard to land, and he asks us, when it is convenient, please to look into the matter.

Of course, we could go the long way around, but it would be both cheaper and pleasanter to take Steve and Annie as guides and cross the mountains. Steve's interest in the trip mounted when he learned that we planned to go to Etna. "We might get to ride in a buggy," he said hopefully.

We think he must mean a spring wagon. Few of the older Indians on the Rivers have ever ridden in a wagon. I do not think Steve has ever been in one. We had hoped to get off the day after the Fourth but for two days Steve has been off hunting for the mules. Steve found them in Orleans. Now they are back; and we are off for Marble Mountain the first thing in the morning. Everything is ready and all is smooth sailing except White Puppy.

We do not know why the Hickoxes called him White Puppy. He is not white and he most certainly is not a puppy. He is a large, rangy dog, with long hair and pointer blood, and we don't know how many different ancestors. He belongs to Luther Hickox. On the days when we have been in Ossi-puk, White Puppy got in the habit of dropping in for breakfast. We would find him lying outside the front door when we opened it in the morning. Still, we looked on him as only a casual acquaintance.

But the last school day in Ossi-puk, when we saddled the mules to ride up river, White Puppy fell in behind us. That would never do. That would never, never do. Our relations with Luther have been of the pleasantest, but we were doubtful whether he would think well of us as dog stealers. We yelled at White Puppy and told him to go home. We continued to yell until we saw White Puppy trotting up the trail toward the Hickoxes. Then we settled back in our saddles and thumped along up river. We stopped a minute at Mark-faced Steve's. We were just out of sight of his cabin when we saw something move in the bushes behind us. It came out of the bushes and wagged its tail. It was White Puppy.

This was serious. We got off the mules and threw rocks at White Puppy. Big ones. Mark-faced Steve came up and joined us and also threw rocks. White Puppy disappeared. We rode on. As we drew into Ronell's Creek, there, lying on the trail waiting for us, was White Puppy. We got off our mules and beat White Puppy. Old-Woman-from-Ronell's-Creek came out and helped us throw rocks. She also told White Puppy just what we thought of him in Indian. It was plain from White Puppy's expression that his feelings were hurt. He put his tail between his legs and drew back out of sight. Then he footed up the situation. He took up a position about a quarter of a mile behind the mules. When we looked ahead, he would creep up closer to the mules. When we looked behind, he would disappear from sight. He was on the trail, waiting for us, when we turned down toward the corral at I-ees-i-rum. He is now on the porch with a loaf of stale bread inside him and a benign expression. We plan to send him back to Luther by the mail-rider. He is to be securely tied up tonight and handed over to Mr. Wright in the morning. For the big day has come, and we are off for Marble Mountain a little before daylight.

All last evening we spent planning the trip with Steve. What we should pack. Where we should camp. Then I thought of something Sandy Bar Tom had told us.

"Plenty of panther up on Marble Mountain?" I asked Steve.

"*Ha,*" said Steve abstractedly.

"Going to pack your gun?" I asked a few minutes later. Steve shook his head.

"Maybe good to have a gun, Steve, if there are so many panthers?" I said encouragingly.

Steve made no answer. After a while he said, "I guess I ain't take no gun."

I sat up. "Steve, why won't you take your gun?" I asked urgently.

Steve sat for a few minutes, looking thoughtful. "Cost too much money," he said finally.

"What do you mean, cost too much money?" said Mabel, coming into the conversation.

"Well," said Steve sadly, "last time I pack my gun, I got to pay four hundred dollars."

Dear, dear. Four dead men. No wonder Steve has a reputation on the Rivers. Maybe, after all, it is better that we should not press the question.

We were up a little before light, breakfasting on coffee and corn pones, when Steve came over to ask if we were ready. The river was so low that he was going to ford the animals, and Jetty had come over to help him. Pete was going to put us across and then take the dugout back to the I-ees-i-rum side. But as the dugout swung into the current, there was something swimming strongly beside it. It couldn't be. Yes, it was White Puppy.

"Pete," we cried, "you promised us to have that dog securely tied up."

"I tie him," said Pete serenely. "I think maybe he get loose."

We struck at White Puppy with the paddle. From the bank, Steve threw rocks at him. Like ourselves, Steve did not care to put too much strain on Luther's good nature. White Puppy dodged the paddle and swam the river a little farther downstream. He evaded Pete's efforts to catch him and was waiting for us when the mules commenced the climb.

It was a climb of nine miles to the top of the first ridge. The trail was obscure. In some places it was no trail at all. It was lucky we had not tried to make it alone. The ground was covered with fallen tree trunks, and across these the mules had to pick their way. You jumped what you could, and when you could not jump you painfully made your way around them. All traces of a trail disappeared. We saw Steve glance around thoughtfully and then look up at the mountain to get his bearings. He chose the easiest lie of ground and we made our own trail.

Every now and then we caught glimpses of the valley and saw the Klamath, now far below us. Then the Klamath and the river valley were gone, and we came out into a great stretch of manzanita and snowbush. There was no sign of any trail, and the bush was so high I could only follow Pet and Daisy and Mr. Darcy, who were ahead of me, by the movements of the top branches of the bush. Sometimes I would catch a glimpse of a head bobbing along, but when it disappeared beneath the bush I would have to follow as best I could. Later, we passed the famous Hay Press Meadows, where five hundred head of cattle can pasture, and then we began to climb again.

We were now following along a ridge upon which some indications of trail appeared. This ridge grew narrower and narrower, until there were only a few high peaks above us. Annie was the first up, then Mabel, and I followed her. On every side were mountains. We were on the top of the world. To our right, lay something that looked like a white cloud.

"Salmon summit," said Steve. "Plenty snow."

Farther on, there was the unmistakable white cone of Shasta, first misty and obscure and then shining out, white and glorious, against a clear blue sky. The trail lay directly along the top of the ridge. The mountains changed as different ridges were lost or came into sight. But hour after hour there was the seemingly limitless expanse. As the shape of the ridges changed or came into view, every mountain we had seen on the Rivers also came into view and then was lost again. Sheldon's Butte, which we see from Orleans. Then the white peak that we tried to photograph at Happy Camp appeared in faint outline on our left. Then Bald Mountain, just below Hoopa.

"That one," said Steve pointing, "he last one before ocean."

As we rode in single file, Mabel pointed to some white rock below the trail.

"Is that marble?" she asked Steve.

"No," said Steve disgustedly. "He snow."

It was snow. At I-ees-i-rum, now far below us, it would be one hundred degrees in the shade. I scrambled down the cliff, wanting to hold some of the snow in my hand. I need not have taken the trouble, for soon it lay on every side of us. At one place the snow was so deep on the trail that we had to get off the mules and walk across it with considerable care, for if anyone slipped on that trail there was no telling where he would end up.

We thought of Ossi-puk and Orleans baking in the heat. We scuffed our feet in the snow and gazed out over the snow-capped peaks on all sides of us.

Annie, on Pet, was well ahead of us, but Steve was some distance behind. Evidently Steve did not intend to stop for lunch. We took a few crackers out of our saddle bags and munched as we rode. Steve called out that Cuddihy's, one of the few camping places in the mountains, lay right ahead of us. As he spoke, there was a hail from just below us, and George McCash and his sister joined us. They had started the night before and had camped in the Hay Press Meadows.

Steadily at the heels of the mules trotted White Puppy. When the entire party rode close together, White Puppy would take the lead. But when the party separated, and Mabel and I rode by ourselves, White Puppy would take up his station at Mr. Darcy's tail, between Mabel and myself. He was polite to the Indians, but that was all. White Puppy was our dog, and he wanted to be sure that everything was as it should be.

Annie had fallen behind with Steve, and George Mc-Cash now rode in the lead. George had no illusions in regard to panthers on Marble Mountain, and he packed a gun. On his last trip across, George had a sharp brush with a panther. He told us how scared he had been and all the things he did that he should not have done, and we laughed so hard we quite forgot to notice that George had not only killed the panther, but that he had held a badly frightened horse and a lantern with his other hand and had shot the panther in the eye, in the shifting light. No mean feat for any man. As we thought about the panther, we were very glad to have George with us. And especially glad that he had his gun. But I did look a little doubtfully at the way George carried his gun. Its muzzle was trained on me. Not exactly on my eye, but right smack on my abdomen. As George jolted along and the gun jolted along, I could see quite clearly down the muzzle. I did not want to bother George with such a small detail, but if George's horse were to stumble, and the gun were to go off, aimed, as it was, right at me, I couldn't help feeling it would be a pity.

The country was changing. We passed beautiful, clear, green lakes, far, far below us. They might easily have been a couple of miles down. Green grass grew on their shores. Then we sighted a jagged twin peak, standing out from the jumble of mountains. It was white, and flashed in the sun.

"Marble Mountain," said Steve briefly.

Marble Mountain is not really marble. As we came closer to it, we could see that it was light-granite color. But it stood away clear from everything else, and flashed more brilliantly in the sun with every mile that lessened the distance to it. We would lose sight of it, and then the trail would wind around and there it would be again, directly ahead of us, white and glistening, the side next to us one great formidable precipice as far down as the eye could see. Later, we rounded this precipice and began to edge our way carefully toward the top. At one place, George made us get off our mules and crawl to the edge, so we could look down. I have never seen such a breath-taking drop. We were not sorry to crawl back again to safety. After that, we drew a little away from the ridge and began winding down a beautiful grassy slope, with the tunbled mountains on every side. They were just beginning to color with the most wonderful pinks and purples when we dropped suddenly into a little dell. There were tall pines around us, and we could hear a trickle of water. This was Cold Springs, where Steve planned to spend the night. We had come fifty miles and had been thirteen hours in the saddle.

Steve made a little fire and cooked while George chopped wood. The other animals were turned loose, but not Maria and Mr. Darcy. They looked as fresh as when they had started. We sat up behind the camp and held their lines while they grazed. We were in no mind to have them give us the slip and make their own way back to Witchpec.

Indian cooking is unhurried. Steve was still far from ready when Luther Tom rode in, followed by two down-river Indians. That made more people among whom to divide our rather scanty supplies. But we shared and shared alike. I got a mug of coffee and a small piece of fry-pan bread, and was thankful for it.

As we lay on the fir boughs that George had cut for us, we should have been counting our blessings, but it was far otherwise. In the first place, Luther Tom and the two down-river Indians and George and George's gun were all camped about a quarter of a mile away. We tried to persuade White Puppy to stay cuddled down beside us, but White Puppy developed other interests. All night the mules shifted and snorted, and we thought of panthers. Steve had only made a tiny fire. It went out within an hour, and we lay by ourselves in the darkness.

But it was neither the darkness nor the thought of panthers that weighed most heavily upon us. A black cloud lay between ourselves and Steve. Steve had made a bargain and had gone back on it. Steve had waited until we were on the trail, and it was too late to turn back, before he told us. Steve had planned with us to travel a reasonable number of miles before we stopped to camp, but his pride was too much for him. He had made fifty miles over the mountains, a thing no sane man would have done, and, although no harm had been done to the mules, Annie's horse was in bad shape and might not last out the trip. Our thoughts were very black. What though there might be panthers eying us from the screen of underbrush? Steve was our friend, and Steve had again gone back on us. We slept and waked and listened to the mules snort and fidget, and then fell asleep again.

It was still dark when Steve roused us. There was faint soft light in the east. We could see the dark blur of the spot where Steve and Annie had camped. Then there was the sound of singing. Steve and Annie lay watching the light brighten in the east. They were singing the morning song. We lay listening while the song rose and fell and the day came.

"Time to get up," said Steve briskly. We drank a bit of left-over coffee, saddled, and were off.

The morning was still young when the mountains began to fall away and the trail widened and grew smoother.

In another hour we had come to Shackleford Valley, where a little stream raced down between smooth, grassy banks. There were tall mountains above us, and great, parklike trees. It was decided that Steve and Annie should turn aside to camp with some Indian friends, and give Pet some time to rest, while we rode on into the valley by ourselves. With bitterness in our hearts, we paid Steve the full amount he had asked. Steve took it and rode off. Then he wheeled his horse and came back. He did not look at us but he thrust two gold pieces into my hand.

"I think all right," said Steve.

Then he smiled and, with all his old swagger, rode away. Everything was all right. Steve had played fair and kept the agreement he had made. Scott's Valley was before us, and we put our mules to the gallop and rode down the trail.

Ever since we had left the Hay Press Meadows, there had been dust on the trail, for we followed in the track of five-hundred head of cattle. But the dust in the mountains was nothing to the dust we found in the valley. It lay thick on everything. After only seven miles, we were pale-yellow wraiths, and it was hard to tell what might lie underneath. Apparently it meant something that we had been seventeen months on the Rivers. We might not know anyone in Etna, but everyone in Etna knew us. The woman in the drugstore, and Mr. Parker, in Denny's bar, and Miss Peters, the librarian, and Mr. Martin, the justice of the peace, all greeted us an intimate friends. We had a bath in a bathtub. Not much of a bath nor much of a bathtub, but none the less a bath, and very welcome. We had dinner in the hotel, and after dinner Steve and Annie and Clo and the two children all came into town, and we had ice cream. The delights of a big city certainly do go to one's head. Oh, and I forgot to say that we had our boots shined, for the first time since January, 1908.

Tomorrow we look up poor old Ruffy. Here in this rich valley, where there are grain fields and fruit orchards, land is valuable, and Ruffy's house is claimed by one white man, the field where he has his garden, by another, and the loft where he keeps his wood, by a third. This is the white man's country, and the Indian has small chance. The idea seems to be to find a location for Ruffy on government land, back somewhere on the mountain. We are supposed to look up the land, have it surveyed, and get Ruffy established on it.

The trouble with us is that all these wagon roads go to our heads. On the way to Ruffy's house we got lost twice. There is so much space here in the valley. You can see miles in any direction. And there are too many roads. They seem to go everywhere. Moreover, the mules take the flat, wide country here in the valley in very bad part. They do not wish to trot. They do not wish to lope. For the honor of the Klamath, we did manage to spur them into a bit of showing off as we came galloping in last night; but today they paid no attention to spur or quirt, and went dragging along the smooth, dusty road with their heads down until we were quite worn out with them.

We had just been lost a second time and had found our way back to what seemed to be a sort of main trail, when we saw before us a man in a very damaged wagon, with some crates of berries in the back and a small boy beside him. We panted up a particularly hot, dusty hill after him and asked some questions about the country. Luck was with us and we struck pay dirt. Our man was a surveyor. He knew every inch of government land. It was a find indeed. We arranged to meet him at Ruffy's in the afternoon.

Ruffy had a small, neat cabin with a little garden. It was smooth, rolling country and on all sides of the tiny holding lay great wide fields and orchards. Although it was nearly the middle of July, the little garden was well watered and the fences were well kept up. There were some fruit trees. The little house was painted and had a porch. The Ruffys had loved this little place and had taken care of it. Our hearts sank. Here in this great, rich valley, what chance did the Indians have? It was a bitter business.

Mr. Custer, the surveyor, arrived while we were admiring Ruffy's vegetables. We talked over the situation with Ruffy and explained that he might choose a location on government land in exchange for the little house they were taking away from him. We found it difficult to explain that he had no legal title to his holding. They were taking away his home. That was all that we could make clear.

All the good valley land had long since gone into private hands. We turned off the valley road and struck up the mountain.

Our party consisted of Ruffy, Charlie Ruffy, Mr. Custer, Mabel, and myself. In a very short time, Mabel and I were extremely glad that we did not earn our living as surveyors, even at four dollars a day. We would toil up a perpendicular slope for about two miles, with thick woods about us, and then Mr. Custer would say, "Now just you look about three hundred feet over that way. That is Albert Rice's corner."

When Mabel had looked and I had looked and Ruffy and Charlie Ruffy had looked, without any of us being very clear about just what we were looking at, we would scramble down a precipice on the other side of the mountain and climb a still more ominous- looking slope. Nowhere was there any sign of arable land. After eight corners, each worse than the one before, about which Charlie Ruffy and Mabel and I had tried to look intelligent and old Ruffy had become visibly more alarmed, Mr. Custer wiped the sweat off his face and said thankfully, "Well, I guess that's about all except the corner to that forty over there. You don't want to see that, do you Ruffy?"

"Yes," said Ruffy firmly.

So we went over there and lost Charlie Ruffy entirely and nearly killed Maria and Mr. Darcy. On all sides of us were steep, wooded mountains. There were not so much as a dozen feet of level ground, and nowhere was there any sign of water.

"Well, here we are," said Mr. Custer. "I guess that's about the whole of it. All right, Ruffy?"

"No," screamed Ruffy. "No all right. Bad place. No water. No nothing. All mountain. No like mountain. Charlie Rice say Government crazy."

"You see, I guess he don't exactly understand," said Mr. Custer gently as we slid down the mountain.

Without a word, old Ruffy turned and left us.

"Is that all the available government land?" we asked Mr. Custer as we thanked him and paid him for his services.

"Well," said Mr. Custer, "there's quite a piece back there higher up the mountain, but it's the same sort of thing you've been looking at."

We rode slowly back to Ruffy's. The problem of the Indian in a white man's country stared us in the face. What could Ruffy do under the circumstances? What could we do for him? We were sick at heart.

Ruffy would not speak to us when we rejoined him on the porch. We tried to explain, but he stood with his back to us. After a little while we turned and came away.

But we could not bear to leave the poor old man in such trouble. After riding gloomily down the road for a quarter of a mile, we turned the mules around and rode back again. We said we did not want him to take the bad land on the mountain. Things were very bad for him. That was why we had come. Because things were very bad. Would they let him stay where he was? Even for a little while? If so, we would be glad. If they would not let him stay, we would come back again. We would do just what he wanted us to do. It was very bad land on the mountain but it was all the land the Government had. We understood that he could not live there with no water. We did not want him to take it. We did not know what to do. But if there was anything he wanted us to do, we would do it.

Peace was restored. We sat on the porch and talked Indian talk. We told stories. Ruffy told stories. We told about the people at I-ees-i-rum and Sandy Bar. Ruffy said he could sing pretty good. Drum pretty good. Maybe he come down river next Pic-i-ow-ish. Maybe he sing for us. Steve, he sing pretty good. But Ruffy sing pretty good. Ruffy sing better than Steve. Drum better than Steve. When we left we were friends.

But, for all that, we came away in despair. We had touched something that turned us cold. Was there any chance at all for the Indian in this white man's country? Was there any chance for the Indian where he had no legal status? It was different in the Forest Preserve. That was government land, where the rights of the Indian were protected in some measure. But here in the valley? What would become of Ruffy? Of course, we could write a report. But what good would a report do in the face of such dire human need? We could see Mr. Mortsoff and talk over the whole situation. But when it came to that, what could Mr. Mortsoff do?

It was a white man's world here in Etna. We were white people and everyone was kind. The Indian and his problems impinged very little on this world of the white man. Everyone was friendly. Miss Jessie came over to see us and talked. Mr. and Mrs. Walker came over and talked. Tim, who works in the livery stable, hovered near, evidently hoping for a word. We had about given over any hope of going to bed when in roared the auto stage, with everybody in it howling drunk, and that created such a pleasant diversion that we slipped away to bed without anyone knowing the difference.

We made an early start in the morning and this time camped at Cuddihy's. We had made slow going. Pet was dying by inches. We hoped we would be able to get her home. Daisy was also in poor shape, so Steve walked, and Annie, Mabel, and I took turns riding the mules. We lazied along and picked flowers. Everywhere along the snow line the ground was covered with them.

A month had passed since we had seen flowers on the Rivers. Every hillside along the Klamath was dry and brown, we met no fellow travelers on the way back, with one exception. Mabel and I were riding the mules when we rounded a curve. Right upon us was a string of pack animals and about a dozen men, a good-sized pack train. We dropped off the trail to let them pass, as they were the larger party, and found a level place on a bit of rock. At the sight of so many animals the mules stood with their heads up, and we sat stiff in our saddles. It was like being in a reviewing stand. As each man rounded the turn, he solemnly took off his hat, and we as solemnly acknowledged the salute. By the time the eighth man had passed, we began to feel like a twin Queen Victoria. Ten men in all, two boys, and a dog, and not one smile among them.

Our last stop was at Mosquito Camp. We hoped that Pet could make it on the downgrade, but we were not sure, and Steve and Annie were both in bad shape themselves. We left them the mules, and both Mabel and I raced down the mountain and perched on rocks and stumps to get our first view of the Klamath. The air grew warm and with every mile the heat increased. At length, far below us, we caught a gleam of silver. Steve snatched off his hat and waved to it, and we raced ahead to the next bend, where we could see our own mountains and the full length of the river, quiet in the summer drought.

All the Alberses came to the river bank with us to put us across. But at I-ees-i-rum a heavy blow awaited us. After all the care and love we had given to our sweet peas, a cow had forced the gate, and every single plant had been eaten to the ground.

But the White Puppy situation was most pleasantly settled. We went down to see Luther and told him how badly we felt at what we had done. Luther was more than friendly. They had too many dogs now. Glad if we would keep White Puppy. Don't give it another thought.

So White Puppy is formally installed as a member of the family. Not that he hasn't been a member of the family ever since the day he joined us on our way up river. But it is a comfort to have everyone know it. That is, everyone but White Puppy. There has never been any doubt in his mind.

On the trip across Marble Mountain, the Indians fed him. But that made no difference to White Puppy. Not by so much as a wag of the tail did he recognize George or Steve or Annie. White Puppy is our dog, and with everyone else he maintains his dignity.

With a recognized position in the world, White Puppy assumes an air of considerable importance. He accompanies us everywhere and insists on sleeping where we do. That is all very well for us and for White Puppy, but it does not fit in with Mrs. Richards' scheme of things. When we go to the ranch house in Orleans, White Puppy goes to the barn and howls all night long. It is a very trying situation, and no one understands why we do not do something about it. But those who know White Puppy understand perfectly well why we do not do something about it. White Puppy has his own ideas and he carries them out.

On our last trip to Hoopa, we expected to be gone several days, so we decided to leave White Puppy at the Hickoxes'. As we stood outside the door, talking to the Hickox family, Clarence, who is an old friend of White Puppy's, got a stout rope and tied him up. We rode on down to Orleans and Mrs. Richards and ourselves slept in peace. Four days later, when we came back, there in the very center of the main trail lay White Puppy. He had got loose the day after we left, trotted up to the main trail, and settled down to wait for us. Clarence tried to tempt him back to the house with food, but he would not budge. After twenty-four hours, they took some food and water up to him, but for three days and three nights White Puppy lay on the main trail, waiting for us to come back.

White Puppy wins. When we go to the ranch house, White Puppy goes with us. We are sorry for Mrs. Richards. We are sorry for anyone who finds his ideas at variance with those of White Puppy. But from now on, where we go, White Puppy goes with us.

CHAPTER XXII

The Great Deerskin Dance

At the Hildings', when we stopped over on our way down river, we heard important news. There is a strong probability that Siskiyou County will go dry. Think of it! Siskiyou, a dry county.

"I'm not going to vote," said Mr. Hilding. "I ain't going to vote even if they pay me five dollars and all my expenses. The way things are now, there just ain't no chance for a packer in this country. The men get drunk and spoil your mules. If they get 'em out alive, coming over Marble Mountain in the fall, you're a lucky man. It costs too much money, the sort of men you get."

We grinned and said, "Why don't you vote for a dry county, Mr. Hilding?"

"Well," said Mr. Hilding seriously, "you know I would if I could. That's why I won't vote at all. But it wouldn't look right, me having been in the business." (We thought of the stories of Hilding and his saloon at Orleans, before Mr. Richards had run him out of town. And how Hilding had boasted that no man left his saloon until he had spent his last cent.) "The boys wouldn't understand it, if I voted dry," went on Mr. Hilding, "so I'll just stay home and not vote at all. But I hope they'll make it. Good for everyone on the Rivers, if we was to have a dry county."

At Happy Camp, Mr. Lindsay had sat on his counter and gravely discussed the question.

"Of course," said Mr. Lindsay, "in that saloon of mine,

I'd never sell a drop of whiskey to an Indian, or to a half-breed either, for that matter."

We applauded what seemed to us a highly proper attitude, and went on to a discussion of the character of Indians, in general.

"You find them pretty honest, don't you, Mr. Lindsay?" we asked."

"Yes," said Mr. Lindsay, "you bet they are. Now if I give an Indian a glass of brandy and warn him he mustn't tell, he'll never breathe a word to anyone. But just let me give a glass to a half-breed and he'll talk about it to the first man he meets."

But among the Indians the talk all up and down river was not of a dry county but of the great deerskin dance at Orleans. The deerskin dance is always held at Orleans. And it is "big time." You may hold a brush dance at Kot-e-meen or at Witchpec, for it is only a local affair. But the deerskin dance is different; Karok or Urok, everyone comes to the deerskin dance. Jennie, who helps Mrs. Richards with the cooking at the ranch house, must go back to Sandy Bar to help with the preparations. So must Kate, from I-ees-i-rum, because her daughter has married a Sandy Bar.

"Kate, he go down river," Steve had told us. "Big cooking at Sandy Bar. All day long Solinda (Kate's daughter), he cook, cook, cook. Kate, he help Solinda. Big cooking. Everybody come to deerskin dance."

The last time we had come up river, Mr. Gent, at the company store, had given us a hundred dollars to take to Mr. Lord, who has taken up a prospect at Hayward's Bar. Mr. Lord is back again on the Rivers. Everyone says that once you drink the waters of the Salmon you will always return to the Rivers.

Mr. Lord had come out tired and worried in response to our call. When he found we had brought him the money, he gave a sigh of relief. As he stood there with his hand on Mr. Darcy, he thanked us again and again. He had sent someone down for the money, but he had come away without it. And here it was Saturday, and all his men to pay, and no money.

"You know," said Mr. Lord, "Indians are always dissatisfied if you don't pay them their money."

We did indeed know it.

"But I can't go to the deerskin dance," said Mr. Lord. "Not the way I am fixed here. I'd like to go but I just can't make it."

We had been looking forward to the deerskin dance for some time, but from what we hear now we may be a good deal deeper into it than we care about being.

The last deerskin dance was held two years ago. From what they tell us, it was a bloody affair. There was shooting and knifing, and Steve nearly got killed. It seems that the drinking had been going on steadily all day, Toward evening, Steve ran into three very drunken Indians from Witchpec, one of whom was Johnny Allen. They stopped Steve, and Johnny Allen struck him in the face. Steve knifed Johnny and ran. It was three to one, but fortunately the three were much drunker than Steve, so he made the best speed. He raced for his own up-river crowd, but when he got to his own campfire there was no one there but Annie. Steve dropped panting on the ground, and Annie flung her skirt over him. It was nearly dark and there was only a small campfire. It flickered and made it difficult to see. Johnny Allen had been pretty much knocked out by the knifing, but the two other men had run into some more Witchpec Indians, and they all stormed into the camp and demanded Steve.

"Gone," said Annie.

"Where?" said the Witchpec Indians.

"Karok," said Annie. The Witchpec Indians swerved and raced up the trail. That night the Karok crowd did get Steve, up river. The talk is now that Johnny Allen is out to get Steve, and everyone is warning Steve to keep away from the deerskin dance.

Mr. Babel is justice of the peace at Orleans, so keeping

order would be his responsibility. That would give us a chance to see the dance with our only personal responsibility that of keeping an eye on Johnny Allen and Steve. We rode down to Orleans in high spirits. Mr. Hale is down below, so we found Mrs. Richards alone.

"Mr. Babel is down at the store, isn't he?" we asked.

"No," said Mrs. Richards placidly. "Mr. Babel was called down to Eureka this morning. Mr. Gent has sent word that he couldn't be at the dance, so maybe you better look out for things."

We felt queer all through our insides. We drifted down to the store and listened to the talk.

"Willy Salstrom is going to make things lively," everyone was saying. "They say Willy and his gang are going to shoot up the crowd."

The Indians had been worried when we came in. Drinking had been going on all day. If Willy Salstrom did shoot up the deerskin dance, it would be bad for everybody. Nobody knew just what might happen.

We went back to the ranch house. Dusk was just falling. Everywhere were little groups of Indians. The crowd was beginning to come in. Drinking was going on at the Brizzard store. We could hear shouts and loud laughter. We wondered about Willy Salstrom. If he really planned to charge in with a drunken crowd and wreck things, what chance was there that we could do anything to prevent it?

It was dark when we picked our way down to the river. We had to cross a wide flat where there was no trail, and it seemed odd to be on our own two feet. As we stumbled over stones and roots, we passed little groups of whispering Indians. In the dark, it was hard to tell who might be friends. At the river's edge we stopped and waited. A dugout was ferrying people across. It slipped away from the bank, filled to the water line, as we came up, and we waited for it to come back. Then we saw another dugout with only four or five men in it, and we shoved through the crowd and stepped in. A torch flared near us and one of the men turned. We could see his face quite distinctly. It was Willy Salstrom. We had got into the boat with Willy Salstrom and his gang.

"Hallo, Mr. Salstrom," we said, and we both sat down beside him.

During the crossing, we joked in as easy a manner as we could muster. Once, we were not sure, but once, we thought we heard Willy Salstrom giggle. We prayed to the Lord that what we had heard was a giggle. Long experience on the Rivers has taught us that it is hard to giggle and then go and shoot up somebody.

On the farther bank we could see Indians in ceremonial dress. As the torches flared, we could see that the men were naked to the waist. They had skins wrapped around them, and beautiful bead belts, and strings of Indian money, and either feathered headdresses or headdresses with claws. Then we saw the flash of white deerskins in the torchlight. The deerskins are carried on poles, and they have wonderful beadwork tongues that flap in and out.

The crowd swayed so that we could see the river. A dugout was being pushed off from the bank. Dancers clambered over the sides and stood erect while endmen paddled slowly upstream. We could see the waving white deerskins and the beautiful feathered headdresses as the Indians danced and gestured in the flickering light. Then the singing commenced. Slowly the boat passed us and the paddles rose and fell. The dancing and singing grew more intense.

The paddles were suddenly still, and a medicine man came down the bank. He also was in full ceremonial dress. For a moment, he stood erect, then he plunged into the water, directly in front of the chanting, dancing men in the boat. He came up dripping, climbed back onto the bank, and disappeared in the crowd. The dancing recommenced and the chanting grew louder as the boat again moved slowly upstream. There was now a great crowd on the bank. We surged along, keeping abreast of the boat, and stumbling over rocks and boulders. Torches flared. The chanting and dancing went on. Then the dugout slowly turned and came back. The first event was over.

We tried to see whether there were some of our friends in the crowd, but it was difficult to recognize anyone in the darkness. A dark shape came up and joined us.

"Hallo," said Irish Evans, from up river. He was a little drunk and walked unsteadily. "The Sandy Bars say you better stay around. You know, everyone of those white deerskins is worth over a hundred dollars. There's a lot of money in the stuff they're wearing here tonight, and the Sandy Bars say they don't want no trouble."

While he spoke we saw the men forming for the deerskin dance. It was like the brush dance we had seen the year before at Kot-e-meen. The two chief dancers crouched and danced, crossing back and forth between long rows of dancing Indians who waved white deerskins and kept time to the chanting with the movements of their bodies. This was different from the brush dance at Kot-e-meen. The naked, gleaming bodies, the gorgeous headdresses, the waving white deerskins, with their bright beadwork tongues, and the deep guttural chant made our breath come quick. There was an excitement in it that we had never felt before. Some of the dancing Indians carried flints, and others fisher skins. We could see them intermittently in the flickering light of the torches. The chanting grew louder. We lost all sense of time.

"Pretty good dance," said someone beside us. It was George McCash. He was naked to the waist and had on a beautiful headdress of claws.

"Who's down from up river?" we asked.

"Dunno," said George, "but they'll all be here tomorrow."

In the long pauses between the dances, we drifted around and joked with different groups of Indians. There was a good deal of drinking, but, on the whole, not as much as we had expected. Whenever we heard raised voices, we joined that group and kidded all the leading spirits in the crowd. As soon as things had quieted down, we slipped away and joined another little knot of Indians.

"Pretty good dance," everyone said.

"Yes," we would reply. "Pretty good dance."

The night wore on. We began to breathe more freely. There was no sign of Willy and his gang. We did not dare to count too much on that giggle, but we prayed hard. As hour after hour went by and nothing happened, we began to get painfully sleepy. The activity in most of the groups seemed to have simmered down to only moderate shouts and laughter.

"What do you think?" said Mabel.

We went from group to group, making ourselves as conspicuous as possible. Then, very quietly, we slipped away. Bed at the Richardses' had never been more welcome. We slept like logs, and were back on the other side of Camp Creek soon after daylight the next morning.

The Sandy Bars were openly reproachful.

"But nothing happened," we said.

No, said the Sandy Bars, nothing had happened. No, Willy Salstrom didn't shoot up nobody. No, nobody got knifed. They didn't know we had gone, for a long time. Not till pretty near morning. But suppose there had been a trouble? All the deerskins and everything from Sandy Bar. It would have been bad for everybody.

All the next day the drinking went on. We sat under a little bush, where everybody could see us. We didn't see what we could do if things got really bad and something happened, but if the Sandy Bars wanted us, there we were. Whenever the drinking got pretty noisy on some part of the flat, we went over and joined that group. We would stand there for a while, kidding the crowd, and then we would go back and sit once more under our bush.

In the afternoon, everybody began to move around, and then slowly they left the flat. The final dance was to be higher up Camp Creek. We followed the crowd. All the up-river Indians were coming in. We saw Mart, very drunk.

He kept his feet while we were talking to him, but he slipped away as soon as he could. We exchanged some talk with the Hickoxes. Luther was almost sober. Then we turned and found Kate standing beside us.

"Steve, he come down river," said Kate, her face troubled. "Annie say, tell you Steve, he come down river." Then she was lost in the crowd.

At upper Camp Creek, the crowd of Indians was the largest we had seen anywhere on the Rivers. Everyone we knew was there, but we also passed group after group of strange faces. Every hour or so dances were going on, but the big dance of that day was not to come off until nearly dark. Excitement was in the air. Everywhere, little knots of Indians crowded together, whispering. The drinking was heavy. We stood talking to some of the Sandy Bars as they got the ground ready for the dance.

"Old Indians feel very bad," said the Sandy Bars. "Old Indian Bob, he feel very bad. Say all young Indians, they don't care. They get drunk and they laugh. They don't care. Very bad for Indians when they don't care for Pic-i-ow-ish."

Herman joined us. "Everybody's here," said Herman. "They say there ain't an Indian from Happy Camp to Witchpec who ain't here or on the trail."

Sandy Bar Tom motioned us to a place where the crowd was thickest. The dancers were already in their places. We saw Dumphrey Pepper, and then we saw Steve. Both were in ceremonial dress, naked to the waist, and with gorgeous headdresses. Each man carried a large flint.

"Where is Johnny Allen?" we asked.

Sandy Bar Tom motioned again. The front row of spectators was already seated on the ground. Behind them stood crowds of onlookers, most of them Indians. Seated in the front row, just at the end where Steve must dance and turn, we saw Johnny Allen. Mabel and I squeezed down beside him. It was an old technique, but we had tried it before and it had worked. Fortunately we were closely packed in. You could feel any unexpected movement in that jam. Johnny did not look at us, but I was sure he knew we were there. Johnny's right arm was pressed tight against my side. I jammed myself as close to it as I could. If Johnny moved that arm, I would know it.

Suddenly the dancers moved into place and the chanting began. There were two long rows of moving deerskins, and between these long rows of dancing, chanting Indians, Steve and Dumphrey, crouching low, began to weave to and fro, flints grasped in their outstretched hands. They circled and passed each other in perfect rhythm. Crouching and dancing, they would pass each other, each man continuing his dance until he reached the end of the row. Then he would turn and dance back again. As Steve reached our end of the row of dancers, he passed so close to Johnny Allen and myself that I could have leaned out and touched him with my hand. I heard Johnny Allen draw a long breath, and I felt his arm tense. Then Steve was dancing away, down to the other end of the line. I began to breathe again.

"Hi-yah. Hi-yah," sang the dancers. The white deerskins waved and the little beaded tongues flickered.

Steve had turned and was coming back. He is one of the most beautiful dancers we have ever seen. Dumphrey was more lithe and there was more grace in his movements, but Steve had a power and a dramatic quality that we have never seen in any one else. He came close, passed us, and turned. He was moving back down the line. Again we drew a long breath. The dance went on. Every time Steve passed us and turned, Johnny Allen's arm grew tense. The dance went on for a long time. Whether Johnny Allen was waiting for a suitable moment to strike, or whether he never really intended to strike, we did not know.

Then suddenly the dance was over, and the Indians were moving away.

We hunted up Steve.

"Steve," we said, "they have just brought us bad news. Old man Frame is dead. They want us to go to Somes. But we cannot go while you are here down river. You come here. You dance. You dance better than anyone on the Rivers. But now the dance is over. Will you go back up river? Now, this minute? So we can go to Somes? We cannot go while you are here."

Steve stood for a long time looking thoughtfully at the place where Johnny Allen had been. We stood watching him.

"All right," said Steve at length. "Maybe I go."

We did not move until we saw him join some of the up-river Indians and take the trail for I-ees-i-rum.

Already the crowd was thinning. Some boys staged a small dance but they received no attention. Little groups of Indians began to move away. We heard shouts and loud laughter. It was probable that the drinking would go on all night and for several days more, but the Indians from Witchpec and up river were leaving. We caught a glimpse of the Sandy Bars. They were rolling up white deerskins and carefully putting them away. The great deerskin dance was over. A new year was ahead of us. The world was made.

As we rode back to the ranch house, the smell of smoke lay heavy in the air. Forest fires were all around us. Mr. Hunter and all the foresters, with all the men they could collect, were up on the mountain, putting up a desperate fight of it, and Dave McLaughlin stopped to tell us that fire had broken out on the trail just below Orleans and that twenty men had gone out to fight it.

Early the next morning, we crossed the Klamath for Somesbar. Storm was gathering fast as we rode down to the river. We have never made the Orleans crossing, which is thought to be one of the worst on the Rivers, and we rather hoped that someone would come along who knew the sandbar, so that we could follow him across. We waited and hoped but no one came.

"Oh, come on," said Mabel crossly. "After two years on the Rivers we certainly ought to be able to make a Klamath fording."

The mules took off much more easily than we had hoped.

Maria was in the lead. We were halfway across and were beginning to get some confidence in ourselves when we found that the water was very deep. Some Indian women came out on a cliff on the opposite bank and waved us back. We sheered to the right. That was better. The water fell so that it was no higher than the knees of the mules. Again we began to edge toward the opposite shore. Again the Indians waved us back. But now we could see the ripple quite clearly, and began to follow it. Slowly the bank came nearer. We were across.

"Darn it," said Mabel, "I wish we weren't so dumb about river crossings. Somehow, I just can't seem to like them."

Mama Frame wept when she saw us.

"You never mind me," she said through her tears. "I feel real good now. You go see Margy. Seems as if she took Papa's death real hard, poor girl."

But in spite of what she said, she clung to us.

"Papa was good to me," she kept saying. "Papa was good to me. He used to warm my feet when I cried with the cold. And I was mean to him. Seems as if I couldn't bear him crowding me all the time in bed. But he was just trying to get warm, poor papa. You girls will stay, won't you? Sam, he thought maybe he could send for a real preacher. If the weather was so he could wait. But it's real warm for this time of year. Papa's got to be put away soon. So we thought maybe you girls would read the Good Book. Sam's sent everywhere by the mailriders, and we figure Papa will hold until Sunday. That will give everybody up river a chance to get here. It isn't as though we were fixed to do right by Papa. But I guess he'd understand."

Margy was taking it very hard. Her face was bloated from crying, and she was still gasping and sobbing hysterically.

"She ain't eat nothing and she don't do nothing but cry all the time," said Carrie admiringly.

We went over to the store to see whether Sam had some

aromatic spirits of ammonia. Sam hadn't any and didn't think it was important.

"I want you to help me lay out Papa," he said.

Mabel followed him into the darkened room where the old man lay in a decent suit of black clothes. Sam was not satisfied with the position of Papa's head. He said it wasn't straight. Mabel and Sam combed out the old man's luxuriant white hair and his white beard and whiskers. Then a half-breed came in and helped carry Papa Frame into the dining room. All the tables had been cleared away, and they put the coffin on saw horses in the middle of the room. Sam stood a minute caressing the silver handles with his hand.

"If we had time," he said, "I think they might take a little more polish."

In the afternoon we cleaned the house, and Carrie brought in flowers and we made a cross for the coffin. Rain had been threatening all morning and by the afternoon it was coming down fast. Jim Tom stopped to tell us that the river was beginning to rise. If the river rose, we wondered how all the people who planned to come could get across.

Mama Frame wouldn't eat the tea and bread that we took up to her, but she wanted to talk. It was mostly about her early life and about Papa Frame.

He was always moving somewhere else, Papa Frame was. Always somewhere it was worse and harder to get along. Why, once they had been on the coast, and Papa Frame had owned the site of San Diego. But it just seemed that Papa had to move. It was awful hard with little children. Once they had put all they had in a wagon and started across the desert. Papa was driving the team, and he had been up all night, and he got so tired he fell asleep. First thing he knew he'd fell out and the wagon run over him. When Mama Frame got the team stopped and got back to where Papa was, he was sitting up.

"Must have broke my leg," he said. "Here, you help me get in that wagon. Got to make that water hole before we stop."

"I kep' the team going," said Mama Frame, "and Papa was in the back of the wagon. He grunted some but he set his leg and bandaged it with pieces of cloth I'd tore for him.

"I never had no comfort or rest," Mama Frame went on, "until Sam got old enough to take hold. Sam wasn't no more'n a kid when he stood right up to Papa and wouldn't let him move. He could swing a pick with grown men when he wasn't no more'n eleven. After he'd stood up to Papa, Sam, he run the family and he took care of Papa and me."

Mama Frame grew quieter after she had talked, and pretty soon she went to sleep.

The next morning, the rain fell in a steady downpour. Margy was still bad, and while Mabel sat with her I cleaned the coffee pot. It had got to the place where the grounds reached the top of the pot and you empty them out and start over, so I started to dig in. For about two inches it was good going, and then I struck hard pan. I tried a knife. No good. I tried a screw driver. Better. I hunted through Sam's tools and found what looked like a small ice pick. Slowly the mass gave. I heaped in the coffee and set the pot to boil. Those cold, wet, old men were going to have a good cup of coffee if I could get it for them.

About the middle of the morning, Frank Offield rode by on his way to the Forks.

"This doesn't look to me like a shower," he said as he stood on the porch, pouring a little stream of water out of the brim of his hat. "Looks to me as though the rains were coming early this year. Salmon's beginning to rise."

We went inside and watched the rain beating steadily against the windows of the little parlor. In the field across from the hotel, three men were starting to dig the grave. While they worked we heard the sound of horses' feet, as the white men on the Rivers gathered to pay their respects to old Papa Frame.

Mama Frame watched them from behind a lowered shade.

"There's Nelson," she murmured, "down from Mac-i-a-rum. And there's old Andy Merrill. There's Hilding and Dutch Henry coming across the bridge. Papa, he'd be real pleased to know they all come. Papa was white and they are white. He'd be pleased to know they come to see him buried."

We handed around cups of steaming coffee while we waited for the Orleans contingent to arrive.

"You folks are real handy at funerals," said old man Grant as he laid his cup down. "Guess the folks here hope you'll stay around."

Just then Sam came in.

"Hunter's here," he said, "but Babel can't get across the river at Orleans. River's too high for him to get across. You folks all ready? I guess everyone else has got here. We better get started."

We all filed into the dining room where the coffin stood, and the men took off their hats. Only white men had come to see Papa Frame put away. But all the white men except those from Orleans were there. Ross and Fernau and Russell stood just across from me, and Old Bob Elliott, all the way from Siwillup, stood by my side. I didn't have any prayer book but I read the psalms for the burial service from the great old Bible that Mama Frame brought me, and did my best with the prayers and a few words about what a good man Papa Frame had been.

Then I stood back and looked at Mabel. Mama Frame had asked for "Rock of Ages" and "In the Sweet Bye and Bye." They went pretty well, with the old white men joining in, and then Mabel hesitated when she should have started in on the second verse. I looked at her to see what was wrong and caught her eyes. Under the coffin sat White Puppy, scratching for fleas. He scratched long and thoroughly with every eye on him. "In the Sweet By and Bye" petered out and came to an end.

We then ignored White Puppy and stood in respectful silence while Sam screwed on the lid of the coffin, and

Margy shrieked and laid hold of one of the handles to keep the men from taking it away.

The old white men listened to her in silence as they had listened to the prayers and the hymns. It came home to me that each man was thinking that old man Frame was having a better funeral, with his weeping family around him, then any one of them might have, and that they thought him a fortunate man.

There was no time for prayers as the coffin was lowered into the muddy grave. The rain came sullenly down. The men stood with uncovered heads. As we turned and came back to the hotel, we heard the earth thud on the lid of the coffin as Sam and a helper hurriedly shoveled it in.

Mr. Lord stopped to have a word with us before he rode away.

"Now there's a man," said Mr. Lord, "who has made a good end. Here, nice and comfortable, with his family around him. Many a poor devil would be glad of an end like that."

We felt comforted. Maybe Mr. Lord was right.

CHAPTER XXIII

Farewell to the Klamath

Steve is making medicine for us. We have three solid weeks of riding ahead, and this afternoon Steve came in to say that for two days he has been making medicine, and he thinks the mists are going down river. This isn't the Grasshopper Song, Steve told us. The Grasshopper Song is a good song, but he thinks this is even more potent.

"The first time Indian god, he come down river," Steve said, "he stop here just below I-ees-i-rum. On his arm, he got rain sacks. He took sacks off his arm and open them so. All the mists, they come up river and the clouds, they get thick, and pretty soon it rain, rain, rain. It rain and it rain. Then the Indian god, he feel bad and he say, 'Anybody, he know my song, rain he stop.' "

And according to Steve, if the song of the Indian god doesn't stop the rain, nothing else will.

It had begun to rain the day that old man Frame had been buried at Somesbar.

The next morning as we saddled our mules for the up-river trail, the peaceful Salmon of the day before had become a roaring flood. Not a rock or a sandbar in sight.

"You'll never get those mules across the Klamath," said Dave McLaughlin as we came out onto the porch. "Lucky if you get over yourselves."

Well, maybe we couldn't get the mules across the Klamath, but after the days at Somes, with poor Mama Frame and Margy and Sam, we couldn't keep our spirits from rising when we found ourselves again on horseback, and the trail ahead. We made the Youngs' just before noon. As we drew in we could hear the sound of the anvil, and we rode over to a little building where we could see the light from a forge. In reply to our call, a man in soiled shirt and pants came to the door, his face and hands grimed with dirt.

"What are our chances of getting across the river?" we asked.

"I'm afraid your chances are not good," replied the blacksmith in the soft, modulated voice with the faint English accent that only Oxford can give. "But we should be glad to keep you, if you will stay overnight."

It was Mr. Young, son of a family whose name he never mentions, who is married to a half-breed. And never to see England again, if all is true that they tell us on the Rivers.

With no chance of crossing the Klamath at Orleans, we rode to Sandy Bar. Mr. Young walked a short distance with us to show us the trail. Standing on the bluff above the roaring, tumbling Klamath, Mabel put her hand to her mouth, and called. She has all but mastered the sweet. clear call of the Indians. Then we waited. After a long time, Sandy Bar Jim came out of his house and scrambled down the bank to the river. Sandy Bar Tom joined him, and we saw them launch the dugout. When we scrambled down to the bar, we found the dugout across and three Sandy Bars waiting for us. Friends mean something in this country.

"Will you swim the mules for us, Jim?" we asked. "Pay you three dollars to swim them."

"Maybe everybody, he drown," said Jim pleasantly.

"Our risk, if you are willing," we said, and began to unsaddle.

For once, Maria and Mr. Darcy gave us no trouble. Their heads rose high above the icy river, and they swam with easy powerful strokes. It was an ugly crossing, but there are no better men on the Rivers than the Sandy Bars. It took all the three Indians had in them, but in a shorter time than we had expected we made the other side.

We wished we could have told the Sandy Bars how we felt, and what it meant to us that they had risked their lives to put us across. But you can't, with Indians. Whatever the danger, and no matter how fine you may think your Indian friends have been, you may only jest at a bad crossing. So we paid Sandy Bar Jim the money and rode up the trail. But it is not for money but for his friends that a man on the Rivers will risk that flooded Klamath.

With the river behind us, we rode in high spirits to Ossi-puk. We ate with relish and went to bed early. But not to sleep. No, not to sleep. In the night I was roused by a strange noise.

"Maybe a ring-tailed cat," said Mabel, and threw a boot at it.

I lit a candle. In the corner of our room, looking straight at us, was a skunk.

"Do you think he may be annoyed?" said Mabel. "I mean, by my boot?" We lay shivering at the possibilities. It is very difficult to go quietly to sleep with a skunk in your bedroom. We had grown accustomed, at Ossi-puk, to eight or ten little hogs under the kitchen stove and a snake in our coffee pot when we got up in the morning to make coffee. But skunks were different. He didn't seem to be there in the morning, so we crawled quietly out of bed and opened all the doors.

"Darn it," said Mabel, "he's right there behind my kitchen stove."

I-ees-i-rum was fifteen miles away. It was raining, a cold drenching rain. I thought lovingly of a cup of coffee.

"Don't you think," I ventured, "that if you were very quiet you might put on the coffee pot?"

"You want me to light that fire," said Mabel, "and make coffee within three feet of a skunk?"

I said nothing.

"Well," said Mabel, "if he moves, for God's sake, tell me at once."

It was not a restful breakfast. We left all the doors

open, and a note imploring Luther to be careful, and to
shut the doors if the skunk should decide to leave. And
then we rode up river.

As the time for our departure from the Rivers comes
closer, we feel that we cannot bear to leave these people.
It is not only that we have grown to care so much for
them, but the way they clutch at a chance to learn wrings
our hearts. The Orleans school appears to be wildly popular.
It is in an old bunkhouse in a deserted part of the mine.
Once a week we have a marvelous dinner at the ranch
with Mrs. Richards, and then ride down to the bunkhouse
and find school waiting for us. At first, we had only the six
Sandy Bars and poor old Mac-i-a-rum Jim, but now the
room is full of Indians. Sandy Bar Mamie, a stout Indian
woman of nearly fifty with Hoopa-bred children, is the
leading spirit. There have been only relatively few weeks
of the Orleans school, but in that time Sandy Bar Mamie
has made incredible progress. She did not even know the
alphabet when she started, and now she is finishing the Second Reader. Each week she comes back with from fourteen
to sixteen pages studied so carefully that she hardly ever
stumbles over a word. And at one of the last school days,
Sandy Bar Jim came in very pleased with himself because
without help from anyone he was able to write quite clearly.

"I can see a robin and a bluebird in the nest." (A statement on page twelve of the primer which we feel ought to
be seriously questioned.)

The news of our going had brought out big schools at
Orleans and Ossi-puk. But at Orleans the Indians, for the
most part, were silent and not like themselves. Even Mamie
paid little attention to what she was reading. We came away
troubled. Leaving the Rivers was very difficult.

We rode in to Ossi-puk a couple of hours ahead of time,
and found both Mr. and Mrs. Nelson. Fortunately there was
time to make tea for them. It had been a long, hot trail from
their house up at Mac-i-a-rum.

Mrs. Nelson is one of the Perch girls, the sister of Mrs.

Young. Like her sister, she is a half-breed married to a white man, but old Nelson is twice her age. She is a young woman of great dignity and charm, but her face was very sad as she told us that their only child had just died of tuberculosis. That leaves only old Nelson and herself in their house in Mac-i-a-rum, and there is a feud between them and the Indians.

We told Mrs. Nelson how much we admired her sister, Mrs. Young.

Mrs. Nelson was silent a moment and then she said, "You see, she had advantages." She looked at us. "You ride every day, don't you? And you have been to San Francisco. I always hoped I might get there. You know, go places and see people. When I was a little girl and went to school, I used to study geography and go home and dream about the places. And I have lived twenty-five years in the same place."

She went on to tell us about her father, old man Perch.

"He was a politician," she said. And she went on eagerly, "I used to read all the political articles I could find. Women don't care for them, generally."

She was going on to tell us more about herself when the Indians began to arrive for school.

"I think you are busy," Mrs. Nelson said. She laid her hand on the old man's sleeve, and they went away.

But the hardest time was ahead of us. It was nearly dark when school was over and all the Indians had left. Then we looked up, and Á-su-ná-pee stood in the doorway.

She said she had been lurking in the woodshed when everyone arrived, and she couldn't get out without being seen. She would not smile at us. She sat grieving on the little stool by the fireplace. We coaxed her to eat a little, and although she is terribly afraid of the dark she sat for a long time over the fire, crying very quietly. She kept saying, "You stay here. You don't go way."

It was evident that she thought we were going away for a long visit. We did not dare to tell her we were leaving the Rivers. As she went out of the door she kept saying again and again, "You come back Thursday? You come back Thursday?"

We said we would, but Judas Iscariot could not have felt worse than we did.

The Tintins had come to the school at Ossi-puk and had brought us a present of some really old Indian beads and an Indian comb. Essie had stayed behind, when the other Indians left, to give us a very beautiful Indian necklace.

"We will see you when you come down river," they all cried as they waved good-by. "We will see you when you come down river."

Two very teary schoolmarms rode back to I-ees-i-rum.

At the flat above Hayward's Bar, we found Herman and Penonie Harry.

"I got land one hundred and thirty-seven feet on river," said Penonie Harry. "How many feet other way to make acre?"

We quit at once being teary. Without any preparation, that is just the kind of question we can't answer.

"We cannot stop now," we told Penonie Harry loftily. "Come to I-ees-i-rum tomorrow." Thank God for the little arithmetic book. With its aid and support we were ready for Penonie Harry in the morning.

Before we had left I-ees-i-rum we arranged for Mr. Petersen to come and have dinner with us. Mr. Petersen is a prospector who lives all by himself in a tiny cabin near Hayward's Bar. There is no one we have ever known who is quite like Mr. Petersen. He is very, very gentle and a little withdrawn, and when he smiles his smile is very warm and sweet. He sat for a long time on our porch, looking out over the river. But he did not seem to be seeing the river or even knowing it was there. We started the phonograph for him, but it seemed to trouble him. He flinched at the sound of the music, so we turned it off. We joked with him as we served dinner, and he smiled his gentle, withdrawn smile. When I tried to change his plate for dessert, he abstractedly held on to it.

"You must let me have this, Mr. Petersen," I said. "I want to give you some pudding and some coffee."

For a moment, Mr. Petersen looked startled, and then he smiled.

"Little lady," he said, "you forgive me. I am away from Denmark a very long time. I forget how we do things there."

After dinner we lit the fire, and after we had sat by it for a long time Mr. Petersen began to talk.

His people were well-to-do in Denmark. They had much more money than King Christian, who, Mr. Petersen said, was very poor indeed. King Christian only had a coachman and a body servant and two girls to cook. Mr. Petersen used to play with King Christian and his sisters, when they were all children together.

"My name was not Petersen in Denmark," Mr. Petersen said. "That is what they call me in this country."

When he was about seventeen, Mr. Petersen first had his dream. He dreamed he was flying slowly through the air. It puzzled him that he could move so easily through the air. He looked up, and above him was a very large kettle. It, too, was sailing through the air, and Mr. Petersen had hold of the bail, or handle. As the kettle sailed slowly through the air, it carried Mr. Petersen along with it. Mr. Petersen and the kettle were not very far above the ground.

It was a strange country over which they passed. Mr. Petersen had never seen any place like it in Denmark. It was a rugged country. There were no fields or farms. There were high mountains and gullies and ravines. A great river raced down through a gorge in the mountains. There were beautiful, clear tumbling brooks. Nowhere were there any houses or any sign of life. The trees were immensely tall. Part of the trunk of some of the trees was a bright orange where the bark had peeled off, and the leaves on the top of some of the bushes were a bright red, which made them look like flowers. The kettle went so slowly that Mr. Petersen could study the character of the country and the trees and shrubs as he drifted over them.

As the kettle slowly drifted along, they left the valleys and the creeks and rivers and went high up into the mountains. The kettle was moving more slowly now, and as they neared the top of a mountain it stopped, and Mr. Petersen dropped to the ground. Directly before him was a sort of hole, or tunnel, in the side of the mountain. He hesitated a minute, and then he stepped into the hole. He was in what seemed to be a tunnel. He could not stand upright, but he was able to follow the tunnel deep into the side of the mountain. He noticed that the tunnel had supports, so that the roof would not cave in.

The tunnel ended in what seemed to be a small room. It was dark, but Mr. Petersen lit a match. In one corner of the little cavelike room was the skeleton of a man. By his side was a large pan and a little pick. There was nothing else in the room but a pile of dirt in another corner. Mr. Petersen went over to the pile of dirt and picked some of it up in his hand. The dirt fell away, and Mr. Petersen saw that what he held in his hand were some pieces of shining gold.

Mr. Petersen was nearly twenty-three when the dream came again. After that second time, it came frequently, again and again. It came so often that Mr. Petersen became restless, and when an opportunity presented itself he came to America. For a time he lived in New York. He was not unsuccessful, and for a while he forgot about the dream. Then it came again. When it began to come frequently, Mr. Petersen left New York and went west. He settled in Kansas and bought a farm and became well-to-do. Once in a long time he would have the dream, but it did not trouble him much. He did well. He had a good house and great barns and stock of all kinds. Then came the tornado. Mr. Petersen was driving his team from the nearest town, about ten miles away, when a great wind tore down upon him. He was thrown from his wagon, and he saw his team dashed against a windbreak and killed. His house and his barns were swept away. When he took stock of the damage, Mr. Petersen had lost all he possessed.

He worked his way farther west. From time to time, he again began to have the dream, until it came regularly every night. He could not forget it. He did not remember very well what happened to him in the daytime. He only waited for the night, when he could go to sleep and live in his dream.

He went still farther west. One day, when he was working on a ranch, he was sent up into the mountains to cut wood for the winter. There he saw something he had seen before.

"What is the name of that tree where the bark has peeled off and the trunk is orange?" he asked the man who was with him.

"That is a madroña tree," the man replied. "There are a great many of them here in the mountains."

Mr. Petersen left his job and went west and north. With every mile, the country grew more familiar. There were the mountains and the gullies and the ravines. There were the tall trees and the madroña and the manzanita bushes, with their red tops that looked like flowers. And then he came to a great, swift-flowing river.

"I knew that river," said Mr. Petersen. "Each night I had seen it in my dream."

The river was the Klamath.

"There is no more to tell," said Mr. Petersen. "I live here and every day I go up into the mountains. I know all this country. In my dream I have seen it many, many times. Some day I shall find the quartz mine that I have seen in my dreams. I think I am very close to it. Every day I see signs that tell me I am very near. I am sixty-five now, but I do not think I have much longer to wait."

He smiled a little wistfully.

"Little ladies," he said, "you are very kind. I did not mean to trouble you with my story. I must go now. You are very kind."

I think one of the things that troubled us most, the day we left the Rivers, was that we were never to see or hear from Mr. Petersen again.

It was our last night at I-ees-i-rum before taking the trail for Happy Camp. Then, with our trunk repacked and safely on its way east, we would turn back again for a trail ride of a hundred miles to Witchpec, cross the Klamath for the last time, stop for an official report at Hoopa, and, with Eureka and the ocean ahead of us, say our last good-by to the Rivers.

Steve and Annie came over in the evening. Steve had never referred to our going away and had carried himself with his usual studied indifference. He had joked and laughed and made no mention of the fact that we were leaving the Rivers. Today, he came in with his accustomed swagger and took down his drum.

"Sing *I-to poo-a-rum, if caro yarmuch* (I'm going away. Ain't that nice), said Annie. It has always been a joke between us, that particular song. Annie sings it whenever we go down river, even for a couple of days, and then looks archly at us and wipes her eyes. But Steve did not look up and laugh as he has always done before. He sat silent for a very long time. He was holding his drum so that we could not see his face.

"*Tani vee, i-to poo-a-rum* (I do not like *i-to poo-a-rum*) said Steve harshly. He drummed loudly for a few minutes. Then he took up his drum and went away.

We did not sleep much that night. Of course, we are hoping that we can come back to the Rivers if, by any wild chance, the Indian Department should approve our plan of a much broader method of meeting the needs of the Indian on the Klamath. But this is quite uncertain. In all the excitement of meeting our people in San Francisco, and going home, we have put out of our minds the fact that we are actually leaving the Rivers. But when we come to face it, we do not see how we can leave Steve and Annie. We just don't see how we can leave them.

The next morning, Steve came in with the rest of the rancheria.

"I want to write a letter," said Steve, "to my cousin in Scott's Valley."

The letter began with some formal expressions, and then Steve dropped his eyes.

"I ain't got no folks now but you," Steve dictated. "My boy, he die and my girl, he die. I don't want to live no more when my boy, he die. Then the schoolmarms come and my heart is good. Now they go away and I don't know what I do."

We were thankful when we were on the trail for Happy Camp. We rode hard but it did no good. We have left other friends behind but we have never felt like this. The way we feel now, it won't be a wholly bad thing if we get drowned in Salstrom Creek and never get out at all.

But before we saddled for Happy Camp, the last blow was still in store for us. Up to the very last we had hoped to take White Puppy out with us. But when we faced it we knew it would not work. White Puppy would never be happy off the trail. White Puppy is our dog. Since the day he followed us up river, White Puppy has never acknowledged the presence of anyone but ourselves. The Indians come and go with never a sign from White Puppy. It is the same with the white men who come to the house. White Puppy treats them as though they were not there.

We hardly dared to look White Puppy in the face after we decided that we must leave him. But when the date of our leaving was actually settled, a change came over White Puppy. When a strange white man came into the room, White Puppy would go and stand beside him. He would not wag his tail, but he gravely considered every man he saw. White Puppy was making up his mind. When we finally decided to give him to Mr. Wright, the mailrider, because

White Puppy so loves to be on the trail, White Puppy made no protest. Mr. Wright put a rope around his neck and led him away. White Puppy gave only one faint little whine and held back a minute. Then he went.

But we mounted the mules in a daze, and though we turned their heads up river we had no knowledge of how or where we went.

CHAPTER XXIV

I-to Poo-a-rum

We made the Elliotts' on the first lap of our trip to Happy Camp with no more than lowering storm clouds.

We no longer question the delay of breakfast at the Elliotts'. Some weeks ago, Eliza and Mrs. Elliott spent the night with us at I-ees-i-rum. They sat on our porch in the gathering darkness, and Mrs. Elliott sang to us in hardly more than a whisper, but her singing is about the most beautiful we have heard on the Rivers.

"This song is when you wake up and see the morning star," Eliza told us.

Well, if that was the song that Mrs. Elliott was singing, no wonder the rest of us had to wait hungrily for our coffee.

"And that one is about the evening star," went on Eliza. "And that one Mother is singing now is about a place just above Happy Camp, you know, that big flat. The song is about the time just after sunset when you see the shadow of the mountain fall across the trail.

"That last one that mother sung is about one of the Sacramento Indians. She came here with her husband, and then he went away and left her, and she says in the song, 'I wonder where he puts his shoes on now.'" (Dressing for breakfast in this country is not too elaborate. For a man, it consists mostly in putting on his shoes.)

But the song we thought most beautiful was the one about O-we, our own mountain. "In the old days," said Eliza, "the Indians say the small peak was a woman, and the big peak, he went and left her and went up river. And she felt so bad she made a song and the song said, 'Oh, my lover, when will you ever speak to me again?' And she cried, and so she made the three furrows down the mountain. And when he heard the song and saw the furrows, he felt bad. And so he turned around and came back to the Rivers. And that is why there are the two peaks just like you see them today."

It was just as we were pulling into Happy Camp that the storm broke, and all day Thursday, as we packed and shifted our things in Mr. Pine's warehouse, the rain came steadily down.

We found ourselves a bit concerned as we unpacked the skirts (seven yards around the bottom) that had been laid away so carefully in our trunk, two years ago in Korbel. May the Lord have mercy on our souls when we appear in them in San Francisco, if the present mode, as presented in the last issue of the *Ladies' Home Journal,* is to be relied on.

But the matter of clothes was not our only problem When we saddled, Friday morning, it had turned warm, and the rain was falling in sheets.

"You won't try to make the Elliotts' in this storm, will you?" asked Mr. Pine. "Why not wait until tomorrow?"

As we had come up river, two days before, on our way to Happy Camp, we had stopped as we always do on the bridge over Clear Creek. The Creek is deep, maybe ten or twelve feet, but it is so clear and green that you can see straight down to every pebble on the sandy bottom. On either side of the Creek are soft, green banks, widening out into green fields, and towering above the green fields are the mountains. We love Clear Creek, and in spite of the need to make Happy Camp before nightfall we had stood for a long time looking down through the beautiful clear water.

But on Friday, as we rounded the mountain on our way back to the Elliotts', Clear Creek was no longer beautiful green, shining water. After two nights and one day of rain, it was a raging river, looking almost as deep and dangerous as the Klamath itself. The water had spread out about ten feet on either side of the bridge, and it lapped and tore at the supports. We dug our spurs into the mules as we thought of the creeks still ahead of us.

Beyond the creek, the trail led up the mountain. As the rain poured steadily down, little trickles appeared in the dry places on the trail. The trickles grew into little runs, and these spread so that, in the low places, water began to cover the trail. Still it grew warmer. The snow must be melting fast in the mountains. In spite of the rain, we stopped at a deserted cabin to feed the mules and share our lunch with two very nice pussycats. A little later, Mabel's watch stopped, and though we rode hard we lost track of the time, and dark found us still an hour out of the El-liotts'.

Coon Creek had to be forded. It was pitch dark when the trail turned sharply downhill and the trees met over our heads. But there was no fear of panthers on a night like this. The next instant, we were in the rushing waters of the creek, but it was not as bad as we had expected, and Mabel suggested fording Siwillup, as it was so late, instead of taking time to go around by the bridge.

At Siwillup, the mules took the water readily enough, in spite of the darkness. We splashed across and had nearly made the other side when Maria took a deep step, and in another minute the water was up to my waist. I heard a splash from Mr. Darcy, and then we were out, and the mules were pulling themselves up the bank.

Bill Elliott came out as we unsaddled.

"I guess you found the water pretty high," he said. "I'm kinda afraid of the Rock Creek bridge. Maybe you better stay over here until the storm is over."

All night it rained. We waked to hear it beating steadily down on the roof over our heads. Above the noise of the

rain was the roar of the Klamath. We would sleep for a
while and then wake up and listen to it. It grew very warm.
As we were eating breakfast a half-breed came in.

"Not much snow left in the mountains," he said.

While we were saddling the mules, the rain beat in
our faces and pounded on the roof of the barn. But the
roar of the river was louder.

Two hours out of the Elliotts' we crossed Dillon Creek.
It tore down through the gorge and was higher than Clear
Creek had been the day before. We rode hard and prayed
that the bridge at Rock Creek would hold—at least until we
got there. It was noon when we had our first glimpse of
Rock Creek. The water was spread out on all sides. Under
the bridge, it leaped and roared in a stretch of tumbling
white foam. It tore at the supports, but the bridge still stood.
The mules did not like the bridge but they took it. Then,
praise God, we were safe on the other side.

With Rock Creek behind us, we were nearing home.
A short distance along the trail, we met Steve, dressed in
oilskins, and with a string of fish in his hand. He waved
at us and promised us some for dinner. We were no sooner
in the house than Annie came over with cleaned fish and
venison. In the afternoon, in spite of the pouring rain, all
the rancheria came over.

After the others had gone, Steve and Annie stayed for
a last evening of songs before the fire. Generally we are
all carried away by the music, but as she sang our favorite
songs Annie cried quietly to herself, sitting back so she
was out of the firelight, and though Steve would rouse himself and sing anything we asked for, between times he
sat motionless, with his drum on his knee, looking into the
fire.

The next day all was confusion. As soon as we were up,
the house was full of Indians. We did our last packing while
twelve people looked on. I-ees Old Woman, for whom we
have done almost nothing, cried all the time. Whenever we
passed her, she would get up and throw her arms around

us, and sob. When at last we were ready and the mules were saddled, everyone said good-by very quietly and went off down the trail to the rancheria. Only Steve and Annie stayed. Steve roped our things for us while Annie swept the floor and cleaned the kitchen. They both stood by the gate, waving at us, as we rode up the trail. The rain beat down upon them, but there they stood, until there came a bend in the trail and we were out of their sight.

We were so upset at leaving them that we forgot all about the rain and the rising river and the trail ahead. But just as we turned into the main trail, a strange man rode up.

"I hear you fellows are going down river," he said. "Got any menfolks?"

We said we had not.

"Well," he said, "I stopped to tell you that the river is over the trail. I had to cut my way over the mountain. I guess you better follow my tracks."

We tried to tell him how grateful we were but he turned his mule and splashed away.

The river was over the trail and no mistake. We blessed the mules as we led them around a perpendicular bank. They might be mean but they knew how to keep their feet. It took us three quarters of an hour to cover ground that we had many times covered in five minutes. We worked our way along, holding on to trees and scrambling through brush while the river roared directly below us. That was the worst bit of trail; the rest of the way to the Johnsons' was relatively easy. But at the Johnsons' we met our first disappointment. Neither love nor money could persuade either Charlie or Fred to put us across the river so we could say good-by to the Hildings. We were hard hit. And the worst of it was that the crossing at the Johnsons' was an easy one. If we could not cross at the Johnsons', there was little chance at Ossi-puk or Kot-e-meen. That meant we would leave without seeing Essie. We could not bear to go away without seeing Essie. And what about Á-su-ná-pee? Could she possibly make it down from her cabin on the mountain in this storm? When we rode up to Mr. Petersen's and found his house closed and Mr. Petersen gone, we broke down and wept.

We had barely reached Ossi-puk, when Luther came down in high boots to say we must come up to his house. The creeks were pretty high and he had been fixing bridges so we could cross. There was a warm welcome for us when we got in. Jessie was cooking for ten, and both she and Mrs. Hickox openly grieved because they had not killed a chicken for us. But they thought we could not possibly get through. Mrs. Hickox gave us two beautiful baskets as a good-by present.

All night it rained and the strange warmth continued. The noise of the Klamath is very plain at the Hickoxes'. Every few hours either Mabel or I would wake up and listen to it. You do not think of the Klamath as a river when it is in flood. It is a great evil force. It is alive, and it means you ill. You know why men used to pray to the gods when they lived on the Rivers. Powerful and unfriendly forces are all around you. They will do you harm if they can. The deep roar of the Klamath beat down on us like the rain on the roof. We turned uneasily in our beds.

Mrs. Hickox was up and had breakfast for us before it was light. With every hour the roar of the river grew plainer. Luther came in while we were eating. He told us the river had risen three feet since the night before. But we would have known that by the sound. We had to cross back over the two little creeks to get the mules. The little bridges had been swept away, so Luther flung poles across and gave us another pole to steady ourselves with. It was not a pleasant crossing. Later, when we had to ride across the same creeks, the mules sat back on their haunches, and the men had to drag them across with ropes.

"You'd better stay," said Luther. "You can't make it. The water will have washed out the trail, and that creek at Han's is sure to be bad."

Things did look bad. For an hour Mabel and I rode in black depression. We thought of Essie and Á-su-ná-pee and Mr. Petersen and Steve and Annie, and the tears rolled down our cheeks. It was almost a comfort to see Han's creek ahead of us, and Han's creek was not so good. But it was not as ugly as Rock Creek had been. The water was over the trail, but we crawled up the bank and managed to work our way from tree to tree, holding on to the ropes of the mules, who splashed or swam through the water below us.

By the time we reached Orleans we were in a little better spirits. The worst of the trail ought to be behind us. Anyhow, we had made Orleans. Maybe we would get through after all.

All the way down river from the Hickoxes' it had rained. There was no break as night fell. The Klamath is not as close to the ranchhouse as it is to the Hickoxes', but as we lay awake in the night there was no mistaking its increasing roar.

"You are fools," said Mr. Hale at breakfast. He got up, picked up his transit, and went out.

At the store, Mr. Gent said jovially that we ought to be tied. Then he, too, went about his business. We saddled and rode out of Orleans.

We got through Orleans Creek. We got through Camp Creek. Our spirits rose. What if it did continue to rain? Things were going well. We came to Salstrom Creek.

There was no sign of the ford across Salstrom Creek. Salstrom Creek was three times its natural size. It was a stretch of white, tumbling water carrying everything before it. There were whirlpools and eddies. The water bounced back from rocks and boulders. And above the roar of the water was the grinding roar of stone against stone as they were swept downstream.

The mules took one look at Salstrom Creek and refused to take it. We tried every device we could think of. Then we went back to the Salstroms' for men and ropes.

Old Joe Salstrom had never been a friend of ours. There is a feud between Old Joe and the ranchhouse, and we are friends of the ranchhouse. Old Joe must be over sixty. He is the most splendid-looking man we have ever seen. He speaks slowly, with a faint accent. He has presence and dignity. You cannot imagine anyone taking a liberty with Old Joe Salstrom. We have only spoken once with Old Joe Salstrom. It is not easy to be friends with two sides of a feud on the Rivers. That is, if they are white men. But when he heard we were in trouble, Old Joe dropped what he was doing. He came down to the bank of the creek with us. Again we tried to make the mules take the water. Old Joe has lived twenty years on the Rivers. He tried everything he could think of. Finally we all stopped to draw a fresh breath.

"The mules are right," said Joe Salstrom. "It is your own affair, but I should like to ask if you must go today?"

We told him we had arranged to meet our families in San Francisco, on the twenty-seventh of the month. There was no way to telegraph. If we were not there on the twenty-seventh, both families would be profoundly worried.

"Well," said Joe Salstrom, "I advise you not to go."

"Wouldn't you go if you were in our place, Mr. Salstrom?" we asked.

"No," said Old Joe, "I wouldn't."

We went back with him to the house. We were licked. Rivers in the Karok country were an evil, malevolent force. We had known they were out to get us since the night we lay sleepless at the Hickoxes'. Now they had. We couldn't make the Forks of Salmon because we should have to cross the Klamath. We couldn't even get back up river to I-ees-i-rum. The creeks would be too high. We were licked. Only a miracle could get us across Salstrom Creek, and we prayed for a miracle.

And then we thought of Willy Salstrom.

For years, Willy had been the terror of the Rivers. He

was the badman of the Klamath and the Salmon from the Forks of Salmon to Witchpec. There was nothing that Willy Salstrom could not and would not do to man, woman, or beast. That is what they said on the Rivers. There was nothing that Willy Salstrom was afraid of. There was nothing he would not attempt. He had done, many times, what no other man, white or Indian, had done on the Rivers.

We sent for Willy Salstrom.

We were sitting in the Salstroms' parlor when Willy came in. Willy was tall and slight. He was young, and his face was hard. He did not look at us when he came in. When he sat down, he kept his face averted.

Did he think he could get us across the creek?

Maybe. He did not know.

Did he have a mule that would take the water?

He guessed so.

With the Klamath as high as this, the water might be over the trail at Big Bar. Was there a trail up over the mountain?

He guessed so.

He still refused to look at us, and after a few minutes he got up and stalked out.

The Salstroms served a good dinner but we found it hard to eat. The women waited on us. Joe Salstrom ate without talking. Willy and two other men sat with their eyes on their plates. After dinner we went out on the porch, watching the rain. Old Joe stood with us. Suddenly Willy came out the back door. He went to a shed and led out a mule and threw a saddle on its back. We ran to our own mules and saddled. As we mounted, Old Joe came out and laid his hand on Maria's neck. He turned to Willy.

"You take these ladies to a safe place," he said, "or you bring them back safe to me."

The place Willy selected to cross the creek was down near its mouth. The creek was wider there but the noise of the grinding boulders was less loud. We held our breath while Willy pointed his mule's head at the water. But no mule on the Rivers quarreled with Willy Salstrom. Willy barely turned his head toward us.

"Take your feet out of the stirrups," he said. Then he rode into the creek.

If an animal goes down with you in a crossing, you don't want your foot caught in the stirrup. The bank shelved off where our mules stood. Maria looked at Willy's mule as it splashed in, hesitated, and then drew back. Mabel was directly behind me, on Mr. Darcy. Without any warning she gave him all she had with her spurs. Mr. Darcy jumped forward and bumped hard against Maria. Maria fell off, down the shelving bank. Once in the water, she followed Willy's mule. **Mr. Darcy followed Maria. Nothing** would keep Mr. Darcy from following Maria. The water swirled by us. The mules stumbled a little but they kept their feet.

We were across Salstrom Creek and on the other side.

We clattered up the bank and back onto the main trail. No one minded the rain. We called out to Willy and asked a question. Willy answered it. We asked another question. Will turned half around in his saddle, looking back at us. We began to talk.

We talked and joked. All the gossip of the Rivers. The things everybody talks about. Willy told stories. Good stories. As he talked, we saw that his face was not hard at all. It was young and open. There is nothing to do on the Rivers, if you have more than the average force and fire and intelligence. Nothing to do but be a badman and scare everybody.

A few miles farther along the trail we heard the sound of a horse's hoofs, and Mr. Hunter came into sight. He had been up the creek staying with a friend, and now he was going a mile farther downstream to spend the night with Red Cap Johnny. There flashed through our minds the stories we had heard. Mr. Hunter's wife—— Mr. Hunter ought to kill Willy Salstrom. But not while Willy Salstrom was there with us on the trail. Mabel spurred Mr. Darcy up beside Willy. I called out to Mr. Hunter.

"Mr. Hunter," I said. "Just wait a minute. I want to speak to you. We left some phonograph records for you at I-ees-i-rum. I wanted to ask you——"

Mr. Hunter looked at Willy Salstrom and then at us. He appeared confused.

"I am not sure I put in your pile just the records you wanted," I went on. Mr. Hunter still seemed uncertain.

"And I have a message for you from Herman Albers about his homesteading," I said, thinking fast.

I looked ahead. Mabel and Willy were just rounding a bend in the trail. In another moment they were out of sight. Mr. Hunter let out his breath with a sigh.

"Well," he said, "we're sorry to lose you folks." And he rode on.

At Big Bar, we left the main trail and started on a six-mile detour. It was straight up the mountain. No trail. Horses could not have made it, but mules could. As we came out of the woods, on a wide stretch at the top of the mountain, the daylight was almost gone. It was a bad bit, stony and cluttered with the tailings of an old mine. It would have been hard for anyone to find the trail, but Willy, without hesitation, rode forward. Suddenly there was a breath of cool air. Then a little breeze. In the west was a broad band of light. The weather had changed.

We clattered down the mountain and rode into Bluff Creek just as night fell. Willy would have gone on with us into Witchpec, but the two men at Bluff Creek said it was a clear trail except for a few landslides.

We shook hands and said good-by.

"We will never forget you, Willy," we said. "We will never forget you." And we never have.

"I can't take no money from you folks," Willy said when Mabel tried to pay him. But he shyly accepted our best quirt as a good-by present.

It was too dark to see the trail as we rode on to Witchpec. We did not know that part of the country very well but the mules did. We slid a little passing over the slides, and there was more rain, but it was not really late when we saw ahead the lights at the Moonharts'.

We got off the mules and tied the lines to the fence. Mr. Moonhart came out on the porch when he heard the barking of the dogs.

"And what are you doing here at this time of night, and in this weather?" he asked sternly when he recognized us.

We told him.

"You come from Orleans?" he inquired.

We said we had.

Several men were sitting around the stove as we came in. Mr. Moonhart sat down, taking his time about it. He stretched his legs out in front of him.

"And that's a joke on Gist," he said. "These women came down from Orleans and the mailrider couldn't make it."

The next day, it was Mr. Gist himself who put us across the Klamath. We were afraid he would hold against us our getting down from Orleans, but he took it all in the day's work.

As we stood on the bank of the Klamath on the Witchpec side, we said good-by to Maria and Mr. Darcy, and then we stepped into the dugout and were paddled across. The river was high, but the Indians at Witchpec can take it. We found other horses and by noon were in Hoopa. As we walked over the beautiful campus on our way to the Mortsoffs', the clouds broke away and the sun came out.

The following day was our last on horseback. It seemed odd to be following the same trails over the grassy hills that we had seen two years before, when we first learned what riding meant on the Rivers. Then Bair's came in sight and we changed horses for the stage. For a couple of hours the road was rough, and Mr. Denny picked his way over ruts and through mudholes. Then before us was the divide, and the ground began to drop away.

There were houses and barns and glimpses of the valley, and the road grew harder and smoother. Soon the reins were tight and we were on the downgrade, going faster and faster as the horses picked up speed. Ahead of us the clouds were pink and orange as we drove into the sunset.

Suddenly, far to the west, something glimmered in a broad band of shining light.

"It can't be," Mabel cried out. "Oh, it can't be the Pacific!"

"I guess it's the ocean, all right," said Mr. Denny as he swung across a bridge and rattled into Blue Lake. A factory was in front of us. A steam whistle blew for six o'clock. There were stores and restaurants and white people, crowds and crowds of white people.

Far behind us were the mountains. We could see them, tall and shadowy, in the twilight. But there was no break in them as we looked back. The mountains had closed behind us, shutting us out from our life on the Rivers. We were no longer members of the Steve family or of the Essie family. We had said our last good-by to Á-su-ná-pee and to the trail and to Maria and Mr. Darcy and White Puppy. We were white people in the white man's country.

We were down below.

Afterword

Terry Supahan

"Steve Supahan was my dad's brother. Joseph was my father and Peter my other uncle. All born at the village of Eye-ethreem meaning Grape Flat.

Medicine was spoken as a prayer and was used often every day in Karuk religion. Winter evenings were for teaching, [and] my brother and sisters sat around our Dad and tried to memorize word for word until we could tell the whole story, or prayer, without a mistake otherwise we were considered feeble-minded.

I guess that is why I can't remember most of what I was taught.

Aunt Kate was Medicine Woman. She performed miracles in healing.

This book was put together when I was 5 years old and I remember being baptised [*sic*] as a Catholic.

I went salmon dipping with my Uncle Steve Supahan one eve, [and] had two pack horses loaded [with fresh-caught salmon] in just a little while. This year my family [only] got one small one.

From the time I was born [in] 1907 until now 1983, I have seen lots of changes good—some bad.

I could have had a good education, but an educated Indian was never recognized."

Leonard Super

Our uncle wrote this into my copy of *In the Land of the Grasshopper Song* in 1983, when he was almost eighty years old, and yet he felt "feeble-minded" that he could not remember everything he was told when he was five years old! The oral tradition has always been a very strong part of my tribe's lifeways: preserving stories, passing on important information, and praying directly, in our religion, to our ancestors and spirit guides. But in his way, our uncle wanted to pass on important knowledge and information that he wanted his descendents to know.

In the Land of the Grasshopper Song has always been an important book to our people. Uncle Leonard used to say, "A long time ago, and even before that . . ." to speak about the ages and timelessness. The Karuk Tribe, like many tribes in California and throughout the West, never did receive the reservation that was promised by treaty but never ratified by Congress. This book represented to the outside world our history—that we did indeed exist—and it captured our good humor, our good looks, and our tough-mindedness. It told, in part, our story as a people that forged a beautiful life in the river canyons and mountains of what is now northwestern California. It told the world that we survived.

I was going to college in Portland, Oregon, in the 1970s when my girlfriend read *In the Land of the Grasshopper Song*. She asked me if I knew I-ees Steve. I said no, that was way before my time. "He sure seems familiar, like I have met him before," she said, "and his humor and teasing sounds like somebody that I have met before for some reason." "We'll ask Uncle Leonard and Auntie Vi," I said, "the next time we go downriver. They've probably heard of I-ees Steve before."

So, on my next trip home I asked Uncle Leonard, "Hey Unk, have you ever heard of a Karuk Indian named I-ees Steve?"

"Sure," he said, "that was my uncle."

CPSIA information can be obtained
at www.ICGtesting.com
Printed in the USA
LVHW02s1244270718
584954LV00006B/6/P

9 780803 236370